Peasants of Costa Rica
and the
Development of Agrarian Capitalism

Peasants of Costa Rica and the Development of Agrarian Capitalism

Mitchell A. Seligson

THE UNIVERSITY OF WISCONSIN PRESS

Published 1980

The University of Wisconsin Press
114 North Murray Street
Madison, Wisconsin 53715

The University of Wisconsin Press, Ltd.
1 Gower Street
London WC1E 6HA, England

Copyright © 1980
The Board of Regents of the University of Wisconsin System
All rights reserved

First printing

Printed in the United States of America

Library of Congress Cataloging in Publication Data

Seligson, Mitchell A.
Peasants of Costa Rica and the development of agrarian capitalism.

Bibliography: p.
Includes index.
1. Peasantry—Costa Rica—History. 2. Land tenure—Costa Rica—History.
3. Agriculture—Economic aspects—Costa Rica—History. I. Title.
HD343.S44   301.44'43'097286   78-65015
ISBN 0-299-07760-8

To James M. Malloy

The peasant knows very well what he wants . . . his dream of living on his own land by the work of his hands, in complete independence and with no obligation to anyone.

—Boris Pasternak,
Doctor Zhivago

Contents

Illustrations	xi
Tables	xiii
Foreword by Richard Newbold Adams	xv
Preface	xix
Introduction	xxiii

Part I: The Evolution of the Peasantry

1 Colonization and the Rise of the Yeoman	3
Poverty Meets the Conquerors	3
Land Tenure and the Development of the Yeoman	6
From Gold to Cacao to Tobacco	11
The End of the Struggle	13
2 Coffee and the Decline of the Yeoman	14
"Brown Gold" Discovered in San José	14
The Early Impact of Coffee	17
Problems of Capitalist Agriculture	22
Summary	48
3 Bananas and the Rise of the Rural Proletarian	49
Coffee Gets Its Railroad	49
The Railroad Transports Yellow Gold	53
Coffee versus Bananas: A Comparison of Forms of Agrarian Capitalism	56
Rural Labor Organizes	64
The Rural Proletarian Labor Unions Mature	73

Part II: The Peasant in the Modern World: The Impact of Agrarian Capitalism

4 The Social Impact of Agrarian Capitalism: Stratification and Insecurity	87
Types of Peasants in Costa Rica	88
Social Stratification among Peasants	95

5	The Peasant's Response to Insecurity: Organization and Land Invasion	104
	Three Types of Peasant Organizations	104
	Peasant Activism: An Explanation	114
6	Government Response to Agrarian Capitalism: Land Reform	122
	First Efforts to Help the Peasant: The CNP	123
	Land Reform Gets Underway	125
	The Impact of Reform	136
7	Conclusion: The Demise of the Peasantry	153
	Agrarian Capitalism in Comparative Perspective	153
	The Alternatives Disappear	162

Appendix 1: Note on the Definition of Peasants   173

Appendix 2: Rank-Order Techniques   176

Appendix 3: The Problem of Inconsistency   178

Appendix 4: Attitude Scales   181

Works Cited   182

Index   213

Illustrations

Figures

1	Population Distribution, Early Colonial Period	6
2	Coffee Exports, 1832-1970	20
3	Population Distribution, 1824	28
4	Population Distribution, 1864	29
5	Population Distribution, 1927	30
6	Banana Production	54
7	Two-Dimensional Plot of Preferences and Subjects	101
8	Hypothesized Relation Between Trust and Efficacy	115
9	Trust Among Types of Costa Rican Peasants	118
10	Efficacy Among Types of Costa Rican Peasants	118
11	Trust and Efficacy Among Types of Costa Rican Peasants	119
12	Change in Land Distribution by Cantons, 1963-73	150

Plates

1	Typical Costa Rican Oxcart Used for Hauling Coffee	78
2	Female *Peones Sueltos* (Day Laborers) Working on a Sugar Harvest	78
3	A Coffee *Recibidor* (Receiving Station) in the Central Valley	79
4	Harvesting Coffee	79
5	Preparing for the Weigh-in After the Day's Coffee Harvest is Complete	80
6	A Cluster of Migrant Workers' Shacks on a Coffee Hacienda	80
7	Freshly Cut Banana Stems Being Transported to the Packing Plant on Overhead Cables	81
8	Two-family Homes Provided by the United Fruit Company for its Workers	81
9	A Squatter Settlement Carved out of the Jungle	82
10	A Squatter's Shack Surrounded by Young Coffee and Plantain Plantings	82
11	A Squatter	83
12	Mass Being Celebrated by a Franciscan Priest in a Remote Village	83
13	A Rural Military Outpost	84
14	A Coffee Farmer and His Family	84

Tables

1	Population Growth in Colonial Costa Rica, 1563-1720	4
2	Land Purchases, 1700-1849	26
3	Coffee Exports, 1940-50	35
4	Characteristics of Land Tenure Types	90
5	Ranks of Peasant Types	97
6	ITCO's Colonization Program	127
7	Trust in Government Comparisons	140
8	Political Efficacy I Comparisons	142
9	Political Efficacy II Comparisons	143
10	Future Orientation Comparisons	145
11	Land Distribution in Costa Rica, 1963 and 1973	147
12	The Peasant Agricultural Enterprise Program	151

Foreword

For too long the countries of Central America have been of minor interest to North Americans. They are small, and concern with them has tended to depend on how they are perceived to affect our national security and minor economic interests. Before World War II they were regarded as the "banana republics," nations that, if not handled by O. Henrian consuls, could be "run" by a small force of United States Marines. When Guatemala succeeded in forging the first major social revolution of the postwar period, the United States simply shifted from the Marines to the CIA and squelched the effort. Today, the heritage of an earlier Marine regime continues a situation in Nicaragua that has everyone but a few United States business interests in a state of indignation. El Salvador, the nation with the densest population of the continental Western Hemisphere, is ruled by an oligarchy-backed military regime that seeks no real solution to the immense problems that confront its citizenry. In most of Central America and Panama the general rule is a military rule.

The only apparent exception to this picture has been Costa Rica. This nation has long been without a significant military force. It has promoted and sustained a myth of being a country of yeomen where a white population has maintained a democratic government and way of life in sharp contrast with conditions elsewhere on the isthmus. But many have long recognized that this myth helps obscure facts that would place Costa Rica much closer to its Central American neighbors than is generally accepted. Work by Costa Rican scholars such as Rodrigo Facio and Samual Stone has made clear that power in Costa Rica has been concentrated since the original European conquistadors settled there, and that much of its "solitude" is closer to that of García Marquez than to Shangri La.

In a world that seeks understanding in simplistic political economic dichotomies, Costa Rica presents some real difficulties. It has been run, by and large, as a political democracy that contrasts sharply with its neighbors, but fundamentally, its history has paralleled their history. The parallel, however, has tended to be softened and offset temporally. Problems that became harshly evident with the massacre of the early 1930s in El Salvador were paralleled by the first serious agrarian strikes in Costa Rica. The revolutionary era that followed World War II and that brought an opening to communist activities in Guatemala brought an anticommunist regime to Costa Rica. In reaction to mounting agrarian pressures, the military came into complete national control in Guatemala and El Salvador in support of agrarian capitalist economies. No apparent room was left for serious solutions to the plight of growing populations of the poverty-stricken. These pressures have been much delayed in Costa Rica; but agrarian problems are mounting, and it will not be surprising to see rearmament and a shift toward more centralized rule.

Mitchell A. Seligson attempts here to bring into better focus some of the issues that make Costa Rica apparently different from and yet fundamentally similar to its Central American neighbors. Although we will have to look further for the answers to some questions, this is a book with very important strengths, and it is important that we take the opportunity to learn from them.

Seligson has constructed a review of both the circumstances that have produced the myth of Costa Rican agrarian democracy and the events that have made that notion anachronistic for over a hundred years. He makes clear that the agrarian capitalism that has assumed a military facade elsewhere has, in Costa Rica, succeeded in developing thus far without that front. But he also makes clear that the mask of militarism is being constructed now in a fashion that may rapidly bring it into greater harmony with its neighbors. He argues that security was founded on national export trade for a century and a half. This security is evaporating through increasing dependence on international markets and concentration of land in the hands of those who do not work the soil. His analysis makes very clear that agrarian capitalism under pressure of growing marginalized populations cannot, in the long run, be expected to support a thoroughly democratic political life. It exposes how a government will become bifurcated. On the one hand there are elements trying to sustain a democratic way of life through special agencies and sympathetic governments. On the other hand, the government itself survives by continuing to align itself with capitalist interests and, in so doing, essentially neutralizes its own democratic impulses in support of those interests that answer to the capitalistic concentration.

The book brings into perspective, albeit incompletely, how these processes have worked in Costa Rica. On the basis of contemporary interviews, it argues that important security has been found in plantation labor, while at the same time making clear that such labor has been so unsatisfactory in the recent past as to be the central condition lying behind the emergence of continuing strikes, and more recently, land invasions. It argues that the relatively calm history of Costa Rica is in part due to the fact that the meseta central population was ethnically homogeneous. Difficulties became more apparent when ethnically distinct populations came onto the scene. Blacks and Chinese were the first to become objects of prejudice, but Levantine Europeans, Italians, and others received their share. It is not made clear, however, what defines an ethnic population to the people of that country; the issue of ethnicity is raised, but we come away with no clear notion of how the Costa Rican perceives it.

A quarter of a century ago, I wanted to complete a survey of rural Costa Rica that Harry Tschopik, Betty Adams, and I had initiated a few months before. The then Director General of Public Health of the country forbade me to continue the survey. Costa Rica was, as he expressed it, an "Aryan" country and its cultural and psychological characteristics were perfectly well known. Mitchell Seligson's work suggests that the ethnic and cultural problems of the country are manifold and not sufficiently well known. Costa Rica has always been part of Central America geographically; this work leaves little doubt that it is also part of that region in terms of development and social problems.

Richard Newbold Adams

Austin, Texas
January 1979

Preface

Research on peasants has suffered from a strict adherence to disciplinary boundaries. This book attempts to bridge the gap between the disciplines by presenting a comprehensive view of the evolution of peasant society in Costa Rica. The standard analytical tools of the political scientist are used here, including survey research and aggregate data analysis. These data are presented, however, in historical context: attitudes of contemporary peasants are interpreted in light of the historical developments which have produced them. The tools of the sociologist, particularly class analysis, also see service in this book, but they are adapted for use in peasant society. Finally, the detailed analysis of case studies used by the anthropologist is applied to some aspects of the Costa Rican setting. It is hoped that through a combination of methodologies and approaches a clear picture of the evolution of Costa Rican peasant society will emerge.

Long before I became aware of divergencies in disciplinary perspectives and methodologies I had become fascinated with peasant life. Many individuals and institutions helped cultivate that fascination, and to them I owe many debts which I will never be able to repay adequately. Fortunately, in marked contrast to many of my Latin Americanist colleagues who are forced by the harsh political realities common to much of Latin America to acknowledge only anonymous sources, I am able to thank most of my informants. Violations of civil and human rights in Costa Rica are still an exception to the rule. May this never change.

My interest in peasants was first stimulated by an eye-opening summer spent with the American Friends Service Committee working on a Mexican *ejido* near the town of Pénjamo. Thus it is to the Friends that I owe my appreciation for having given me the opportunity to see for myself the hardships of peasant existence. One brief summer of contact with peasants, however, is of course far too short a time for one to gain an in-depth understanding of their lives. Whatever deeper appreciation I have for them was instilled in me by the villagers of Agua Buena de Coto Brus, the storybook mountaintop hamlet where my wife and I lived for nearly two years during our service in the Peace Corps. I particularly would like to thank Francisco Mejía M., Blanca Rosa de Mejía, Gabriel Castillo, Jovita Cordero de Castillo, and Ernesto Araya Solís for their unfailing friendship and their efforts in helping an outsider to better understand Costa Rican peasant society.

Many Costa Ricans gave generously of their time. Among those who went beyond the call of duty were Lic. Oscar Arias Sánchez, Lic. Rodolfo Cerdas Cruz, Dr. Samuel Stone Z., and Lica. Elena Wachong Ho, all at the Escuela de Ciencias Políticas of the Universidad de Costa Rica at the time of the study. Also of assistance at the University were Lic. Eduardo Lizano Fait of the Departamento de Economía, and Lic. Miguel Sobrado of the Departamento de Ciencias del Hombre. At the Costa Rican census bureau, enormous help was provided by Lic. René Sánchez Bolaños, Director; Ramón Luis Arguello Vargas, head of the 1973 Population Census; and Alvaro Garreta Quiroz, head of the 1973 Agricultural Census. All of the following individuals were more than generous with their time and I owe them each a great debt: Zahyra Agüero de Fallas, widow of Carlos Luis Fallas; Richard H. Beck, President of the Cámara de Industrias de Costa Rica, and Mario Carvajal, executive director of that organization in 1973; Lic. Alexis Gómez Guillén, Vice President of the Junta Directiva of the Instituto de Tierras y Colonización (ITCO) from 1970 to 1974; and Lic. José Manuel Salazar Navarrete, Executive President of ITCO from 1975 to 1978; Lic. Ennio Rodriguez, Lic. Juan Rafael González Cordero, and Lic. José Angel Vargas, directors of ITCO's Departamento de Planificación between 1973 and 1976; David Heine and Eduardo Zúñiga of the Peace Corps; Guido Liercci of the Comité de Bienestar Comunal de San Vito de Java; Lic. León López Corella of the Centro de Orientación Familiar; Lic. Carlos Ramírez Mata of the Dirección Nacional de Desarrollo Comunal (DINADECO); Lic. Oscar Saborío, Diputado in the Asamblea Legislativa; Lic. Alberto Salas Medina of the Oficina del Café; and Lic. Miguel Gómez B., director of the Unidad de Opinión Pública, Oficina de Información, Casa Presidencial. A special thanks goes to Dr. Rogelio Pardo Evans of the Clínica Bíblica, whose ministrations fended off the numerous infirmities my wife and I acquired in the countryside, and to Ulises Blanco Mora for giving us a hand with the interviews in the most remote sample segments.

North Americans working in Costa Rica at the time the research for this study was conducted gave a fellow countryman a helping hand on many occasions. I am most appreciative to John A. Booth of the University of Texas at San Antonio and John C. Hammock, Director of Acción Internacional Técnica, both of whom were doing research for DINA-DECO from 1972 to 1974. Others who provided helpful assistance include Minor Anderson, Director of the Peace Corps in Costa Rica; Chris Baker of the State University of New York at Albany; Theodore Creedman of the Universidad de Las Américas, Puerto Rico; Ian Rawson of the University of Pittsburgh; John Quebedeaux of the U.S. Census Bureau/A.I.D.; and Jim Rowles and Oscar Salas Marrero of the Agrarian Law Project of Stanford University.

I would also like to express my appreciation to several scholars at the University of Pittsburgh who provided invaluable assistance. James M. Malloy (*mi patrón*) shared with me his deep insights into Latin American politics and encouraged my work at every step of the way. It is a small token of my appreciation to dedicate this volume to him. Paul Allen Beck spent countless hours reviewing my work, helping me to sharpen the analytical focus, and Carmelo Mesa-Lago provided invaluable assistance in understanding Latin American political economy. Most helpful in the design of the project were Carl Beck, Ray Corrado, Michael Margolis, Morris Ogul, Reid Reading, Phil Sidel, and Arthur Tuden, all of the University of Pittsburgh. Charles Cannel, Martin Frankel, Leslie Kish, and Arthur Miller, of the University of Michigan, assisted in questionnaire and sample design, and John D. Powell of Tufts University and Thomas E. Greaves of the University of Texas at San Antonio provided helpful comments on the study in its design phase. Enrique A. Baloyra, of the University of North Carolina at Chapel Hill, read an early draft of the work and offered helpful criticism. At the University of Arizona my colleague Edward J. Williams made numerous helpful suggestions in improving the book's organization, and Elizabeth Perry helped in conceptualizing the theoretical material contained in the introduction and chapter 7. Helpful comments on chapter 4 were made by Clyde Coombs, Otis Dudley Duncan, Olen E. Leonard and Herbert F. Weisberg. Richard J. Moore provided useful insight into some of the analysis presented in chapter 5, and Vine Deloria and George Primov were kind enough to comment on the ethnicity discussion in chapter 7. Marion Schwarz was indispensible in modifying and converting the Gini index and multidimensonal scaling programs. She also created the data file analyzed in chapter 6. Susan Dalbey and Peggy Ellig patiently and skillfully typed and retyped the manuscript.

My wife, Susan Berk-Seligson, participated in every phase of the project. She conducted nearly half of the 531 interviews analyzed in Part II, prodding me on to one last one when my stamina would fail at the end of a long, frustrating day. Susan spent several hundred hours with me editing, coding, checking, and rechecking the interviews by the light of our Coleman lantern. If this book has any coherence at all, it comes as a result of our endless hours of discussion about it and her willingness to re-read it more times than I could stand to. As I edit these words, Susan is putting the finishing touches on her doctoral dissertation. I doubt that I have been as helpful to her as she has been to me.

I would like to thank the editors of the *American Journal of Sociology* and the *Journal of Developing Areas* for permitting me to reprint portions of articles I published in those journals.

Several institutions generously supported this research project. A two-year grant from the Foreign Area Fellowship Program of the Social Science Research Council (with funds provided by the Ford Foundation) supported the field work from 1972-74. A summer spent in study design at the Survey Research Center at the University of Michigan was made possible by a Danforth Foundation Graduate Fellowship. Danforth also provided additional funds to support the research and writing of this book. The University of Arizona Foundation provided a timely grant for the purchase of the computer programs utilized in chapter 4, and the Institute of Government Research of that University provided released time from teaching responsibilities to complete the work. The data reported in chapter 6 were gathered by Elena Wachong Ho and me in 1976 under a generous grant from the Ford and Rockefeller Foundations' Joint Population and Development Policy Research Program. In Costa Rica ITCO provided abundant institutional support for that project. An additional short trip to Costa Rica in 1978 was made possible by ITCO, the Programa Centroamericano de Ciencias Sociales (CSUCA), and the Latin American Center of the University of Arizona. The final editing of the manuscript was completed while the author held a Martin Research Fellowship at the Harry S. Truman Research Institute of the Hebrew University of Jerusalem, Israel. None of the opinions or conclusions stated herein, however, are the responsibility of any of these foundations or of any of the individuals mentioned above. That responsibility is completely mine.

M.A.S.

Mount Scopus, Jerusalem
January 1979

Introduction

Peasants[1] rarely write their own story, but they do have one to tell. Whereas for many years scholars have treated them as peripheral to the main currents of history, it is increasingly recognized that peasantries play a crucial role in the evolution of modernizing societies. As Barrington Moore, Jr., [1966:453] points out, it is no longer "possible to take seriously the view that the peasant is an 'object of history,' a form of social life over which historical changes pass but which contributes nothing to the impetus of these changes." For centuries peasants were footnotes to major political developments, largely isolated from changes occurring outside the village. Major shifts in the international economic system, however, have brought peasants, often against their will, into contact with the outside world.

The basis of peasant isolation was economic. Peasant agriculture was subsistence in nature and many peasants had no contact with the market system. With the growth of cities, a demand for foodstuffs was created and surplus production began to be sold in urban centers. Nevertheless, contact between peasant and non-peasant remained low.

It was not until the development of export-oriented agrarian capitalism that the relationship between the peasant and the outside world underwent a fundamental transformation. The international market penetrated the mud walls and bamboo hedges of peasants villages all over the world, bringing with it profound changes in the fabric of peasant life. In many areas of Asia, Africa, and Latin America, large-scale cultivation of internationally marketable commodities such as bananas, cacao, coffee, and tobacco meant that for the first time there existed a heavy demand for peasant production. Peasants found themselves being subjected to new and ever-increasing pressures to produce a surplus for the

---

[1] Considerable controversy surrounds the definition of peasant. As is explained in appendix 1, a broad definition is used in this book, one encompassing landed and landless country folk.

highly lucrative international market. Moreover, an entirely new form of agrarian organization, the plantation, was developed in order to achieve levels of production not possible in small scale production. Land once seen by peasants as a birthright was converted into a commodity the possession of which was denied to many. Some of the new changes in economic order brought with them new opportunities. Some fortunate peasants found that they could earn handsome profits on the sale of their goods, purchase land, hire servants, and obtain a small measure of economic power. But for the bulk of the peasantry, capitalism resulted in increased pressure from overlords and the international economy. Exploitation, characteristic of the peasant way of life, was exacerbated as market forces extracted ever larger surpluses from the work-weary peasants.

Only in recent years have researchers taken a careful look at the impact of agrarian capitalism on the peasantry. As a result of the work by Steward et al. [1956], Stinchcombe [1961], Moore, Jr. [1966], Wolf [1969], Womack [1968], Tullis [1970], Migdal [1974], Paige [1975], Scott [1976], and Duncan and Rutledge [1977], to mention only a few of the best-known studies, it has become clear that the development of export-oriented agrarian capitalist production has had a devastating impact on the peasant and his way of life. We have also learned that some peasants, in response to export agriculture, have become involved in rebellion:[2] "The twentieth century has been the century of peasant revolution" [Migdal, 1974:226].

This book, however, is largely about non-rebellion. It is about peasants who are caught up in the same forces which have ravished peasant societies all over the globe, but who have not rebelled. Indeed, a central purpose of this book is to serve as a corrective to the literature which too frequently has drawn our attention away from the day-to-day nonrebellious nature of peasant life to focus instead on the rare instances of peasant uprisings. As James C. Scott [1976:203] so correctly points out,

> To speak of rebellion is to focus on those extraordinary moments when peasants seek to restore or remake their world by force. It is to forget both how rare these moments are and how historically exceptional it is for them to lead to a successful revolution. It is to forget that the peasant is more often a helpless victim of violence than its initiator. Most important, it is to forget that aside from these "moments of madness" (and even during them!), much of the day-to-day reality of peasant life is the effort of the family to assure itself an adequate food supply.

[2] I refer to rebellion rather than full-scale revolution. Following Scott [1976:194], I prefer to limit my discussion to the narrower of the two phenomena because a discussion of revolution would take me beyond the scope of this book. I view the term *rebellion* as equivalent to Paige's *revolt* [1975:40-45].

Introduction

But how is it possible to explain "the *absence* of revolt in the context of exploitation and misery" [Scott, 1976:194]? How can we understand the failure of peasants to rebel against the loss of land, jobs, and income and against a reduction in their food intake? Scott points to several factors which militate against peasant rebellion. When the changes are gradual and spread slowly over the masses of peasants, the probability for rebellion is greatly reduced. The scope and suddenness of the forces of change have an impact on the probability of rebellion. Following Barrington Moore Jr. [1966:474], Scott argues that only when there is a rapid change which affects a large body of the peasants do we have one essential cause of rebellion. This view, in part, reflects the theories of revolution suggested by Davies' [1969] "J curve," Tanter and Midlarsky's [1967] "revolutionary gap," and the more recent efforts to apply the mathematics of "catastrophe theory" to revolutions. That is, each of these theories focuses on the suddenness of the change as a crucial determinant of revolution.

Agrarian capitalism is rarely introduced with great suddenness, although Scott does not indicate how short a period of time a "sudden change" might be. By its very nature agrarian capitalism is a relatively slow process, taking place over decades, sometimes involving generations of peasants. Agriculture is a trial and error enterprise; crops that grow well in one region, with certain conditions of rainfall, temperature, and soil, will not necessarily do well in another zone. Hence, the planting of new crops takes place slowly as entrepreneurs become familiar with the crop and its "likes and dislikes." Furthermore, production and shipment of these crops for export invariably necessitates the creation of a fairly elaborate infrastructure which may include roads, railroads, docks, and storehouses. The accumulation of sufficient capital to provide this infrastructure takes time, and is frequently derived from the profits of the agricultural enterprise itself rather than from an infusion of capital from other sources. Production tends to grow in proportion to the profits produced by the crops themselves.[3]

---

[3]On the other hand, the termination of agrarian capitalist production can take place in a very short period of time, sometimes in a matter of months. Agrarian capitalists are extremely sensitive to world market price fluctuations and the availability of better growing conditions elsewhere. The Caribbean offers testament to the suddenness with which agrarian capitalism can "pack its bags." Producers there terminated sugar production and moved to other islands as they found that soils declined in fertility and crop production fell off. The development of artificial rubber halted natural rubber production in Manaus and left that city an elegant reminder of the ephemeral wealth of the region. In Costa Rica, as will be shown in chapter 3 of this book, changes in world economic conditions coupled with crop diseases resulted in a hasty withdrawal of banana production from Costa Rica's Atlantic coast in the 1930s.

The second factor which helps explain non-revolt is, in Scott's terms, the employment of "adaptive stategies." These include escaping the impact of agrarian capitalism through migration, social banditry [Hobsbawm, 1959], and opportunities created by elites (e.g., food relief programs). In the case of Costa Rica, migration to virgin rural areas historically proved to be a major method for escaping the hardships brought on by agrarian capitalism and must be seen as a primary factor in explaining non-rebellion (see chapter 2). The settlement of most virgin territory, however, has tended to weaken migration as an adaptive strategy. Although social banditry is virtually unknown in Costa Rica, land invasions are increasingly common (see chapter 5) and may become the primary adaptive strategy of the future. Opportunities created by the elites, in the form of land reform, have not come into play until fairly recently, and not until the last few years have they had any impact at all (see chapter 6). Squatting and land reform would appear to be the main adaptive strategies which may help forestall rebellion in the future. The viability of these strategies, however, largely depends on the state. If it chooses to suppress land invasions and terminate land reform programs, the Costa Rican peasantry is quite likely to turn to rebellion.

The risk factor is the third element which favors non-rebellion. Scott [1976:225-40] argues that when the coercive power of the state is high, rebellion is tantamount to suicide. Under such circumstances only peasants who have no alternative will embark upon such a course of action.

Until very recently, the risk factor has been minimal in the Costa Rican case and therefore would appear to favor peasant rebellion. However, the extreme weakness of the military establishment in Costa Rica has made the harrassment of the rural population a rarity and police brutality almost unknown. Indeed, rural folk culture views the policeman as a buffoon: illiterate, incompetent, and harmless [Salguero, 1976]. Consequently, the near absence of repression in rural Costa Rica gives the peasant less cause for rebellion. Unfortunately, both the image and the reality have been undergoing change since 1970: the rural police have been centralized into a "Guardia de Asistencia Rural;" the military police have been increased in size and effectiveness; and permanent rural military outposts have, for the first time, been set up in areas which have recently exhibited peasant unrest. Threats of invasion from Nicaragua have increased military spending and preparedness. If a leftist regime

---

It can be seen, then, that the introduction of agrarian capitalism is rarely sudden. The halting of capitalist agriculture, however, is frequently very sudden and is probably a more common cause for peasant rebellion than is its introduction. It is necessary to modify Scott's view somewhat by recognizing that whenever either the introduction *or* withdrawal of agrarian capitalism is sudden the conditions for rebellion may be said to exist.

were to come to power in that country one could anticipate a dramatic shift in the nature of the Costa Rican regime. While the coercive capacity of the Costa Rican state remains low compared to that of most other Latin American nations, its growth cannot be ignored.

The Costa Rican case reveals a fourth factor (not mentioned by Scott) which helps militate against peasant rebellion, one which is crucial to understanding the impact of agrarian capitalism on much of Central America. While export agriculture often results in the attenuation of one mode of peasant economic activity, paradoxically, it opens new doors as well. While many peasants lose their land during the expansion of agrarian capitalism, some of these same individuals find steady work on the very land which they have lost to the newly formed commercial haciendas and capital intensive plantations created by export agriculture. However, according to many observers, the loss of land involves a crisis of inestimable proportions for a peasant. Indeed, the distribution of land has been viewed as a central cause of rural violence [Russett, 1964; Mitchell, 1968, 1969; Zagoria, 1971], and poverty [Griffin, 1976]. If these researchers are correct, the wage labor alternative created by export agriculture would do little to forestall rebellion. However, if one looks more closely at the meaning of land in peasant society, as is done in chapter 4 of this book, it becomes clear that land ownership is simply one means (although a very important means) for a peasant to subsist. Scott [1976:6-12] argues convincingly that the "moral economy" of the peasant is rooted in the "subsistence ethic," i.e., behavior and moral code that are produced in a society whose fundamental daily problem is that of physical survival. Scott illustrates his point with Tawney's [1966] statement that "the position of the rural population is that of a man standing permanently up to the neck in water, so that even a ripple is sufficient to drown him."

In my view, peasants can keep their "heads above water" in many ways, one of which is owning a small plot of land; another is having steady work on a commercial hacienda or plantation. I would argue, furthermore, that most peasants perceive this economic reality and act accordingly. Hence, when they are confronted with the loss of their land, they may be more willing than some have thought to accept the alternative of wage work *if such work is available.*

In a more general vein, it would seem that all too much emphasis has been placed on the bucolic notion of the peasant's love for his land. Redfield [1956:112] writes of the peasant's "intimate and reverent attitude toward the land." Is it the land that the peasant "loves" or is it his survival? I would suggest that it is the latter and that if researchers were to follow Scott's lead and recognize the subsistence ethic of the peasant they would be more likely to understand why rebellion is such a rare phenomenon among peasants.

Unfortunately, the alternatives created by agrarian capitalism often provide only short-to-medium-term solutions for the problems created by it. So long as these alternatives are available it is possible for the peasant to survive. Under such circumstances rebellion is a dangerous and unnecessarily risky enterprise. In the long run, however, the wage labor alternatives begin to diminish in number as agricultural machinery displaces workers. As the alternatives disappear, rebellion becomes the more likely course of action.

One of the most renowned peasant rebellions, that led by Emiliano Zapata in Mexico beginning in 1910, well illustrates both the importance of the alternatives which agrarian capitalism creates and the ultimate limitation of those alternatives. After 1880, when the *hacendados* acquired new, efficient sugar-milling machines and a railroad, the poorly capitalized *hacienda tradicionalista* gave way to the capital intensive plantation. John Womack, Jr. [1968:46], Zapata's most eloquent biographer, describes the consequences: "Bit by bit the villagers lost their land—like the orchard of Olaque in Anenecuilco in 1877—but they fought on year after year to preserve what was left." Those who could obtained jobs on the plantations. These peasants were largely uninvolved in the revolution which was to follow. Those who had lost their land and had failed to obtain jobs on the plantations were unable to provide for their subsistence. It was these peasants, their backs to the wall, who lashed out. The result was a revolution which was to influence profoundly the course of Mexican history.

The escape valves mentioned earlier in this introduction are the basis for the formulation of the central hypothesis of the study: *When peasant subsistence is threatened, alternatives will be pursued before the course of rebellion is chosen. Only when the peasant perceives that there are no alternatives to subsistence, even alternatives which would mean a significantly lower income, loss of freedom and status, will he (or she) turn to rebellion in some form.* Scott [1976:204] has captured the essence of this hypothesis when he states:

> The peasant inevitably seizes the opportunities that are available to him—even though many of them may be disagreeable. "Opportunities" is too positive a word for the survival strategies I have in mind. The choices may include putting all of the family to work, eliminating valued ceremonial obligations, emigrating, sharing, poverty, seeking charity, or serving in a landlord's gang against one's fellow-villagers; and, as this list suggests, they usually entail great human costs.

Introduction

It is, of course, a matter of individual judgment as to the relative importance of traditional life-style vs. economic subsistence. In my view, Scott places too much emphasis on the negative nature of the alternative "opportunities." He views the "safety valves" as representing a "ransacking of the economic and social environment for those sidelines and connections that will stabilize subsistence" [Scott, 1976:204]. He fails to see that some of the alternatives, while perhaps depriving the peasant of his traditional existence and the values attached to it, provide him with an economic existence more favorable than before.

Furthermore, Scott views alternatives such as "local forms of self help" as " 'water-treading' based on the 'self-exploitation' of labor" [Scott, 1976:205]. In fact, as I have argued elsewhere [Seligson and Booth, 1979b], such local forms of communal self-help can make a significant difference in a peasant's life chances. For example, a peasant's opening a local school so that his children may learn to read and write or his constructing a small bridge or road which will permit him to move his crops to the marketplace are not merely "water-treading" local forms of self-help. Such measures may make a fundamental difference in the peasant's life style and economic existence.

Scott is correct, of course, when he argues that self-help serves elite interests by staving off rebellious activity and may consequently do nothing to offset those fundamental structural inequalities in the system which permit the long term exploitation of peasants. Sharpe's [1977:xv] study of community development efforts in a peasant village in the Dominican Republic comes to a similar conclusion, "that beyond the often-recognized organizational difficulties are critical structural problems that so seriously limit the scope of action of local economic organizations that the value of such undertakings within existing social structures must be seriously reconsidered." Nevertheless, self-help is a much more realistic form of adapting to the shocks of agrarian capitalism than Scott would have us believe, if we bear in mind Barrington Moore, Jr.'s [1966:453-83] admonition that peasant resistance to exploitation brings with it enormous costs and the near certainty of failure. Thus peasants frequently become the very victims of the rebellions which they initiate.

Local self-help may not only serve to make comparatively minor but nonetheless crucial, improvements in the village, it may also hold wider political implications. As Scott [1976:207n] himself admits, "In the West there was often great continuity between local and seemingly apolitical self-help efforts and later political initiatives." While Forman's [1979] observations on authoritarianism in Brazil in the post-1964 period seem to show that such political "spill-over" did not occur, other studies conducted elsewhere in authoritarian Latin America have come to different conclusions [McClintock, 1976; Fishel, 1979; Landsberger and Gierisch, 1979].

Another major alternative which Scott discusses is migration out of peasant society altogether and into the urban environment. Research has shown that in contemporary Latin America a major portion of urban growth is a product of rural to urban migration [Sauers, 1974:19; Shaw, 1976]. While this alternative almost certainly means for the migrant the termination of the peasant way of life and many of the values associated with it, it does not necessarily mean downward social mobility, economic deprivation, and humiliation. Recent research on rural migrants [Perlman, 1976; Moore, 1979] has indicated that contrary to the bleak pictures painted by early observers, rural folk in cities are able to adapt to their new environments quite well and often live better, in many ways, than they once did. This, however, is not the place to discuss the large literature on migration and urban slums. Yet it is important to note that many observers doubt the ability of the urban sector to continue to absorb masses of rural migrants. The urban industrial base in most Latin American nations, especially those in Central America, is so poorly developed and so highly dependent on high technology and low labor production techniques that it is felt that the urban escape valve may be forceably closed off by urban elites and middle classes. From this perspective Latin American peasants will become "demographic surpluses . . . condemned to gradual extermination" [Jaguaribe, 1973:384].

One final alternative is that of agrarian reform. Scott [1976:215-19] discusses the role of the state in providing peasants with alternatives, but views this type of assistance as little more than an effort to "diffuse the explosive potential of agrarian unrest" while avoiding any fundamental redistribution of wealth. Certainly the bulk of the evidence from Latin America supports Scott's contention. For example, agrarian reform in Bolivia and Peru has not given significant political power to the peasants. Yet, large-scale agrarian reform provides peasants with access to land, and thereby increases their security. If one wants to argue that fundamental social revolution is a necessity, then agrarian reform is to be shunned because it demobilizes peasant movements without bringing about a redistribution of power. However, as pointed out above, the costs of such revolution are so enormous that it is difficult to urge peasants to reject land reform in favor of revolution.

Peasant rebellion is a rare event in spite of the obvious economic, social, and political privations which peasants endure. It will be shown that in the Costa Rican case peasants adapted to new situations rather than resist them. Alternatives, some attractive and some much less so, were available to the peasant and they were pursued. As is shown in the concluding chapter, however, population pressure on a finite land area, together with the mechanization of agriculture, a reduction in the number of wage labor jobs, and the saturation of world markets with the country's principal export crops, has resulted in the closing off of many of these alternatives. The conditions militating against rebellion are disappearing.

The theme of this book is the impact of agrarian capitalism on peasant security, with particular focus on the situation in Costa Rica. The study demonstrates how the introduction of coffee radically altered the social status of peasants, the bulk of whom had been yeoman farmers, by forcing large numbers of them to lose their land. Many of these newly landless peasants became rural proletarians on large coffee haciendas, thereby reestablishing the security of their subsistence. Others refused to accept this new status and migrated to other areas of the country in search of new lands. Still others managed to hold onto a small piece of property and used the income from irregular day labor on the plantations to supplement their meager returns from farmimg.

But it was not only the peasantry that was altered by the introduction of agrarian capitalism. The aristocracy found, for the first time, a source of wealth with which to underwrite the style of life it had long desired but had been denied through centuries of colonial poverty. With coffee, the aristocracy obtained the needed economic power to complement the social and political power it already held. As a result, its grip on society became complete.

Coffee, as important as it has been in Costa Rican social history, has not been the only source of agrarian capitalism. Banana cultivation, introduced as a result of the construction of a railroad designed to transport coffee to the seaport, served as an escape valve for the peasants who were being displaced from their lands by the coffee industry. It offered them an opportunity for relatively secure employment. Indeed, the demand for labor on the banana plantations initially saved the country from massive rural unemployment and subsequent peasant unrest. At the same time, however, a new kind of dissatisfaction, stimulated by the inhuman working conditions forced upon the banana workers and by the cruel hand of international economic forces, eventually led to the formation of unions of rural proletarians led by the Communist Party. The unions offered a new challenge to the coffee aristocracy.

Today, with the labor absorptive power of the coffee and banana industries spent, and with the drying up of the frontier lands once so handy an escape valve for the peasant in search of land, conditions in the

Costa Rican countryside are deteriorating. The one remaining alternative is the cities, but the painfully slow growth of industry is barely able to absorb the natural growth of the existing urban population without having to deal with a flood of rural immigrants. Land reform has been attempted, but the effort has been limited. Rural conflict in the form of land seizures is, for many peasants, the only way out of this dead-end street.

The book is divided into two parts. The first treats the historical evolution of the peasantry in Costa Rica. Beginning with colonial times, the narrative of chapter 1 describes the poverty of the colony and the resultant establishment of a relatively homogeneous population of yeomen. The small nucleus of aristocrats which existed were unsuccessful in finding a source of wealth to underwrite their social position until they discovered agrarian capitalist export agriculture in the form of coffee. Chapter 2 describes the introduction of coffee cultivation and the many and varied influences that it had on the society. Enormous wealth was generated and some elements of society progressed. Others however, particularly the bulk of the peasantry, suffered downward social mobility as their land was absorbed by the growing coffee industry. Some peasants made landless by the spread of coffee cultivation took up jobs in the newly organized banana planations, as is described in chapter 3, giving rise to a class of rural proletarians.

The second part of the study explores contemporary conditions in rural Costa Rica. Chapter 4 examines the social stratification in rural Costa Rica produced by the spread of agrarian capitalism. Peasant attitudes toward the stratification hierarchy are explored in detail. Peasant organization, squatting, and the motivations thereof are discussed in chapter 5. The government's response to land tenure problems is presented in chapter 6. The final chapter compares the Costa Rican experience with that of other nations, and attempts to explain the peculiarities of the Costa Rican case.

In the pages that follow, a non-peasant will attempt to tell the story of one peasantry that is undergoing the trauma of being thrust into the world of capitalist agriculture. The final product, like all works which are ghost written, suffers from untold errors. I can only apologize for them; they cannot be avoided.

Part I
The Evolution of the Peasantry

1 Colonization and the Rise of the Yeoman

A provocative work on the theory of modernization [Riggs, 1964] argues that traditional society can be compared to a narrow beam of light. At this stage of development the societal divisions so noticeable in our modern world (class, occupation, education, and income) are simply not present. Traditional society is a "fused" society. As modernization progresses, social differentiation begins to take place much in the way the fused beam of light is broken up into its spectrum of colors as it passes through a prism.

Throughout the colonial period, Costa Rican society looked much like that beam of light with minimal social divisions. In this chapter that fused society is described. In the following two, the beam is passed through the prism of agrarian capitalism.

Poverty Meets the Conquerors

Costa Rica developed differently from its neighbors in Latin America. In many neighboring countries an abundance of gold, silver, and Indian labor, at least in the early years of the colonization, provided the capital necessary to underwrite an aristocratic style of life for many Spanish and Portuguese settlers. Hence, most analyses of the development of Latin America highlight the clear-cut social and economic stratification which characterized colonial society and which persists right up through modern times. Indeed, Latin America frequently has been called a "dual society" in which the masses are abysmally poor and the elites enormously wealthy [Lambert, 1971:114-48].

Largely as a result of the crushing poverty of the colony, Costa Rica's evolution was markedly different from that of her neighbors. The economic duality which separated the elite from the masses in the rest of

Latin America did not emerge in colonial Costa Rica. As will be shown in this chapter, the differences which did exist were largely social, and it was not until the introduction of agrarian capitalism in the nineteenth century that major economic differences bifurcated the population.

Costa Rica had neither precious metals nor an abundant Indian labor force. Although there are conflicting reports as to the number of Indians inhabiting Costa Rica at the time of the conquest (see note to table 1), there is little doubt that their numbers declined precipitously after the Spaniards arrived. Table 1 reveals a sharp drop in the Indian population in the early years of the colonization and further reductions in the ensuing years.

Table 1. Population Trends in Colonial Costa Rica, 1563 to 1720[a]

Year	Indian	Spanish	Negro
1563	80,000	---	---
1569	---	---	30
1573	---	55	---
1581	7,000	---	---
1583	4,504	---	---
1645	3,200	200	---
1665	1,600	---	---
1675	2,000	500-700	---
1681	1,600	---	---
1700	---	2,146	154
1714	999	---	---
1720	---	3,059	168

Sources: MacLeod, 1973: 332; Stone, 1975: 55; Fernández, et al., 1976: 8.

[a] MacLeod [1973: 322], primarily basing his estimates on the same sources used by Stone [Thiel: 1902], comes up with quite a different estimate for some years. The major differences between these is as follows: MacLeod, a member of the "Berkeley School" (those who hold that the decimation of the Indian population in Latin America was much more severe than was previously thought), believes that in 1563 there may have been as many as 80,000 Indians in Costa Rica, whereas Stone reports 17,166 for the year 1569. The discrepancy lies in the interpretation of the colonial population estimates. MacLeod's figure is arrived at by counting the number of Indians as "Indian Tributaries" (heads of families) and multiplies this figure by 4 (the estimated average size of the family). Stone, on the other hand, accepts the figure given by Thiel. MacLeod's estimate of the Indian population in the year 1581 is 7,000 as compared with the Thiel estimate of 17,166 for 1569.

The causes of the population decline are generally understood. MacLeod [1973:99] finds evidence of an epidemic in Costa Rica as early as 1573, and suggests [1973:205] that even the early Central American epidemics of 1520, 1531, and 1545-48 may have affected the indigenous population. It has been established that "the pandemic of 1576-81 . . .

reduced the Indian population of highland Costa Rica to a very few, and from then on the area was to become chronically starved of labor" [MacLeod, 1973:205-6]. Sadly, the impact of disease did not confine itself to the sixteenth century but continued right through the colonial period as Gibson [1970:93] reports:

> The population history of the 17th and 18th centuries, and particularly the period between 1611 and 1660, is a history of the disappearance and destruction of the Indians—either by epidemics, or by being taken prisoner and moved from one location to another for labor purposes. Five severe epidemics occurred in the seventeenth century: 1614, 1645, 1654, 1690 and 1694. The first had a devastating effect—seven towns whose combined population was about 1,000 before, totaled but 240 afterwards. The last three epidemics were widespread smallpox epidemics. . . .
> During the eighteenth century the Indians fared no better than previously. Attacks upon villages and kidnapping by pirates decimated the population along the Atlantic coast. . . . Epidemics ravaged the Indian population again in 1737 and 1781.

Disease, over-work, and general mistreatment by the Spaniard produced in Costa Rica, as in most areas where the Spanish colonized, the destruction of the Indian.

The colonists found that there was very little gold in Costa Rica. The early settlers heard rumors from the Indians of fabulous mines, but none of any consequence was discovered. The gold that was found came from the streams and could only be extracted through gold-washing or panning. Since this method required a considerable amount of labor, and Indians were in short supply, little gold was extracted from Costa Rica's many rivers. Only in Honduras and Northern Nicaragua was there sufficient gold in the streams and rivers to make the enterprise worthwhile, and Spain concentrated its efforts in those areas [MacLeod, 1973:57]. Within a decade or two of the conquest Costa Rica was notorious for its lack of significant amounts of gold, making it unattractive for the prospective settler.

The colony's isolation from the outside world added to the problem of population decline. Nearly all of the people lived on the *meseta central*[1]

---

[1] The meseta central is an intermountain plateau with an elevation varying between 3,000 and 4,000 feet. Thus, despite the fact that it is located only a short distance from the equator, its climate is cool (70 degrees fahrenheit, on the average), moist, and springlike all year round. Furthermore, since the surrounding mountains are volcanic in origin (the last major eruption occurred on March 13, 1963 [Lundberg, 1968:27-29]), the soil is composed of rich volcanic ash. As a result of its magnificent climatic and soil conditions, the meseta has been a favored place of settlement throughout Costa Rica's history. The total area of the meseta is small, however, amounting to 6 percent of the total land area of the country [Dirección General de Estadística y Censos, 1973a:1].

(see figure 1), cut off from both the Atlantic and Pacific Oceans by mountains. There were few roads and no ports; the country developed, or more accurately, stagnated, in isolation.

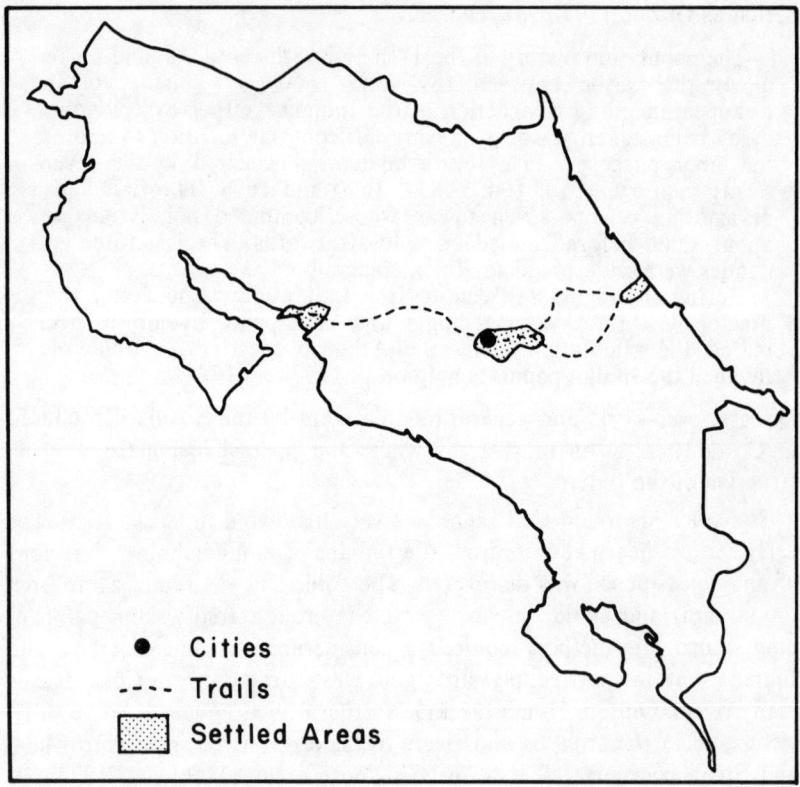

Figure 1. Population distribution, early colonial period
Adapted from Nunley, 1960:16

Land Tenure and the Development of the Yeoman

The absence of gold, a small and shrinking Indian population, and geographic isolation did have one positive consequence: the development of a strong yeomanry. Given the realities of poverty, the colonists turned their attention to farming. Each new settler found himself a plot of land and began to work it. The colonists did not settle in villages the way they did in many other parts of the New World. Rather, they preferred to set up homesteads which were isolated from the other settlers. Each homestead gave birth to a yeoman farmer, independent, self-sufficient, and poor. Despite numerous attempts on the part of the Crown and the Church to concentrate the population into cities, it proved impossible to do so. Up until the beginning of the eighteenth century, Cartago (with a population of 2,353) was the only permanent city in the country [Nunley, 1960:79]. The rest of the population ended up in widely separated farms scattered all over the meseta.

There were two basic reasons for the pattern of dispersed settlement. First, the Spaniard, after establishing his settlement, was forced to remain "down on the farm," because the Indian labor force was rapidly shrinking in size. The colonist was not permitted the luxury of living in town, since his labor was desperately needed on the farm. The second factor instrumental in impeding the formation of towns (and related to the lack of a substantial Indian work force) was that there was almost no surplus of agricultural products for export, and consequently, there was no reason for the establishment of trading centers for the sale of such goods. As a result of the dispersed colonization pattern and the lack of trade with the outside world, farms developed as virtually self-sufficient entities. As one scholar [Saenz, 1969:16] reports, "production was thus directed to providing for the local necessities; this resulted in the formation of subsistence farms thinly scattered over the meseta central. . . . In such isolation the colonial economy completely disintegrated and it became in the fullest sense of the term a subsistence economy."

The pattern of dispersed colonization continued up through the end of the colonial period. Efforts were repeatedly made by the Church to resettle the people in Cartago and Esparta, in order for them to establish churches. The Church even went so far as to threaten with excommunication all those Spaniards who continued to live in dispersed settlements [Sandner, 1962:36], but the threats went unheeded.

In contrast to many other areas in Latin America, the colonial hacienda was a minor feature in Costa Rica, and did not take root at all in the meseta. Recent research by Meléndez (1977a:70-79) does report the existence of haciendas in colonial Costa Rica (along the Pacific lowlands and the peninsula of Guanacaste). However, the shortage of Indian labor made the haciendas economically nonviable. The few which managed to survive were further weakened by a change in the laws governing the *encomiendas* which went into effect around 1620. According to the new regulations Indians were no longer obliged to provide labor for the colonists, but were instead subject to taxation (Meléndez, 1977a:71). By 1720, when the Spanish population had grown to a little over three thousand, the total Indian population was less than one thousand [Macleod,1973:332] (see table 1).

Slave labor might have been a viable alternative to the shortage of Indian labor, but the general poverty of the colony prevented the importation of any significant number of slaves. A search in the historical archives failed to turn up more than a scattering of references to Negroes in the sixteenth century, and their total population never exceeded two hundred in the colonial period (see table 1) [Meléndez, 1972:13-52; Riismandel and Levitt, 1976:102]. Slavery was abolished entirely in 1824.

Aside from the limited number of haciendas reported above, the basic pattern of land tenure in colonial Costa Rica was dominated by the small farm. In the cool highland region where nearly all of the colonists chose to live, there were simply not enough Indians to sustain the development of large-scale hacienda agriculture. The encomiendas which were granted in the early period of colonization (beginning in 1569 [Macleod, 1973:125]) were broken up among the heirs of the conquerors, Costa Rica not following the custom of primogeniture [Meléndez, 1977a:90].

The lack of success of the encomienda system, however, did not prevent the colonists from acquiring legal right to parcels of land. Acquisitions were made in two ways. First, beginning around 1575, the Crown started distributing land to the *conquistadores* in lots called *peonías*, (forty- to eighty-hectare plots) and in large chunks called *caballerías,* which were some five times larger [Salas Marrero and Barahona Israel, 1973:200]. It was in this way that the first large landholdings were acquired. For those who were not related to the small elite group of conquerors, a different system of acquisition was devised. Traditional Spanish law, derived from Roman law, recognized the right of "peaceful, continued possession" as a means of gaining title to a parcel of land. Essentially, through the process called *prescripción posesiva*, an individual who could prove residence on a plot for ten years was granted title to that land after paying a specified sum to the Crown [Salas Marrero and Barahona Israel, 1973:200-201]. Under this system it was theoretically possible to obtain secure title to vast areas of the countryside. However, this was not what in fact happened in Costa Rica since, without Indian or slave labor, there was no motivation for the settlers to acquire more land than they could work. In fact, ownership of large tracts of unworked land was viewed as a potential liability, because it subjected the owner to Royal taxation.

Out of this system of land tenure grew a tradition in which "settlers had a 'natural right' to the use of as much land as necessary to subsist" [Saenz, 1969:19]. Land was viewed as essentially limitless in supply, while the demand for it made by the tiny colonial population was almost nonexistent. As a result, there was simply no market for agricultural land, and possession was denied to no one.

The availability of land was what attracted the few Spanish migrants who eventually came to Costa Rica. Samuel Stone notes that those who were contemplating migration to Costa Rica were aware of the fact that it offered them little in the way of wealth or a comfortable life:

> ... the majority of the people who migrated to Costa Rica came from the poor peasant classes (generally from Andalucía), attracted by the idea of becoming landowners. Even before beginning the trip they knew that they themselves would have to work the land, and that the province of their choice would reward them with neither glory nor riches. [Stone, 1975: 107]

What Costa Rica did offer, however, was land, and for those landless workers in Spain who longed some day to be propertied, Costa Rica offered fulfillment of their dreams.

Since throughout the seventeenth and eighteenth centuries Costa Rica was dominated by the family farm, it has been customary to claim that the country did not have class distinctions of any kind. The phrase "rural democracy" is used over and over to characterize this period of Costa Rica's history [Monge Alfaro, 1966:137]. There is, no doubt, a great deal of truth to this point of view, and any attempt to read into this bucolic life a Marxian class struggle would be totally unwarranted. Not even the aristocratic colonial authorities were immune to the scourge of poverty; the Governor reported in 1719 that even he had to do his own sowing and reaping or he would perish [Jones, 1935:56]. He also stated that since there were no produce markets of any kind, it was not possible to buy anything. The little commerce that did exist was usually conducted under the barter system, with the cacao bean representing the only form of "legal tender" for cash deals [Fernández Bonilla, 1886:V, 475-77]. The bean was actually established as legal currency in 1709[2] and continued to be used for that purpose up through the middle of the nineteenth century [Fernández Guardia, 1967:57; Facio Brenes, 1972:47].

It is necessary, however, to point out that general poverty and the existence of a rural democracy by no means excluded the possibility of

---

[2]According to another source, the year 1710 is given [Valerio Rodríguez, 1953:50]. It is interesting to note that the establishment of cacao as legal tender was seen as a significant technological advance, since the bean, which had to be roasted and shelled before eating, was more hygienic than wheat, the previously used medium of exchange. As one observer notes, "One can imagine that, although in those times there was not much talk about hygiene, flour and crackers passed on from hand to hand did not offer the best sanitary conditions ... whereas cacao first had to be roasted and shelled afterwards, thereby eliminating all danger of contamination" [Valerio Rodríguez, 1953:47].

class distinctions. On the contrary, the distinction between the blue-blooded conquerors and the commoners was maintained throughout the colonial days, if not always in terms of clear-cut economic differences, then certainly in terms of social status. What took place in Costa Rica throughout the colonial years was a "downward leveling of social relations" [Saenz, 1969:17] as a result of the general economic poverty of the area. Nevertheless, it is going too far to claim, as does Saenz, that, "such social and economic differences which existed among the population in the first year of the colony eventually disappeared so that the social organization was modified to one in which class differences were very slight or nonexistent" [1969:17], or, as does Monge Alfaro [1966:137], that Costa Rica was "A rural democracy: there were no castes, nor slavery." Actually, even though land was relatively easy to obtain, there are reports of poverty-stricken landless colonists [González, 1973:2]. A much more accurate appraisal of the situation is given by Stone [1971a:108], who puts it this way: "In summary, the society can be divided into two categories: the elite . . . (that is, the nobility) and the rest of the population which lived in extreme poverty." The importance of this distinction should not be ignored, since it was the basis for the future development of Costa Rican social classes.

Evidence for the two-fold typology of classes proposed by Stone is given by the Costa Rican political scientist Oscar Arias Sánchez [1971]. Arias argues that the notion of universal poverty in colonial days should be reexamined in light of several facts. First, he points out that as in other areas of the New World, the blue-blood conquerors were accompanied by their commoner servants. These blue-bloods, however, did not come from the highest orders of Spanish nobility; rather, they were "Spaniards of second level noblemen or sons of noblemen or knights, who, upon setting foot in the Indies, acquired the noble title of conqueror and were aristocracized" [Arias Sánchez, 1971:59]. The newly anointed noblemen were, as are most *nouveaux riches* groups, quite anxious to assert their newly found position. As regards their life-style, they were able to live much more comfortably than the rest of the population. Cartago became the center of operations of this class. A visitor to that city in the seventeenth century noted that there were a number of wealthy citizens who carried out direct trade with Spain and who owned at least a few slaves [Arias Sánchez, 1971:60-61]. Yet their central problem was the lack of a sizable fund of exploitable wealth in their newly found home. The country was so poor that it was impossible for this group to amass anything like the fortunes which poured into the coffers of the aristocracy of Mexico and Peru. By comparison, the Costa Rican aristocracy was a pauper class. In essence, then, there was a classic situation of status incongruity, one which forced the blue-bloods to try a number of schemes designed to obtain for them the economic wealth they so eagerly sought. The chronology now turns to those schemes.

From Gold to Cacao to Tobacco: The Search That Lasted Centuries

The aristocracy, after settling in Cartago, became quickly and painfully aware of the fact that the Indians in that area had no gold to offer and that there were no productive mines in the vicinity. It was rumored, however, that the forbidding region of Talamanca contained some of the richest gold mines on the continent. In addition, a legend grew up reporting of fantastic emerald mines known as the "Tisingal" [Fallas, 1970:322]. In 1605, Diego de Sojo set out to conquer the Talamanca region and bring back its riches. He was successful in establishing a small settlement near the mouth of the Sixaola River along the Atlantic coast, but the Spaniards so seriously mistreated the local Indians that in 1610 they attacked, forcing the Spaniards to abandon the settlement. Meanwhile, in 1608 Gonzalo Vázquez de Coronado attempted to conquer the bellicose Talamanca Indians, but his efforts also failed [Fernández Guardia, 1967:49-53]. Other attempts were made, but at best all they accomplished was the capture of several hundred Indian slaves; no gold was found [Monge Alfaro, 1966:92]. The heavy rainfall, dense jungle growth, and forbidding mountain slopes made full exploration of the region impossible. As late as the 1970s this region has remained almost impenetrable. Small planes which crash in the Talamanca are rarely recovered and, on occasion, stories of witchcraft and eerie tales of murder emanating from there reach the national press.

It was not in the legendary mines of the Talamanca that the Costa Rican nobility was to find its economic sustenance. Having failed in the attempt to obtain gold, they turned their attention to the production of a cash crop that would, on the one hand, provide a high return for little investment and, on the other hand, not require the use of large numbers of workers, since these were in precious supply. Cacao was hit upon as the ideal crop, and planting was begun in earnest in the Atlantic region, in the area around the banks of the rivers Matina, Barbilla, and Suerre. The area was chosen because it had a suitable climate for the crop, it was close enough to the Atlantic Ocean to make export an easy affair [Lindo Bennett,1970], and the presence of the Urinama Indians could guarantee a minimal labor force [MacLeod, 1973:333]. The cultivation of cacao reached its peak in the eighteenth century with nearly 200,000 trees planted [Vega Carballo, 1972:11]. The colonial government did all it could to stimulate production: taxes were abolished, land was granted to all those who started a plantation, and an additional prize of thirty *manzanas* (20.7 hectares) of state land was offered for each manzana of cacao trees brought into production [Lindo, 1970:13].

Despite this promising start, cacao also turned out to be a failure. A major flaw in the scheme was that in locating the plantations close to the sea, the growers subjected them to the constant threat of pirate and Indian invasions. The Zambos-Mosquitos Indians in consort with such infamous English pirates as Henry Morgan invaded the area constantly, killing the slaves who worked there and making off with the crop. Despite these factors, the cacao planters managed to increase production, apparently because they were able to establish a *modus vivendi* with the Indians. What struck the fatal blow to the industry was the fact that in the last years of the eighteenth century cacao haciendas in Rivas, Nicaragua, began producing large quantities of the bean at a lower price [Vega Carballo, 1972:15]. By 1790 the Costa Rican effort was in full decline, and by the early 1800s the plantations were abandoned completely [Saenz Ulloa 1973:636].

Tobacco was the third alternative pursued by the anxious colonial aristocracy. Traditional among the aborigines of the area, it was first exported in 1638 [Fallas, 1972:29]. Since tobacco was labor intensive, it was difficult to increase production and, consequently, did not offer an ideal solution to the problem of capital scarcity. In addition, it is reported that the leaf was of low quality. The final crushing blow to the "tobacco solution" came, strangely enough, as a result of Spain's eighteenth-century wars with England and France, which forced her to look for new sources of revenue in the colonies. In 1752 Spain imposed a state monopoly on the growing and selling of tobacco in Peru in order to increase its revenue [Fallas, 1972:37]. Spain found that controlling tobacco in this way permitted her to extract a considerable amount of new wealth from the colony; she subsequently imposed state controlled sales on Costa Rica, as well, in 1766. From that date until 1792, the lion's share of the profits were drained off and sent to the Crown. As a result, what little hope the local aristocracy had of becoming rich from the leaf was eliminated[3] [Muñóz Castro, 1962].

---

[3]The production of tobacco did not cease with the establishment of state control; on the contrary, it increased, since the operation still proved profitable for the small farmer. The largest harvests were actually obtained beginning in 1785, nineteen years after the imposition of control, when the total amounted to some 7,500 *quintales* (one quintal equals 46 kgms.). A great deal of excitement was generated in 1787 when Spain granted to Costa Rica the monopoly for tobacco cultivation in the Audiencia of Guatemala; a consequence

The End of the Struggle

The unsuccessful search for a sound economic basis on which to underwrite an aristocratic life-style persisted throughout the colonial era. This protracted treasure hunt must have tried the patience of many an aspiring aristocrat. Some returned to Spain, others moved to more fertile colonies, and a few stayed on. Paradoxically, while the failure to find a cash crop proved to be the bane of the blue-bloods' existence, it was a boon to the rest of the population. Specifically, it meant that those who came in search of a small piece of land were able to settle it without much interference from either local aristocrats or the Crown.

Had some means of extracting wealth been uncovered in the colony, the Crown and the local aristocracy would have forced the peasants to do the extracting. The lack of wealth in Costa Rica, however, meant that for the most part they were left to their own devices. Spain simply was not interested in juiceless oranges which could not be profitably squeezed. At the same time, the local aristocracy was unable to establish the huge haciendas so typical in the rest of colonial Latin America. Moreover, since food itself was scarce, it was simply good politics on the part of the Crown to let each new immigrant fend for himself. Had the colonial governors restricted the access to land, they would have been forced to feed the population. Thus, throughout the colonial period, and even extending for some years into the post-independence period, the yeoman predominated. However, the introduction of coffee—the aristocracy's salvation and the peasantry's ruination—was to change all of this.

---

of this grant was the largest harvest of colonial days, reported in 1788, with a total of over 10,000 quintales yielding a record 60,846 pesos distributed among 858 growers. The mean gross income per producer, therefore, amounted to less than 75 pesos. From this sum he had to subtract the following taxes: (1)*el diezmo*, (2)*la primicia*, (3)*tributos eclesiásticos*, (4) *el derecho de alcabala*, (5) *el derecho de entrada* [Fallas, 1972:61]. Fallas calculates that a producer who earned a gross income of 210 pesos was left with 166 pesos after taxes. The Crown earned 100 percent on each quintal [Vega Carballo, 1972:20; Araya Pochet, 1971:83]. What little profit was achieved by the producer was further reduced when, without warning, in 1792 the Real Audiencia removed Costa Rica's export rights in order to stimulate production elsewhere [Vega Carballo, 1972:18]. After independence the new government continued, until 1869, to retain a state monopoly on the growing and selling of tobacco. Consequently, production dropped off, so that by 1883 (the earliest figures available for the Republican period), there were only 284 producers growing a total of 1,477 quintales. For an interesting discussion on the role of tobacco growing among modern-day Costa Rican peasants, see the study conducted by Barlett [1973; 1975:135-49].

2 Coffee and the Decline of the Yeoman

"Brown Gold" Discovered in San José

In 1808 Governor Tomás de Acosta brought coffee seeds from Jamaica [González Víquez, 1933:4-9], although some believe that the bush was known as early as 1740 [Stone, 1975:76]. The introduction of coffee was viewed by the aristocracy as one more attempt to strengthen the economy of the poverty-stricken colony. This attempt, in contrast to the ones which preceded it, was to succeed.

The early expansion of coffee plantings evolved slowly, and little progress was achieved before 1820. There were three central reasons for this. First, coffee cultivation was an unknown skill and few were adventurous enough to try it. Second, no transportation system existed, so that the farmer would have had to plant coffee without being assured of a means to market it. Finally, lack of capital made the required investment extremely difficult. These limitations, however, were to be overcome beginning in 1821, the year that Costa Rica obtained its independence from Spain.

Independence came as a surprise to Costa Rica; while the historic Acta del 15 de Setiembre was being signed in Guatemala, Costa Ricans went about their business in complete ignorance of the event. In fact, it was not until nearly a month later, on October 13, that Governor Juan Manuel de Cañas opened a letter sent by special messenger, and read the historic documents. And it was not until December 1 of that year that Costa Ricans, in the Pacto de Concordia, officially declared their independence [Monge Alfaro, 1966:149-54; Obregón Loria, 1971].

Despite the rather undramatic advent of independence, it soon became apparent to Costa Ricans that the country was, for the first time, free to develop its own sources of revenue. Political independence meant freedom from colonial economic dependence, or so it was thought at the time. In 1821, the town council (*ayuntamiento*) of San José passed a decree providing free state land and free coffee seedlings to any individual who agreed to plant them. This resolution was followed by a similar one from the councils of Cartago and La Unión in the same year, requiring all of the families within their jurisdiction to plant from twenty to twenty-five coffee bushes in their backyards.

These two agreements were the first in a long chain of decisions taken by the government to stimulate coffee production. Later, in 1825, the first chief-of-state of the new republic, Juan Mora Fernández, exempted coffee from the payment of the diezmos tax. In 1831 a decree was issued to the effect that anyone who cultivated coffee on state lands would automatically become the owner of those lands if he worked them for five years [Oficina del Café, 1954:7-8]. In 1840, President Braulio Carrillo decreed that the area called Pavas should be planted in coffee [González Flores, 1933:18]. In addition, don Braulio encouraged coffee production in the areas of Hatillo, Mata Redonda, la Uruca, Zapote, Desamparados, San Juan de Murciélago, and Escazú [Araya Pochet, 1971:80]. Finally, the government contracted with several foreigners for the establishment of agricultural colonies. Unfortunately, none of these was a success, owing to their location in remote, inhospitable regions [Hall, 1976:36-37].

As a result of the steps taken by the government to stimulate production, sufficient quantities of the bean became available for export. It was not until 1832, eleven years after the beginning of government intervention, that production was high enough to make a major shipment possible. In that year a German businessman with offices in San José exported the first substantial quantities to Chile for reshipment to Europe. When the Costa Rican coffee arrived in Chile it was mixed with the locally produced variety and reexported to Europe under the name Café de Valparaíso. Hence Costa Rica was exporting through an intermediary (Chile), which was mixing its lower-priced variety of coffee with Costa Rica's high-quality bean. Consequently, although the quintal (46-kilogram sack) was selling for twenty pesos in Europe, Costa Rica received only three [Monge Alfaro, 1966:203; Salas Marrero and Barahona Israel, 1973:533].

Efforts were made to circumvent Chile and thereby increase profits. The first direct shipments to Europe were made in 1833, when 16,000 kilograms were shipped to Liverpool on the frigate *Emulon* [Vega Carballo, 1973:87], but the bulk of Costa Rica's coffee still went to Chile. Regular exports direct to Liverpool began in 1844, when the British sea captain William Le Lacheur, commanding the *Monarch*, arrived in Costa Rica and began regular exports to the London market. Le Lacheur made contact with Santiago Fernández, one of the aristocrats heavily engaged in coffee growing, and contracted for the export of 5,505 quintales (253,230 kilograms) of the bean. The deal proved successful, with Le Lacheur paying Fernández eight pesos per quintal (less transportation charges from the meseta to the Puntarenas port) [González Flores, 1933:20]. With the establishment of direct, regular shipments to Europe, the aristocracy finally discovered its gold mine, some two and a half centuries after the discovery of Costa Rica.

In terms of profits reaped by the aristocracy, coffee truly was a gold mine. While the peasant producer received a higher price once direct exports to Europe began, the profits of the exporters and importers were colossal by comparison. The producer had to pay for the planting, weeding, picking, washing, drying, packing, and shipping (to the port), and for all this he received from 2 to 4.5 pesos per quintal [Stone, 1975:81 n.4]. Although there is no way to determine precisely the producer's costs, they probably amounted to half of the payment he received [Cardoso, 1975:33]. Transportation to the port alone amounted to 20 percent of sale price [Cardoso, 1973:34].[1] The exporter, on the other hand, received three pesos per quintal for his entrepreneurship, his risks, and the time he spent filling out the necessary papers. Clearly, most of those three pesos was profit. The importer did even better than the exporter. In the case of Le Lacheur, for instance, he made profit not only by shipping the coffee to London, but also by setting up his own import house (John K. Gilliat and Co., Ltd., still in operation) and selling the coffee at approximately twenty pesos per quintal. His profit, therefore, was twelve pesos per quintal, minus the cost of the sea voyage and expenses.

The pattern of profit established at this early date continued, with slight modification, up to the present. Although the government stimulated coffee production, it adopted a laissez-faire policy regarding the regulation of prices between grower, exporter, and importer, a policy unaltered until 1933. The impact that this policy had upon the peasantry cannot be overlooked. Although the peasants produced the crop upon which Costa Rica's economy rested, they reaped little benefit from their labors. The profits were skimmed off by domestic economic elites and foreign entrepreneurs.

[1] These costs could be reduced if family labor were used in the production process, but this, of course, meant that the labor would be taken away from subsistence crop production and put into coffee production. The actual savings therefore were reduced.

The Early Impact of Coffee

Infrastructure Development

The processing and shipping of coffee require roads which can sustain a large volume and weight. In most areas of Costa Rica, since the harvest season coincides with the months of heaviest rainfall (generally between September and early December), roads become a sea of mud under the never-ending parade of oxcarts with their knife-edge wooden wheels cutting into the rain-saturated earth (see plate 1). Consequently, when the first profits of coffee began to roll in, attention was turned to improving the primitive, poorly maintained road network which had been established in colonial days.

In 1843 the Sociedad Económica Itineraria was formed by the largest coffee producers; its function was the promotion of road development. Throughout the colonial period and early years of independence, Costa Rica had almost no road network at all. Actually, the only permanent road was the Camino Real, a mule path from the meseta to Nicaragua. Other paths existed (one south to Panama and the other east to the Atlantic port), but these were frequently washed away in the heavy rains [Hall, 1976:58]. A tax of one real per quintal (46 kilograms) was imposed in 1841 [Oficina del Café, 1954:15], permitting the society to build a road from the meseta to the Pacific port of Puntarenas, completing it in 1846. The opening of this road ensured producers permanent access to the port, which in turn helped to further stimulate production. However, feeder roads from the farm areas to San José were sorely needed. The society worked on this problem as well: roads were constructed north to Sarapiquí and east to Matina and Moin. In order to facilitate export shipments, the ports of Puntarenas, Caldera, and Matina were improved [Araya Pochet, 1971:80-81; Avila Bolaños, 1972; González Flores, 1933:19].

The prosperity produced by coffee was sufficient, even in those early years, to permit expenditures on other, much-needed infrastructure projects. Consequently, the postal service was established, the city of Cartago (damaged by an earthquake) was rebuilt, the streets of San José and Cartago were paved, and the first school of higher learning, the University of Santo Tomás, was opened [González Flores, 1933:19].

Capitalization

The cacao bean, used as the medium of exchange in colonial days and therefore indicative of the uncapitalized nature of the Costa Rican economy, was gradually replaced by other currency. Shortly after coffee production began, the first national currency, called *americana insurgente*, made its appearance, and in 1823 the first silver and gold coins were ordered minted. A small gold mine (Monte del Aguacate) was discovered in 1815 and exploited extensively, beginning in 1820. The mint (la Casa de Moneda) was officially established in 1828 [Núñez M., 1971:123]. With its newly found source of income, the Republic was able to pay its debt to the ephemeral Central American Federation established in Guatemala in 1824 [Karnes, 1961:49]. The public treasury in 1826 increased its annual income by 16,000 pesos, so that it amounted to 24,000. By 1849 the income had reached 120,000 pesos. The principal source of this income was the customs duty levied on the mountains of imported goods that filled the holds of the returning coffee ships [Araya Pochet, 1971:81].

Import Expansion

Other salubrious consequences of the "coffee miracle" were forthcoming. As already mentioned, the ships which returned from the continent brought with them a wide range of new products. Perhaps most important among them were tools for agriculture and construction. These made possible more efficient work in the fields and the construction of more sanitary and comfortable homes. Damp adobe walls began to give way to brick and wood, and windows were installed to bring light and air into the once-dark dwellings. Iron stoves replaced the smokey open hearth arrangement of the past, and porcelain replaced the wooden bowls of poverty. In agriculture the steel hoe, plow, shovel, saw, machete, and ax brought about a revolution of efficiency, while the corn mill and rice winnower freed the housewife from hours of drudgery [González Flores, 1933:20-22]. The ships also brought new materials for more comfortable clothing, books to stimulate the mind, and medicines to cure the body. And with the cargo came immigrants (not a wave, but a ripple) seeking to take part in the newly found wealth. Doctors, lawyers, engineers, and educators: they all came in those golden days of the coffee boom [González Flores, 1933:20-24].

Exports Increase

During the first years of coffee-growing in Costa Rica, up through the 1830s, production was handled with a minimum of technology. The cherries, once picked from the bushes, were left to ferment for forty-eight hours and then were washed in small basins to loosen the pulp. Oxen were used to trample the cherries in order to extract the bean. Unfortunately many beans were damaged in this way, and the export prices suffered as a consequence. The beans were then set out to dry on the patios adjoining the grower's cottage. The labor investment was great, but the capital required was minimal. Each family could plant, harvest, wash, and dry no more than its own labor resources would permit. For the aspiring aristocracy this system had two distinct disadvantages. First, overall production was kept relatively low, far beneath the strong demand on the London exchange for Costa Rican coffee, which was highly valued in Europe for its flavor. Second, because of Costa Rica's small population and almost nonexistent Indian work force, there was little surplus labor available to tend to the large coffee estates that the aristocracy was envisioning for itself. Because of the ready availability of land in the colonial period and the resultant predominance of the yeoman, there were almost no landless laborers available. Expansion of labor-intensive cultivation was therefore impossible. Mechanization of production helped solve the problem of low production and labor shortages.

In the middle of the nineteenth century mechanization of coffee production began. Newly invented machinery was imported and installed in *beneficios* (coffee-processing plants) [Facio Brenes, 1972:44].[2] These machines were capable of processing a huge quantity of coffee in a very short time, and in a way which produced a higher quality product than had been available before (the beans were not crushed). The rapid mechanization of processing permitted the expansion of production by diverting workers from the processing stage to the harvest. Greatly increased exports resulted, as is indicated in figure 2. Production, which stood at only 23,000 kilograms in 1832, reached over 1,000,000 in the 1840s, 4,000,000 in the 1850s, and over 11,000,000 by 1870.

Wages Increase

The mechanization of production through the introduction of the beneficio did not put an end to the problem of labor scarcity. While it is true that the beneficio did free a substantial part of the work force for coffee-picking, labor still remained in very scarce supply during the harvest. As early as 1844 a report of a foreign visitor traveling in Costa

[2]It is difficult to pinpoint the year when this machinery was introduced. Facio [1972:44] puts it in 1856-57, Stone [1969:184] sets the date at 1856, and Saenz P. [1969:25] uses 1858. Apparently both Stone and Saenz are relying on Facio as their source. However, there appears to be some difficulty in accepting a date this late, since a visitor to Costa Rica in 1844, Robert Glasgow Dunlop [1970:117], reports that the largest farms used hydraulic mills and windmills to process the bean. Apparently, machinery was introduced bit by bit, over the years, and slowly gained in efficiency and capacity, so that by the 1856 date, probably a large percentage of the coffee was produced in beneficios. This is the view that Hall [1976:49] and de Andrade [1966:139] take. They note that the wet method (*beneficio húmedo*) of coffee-processing was introduced from the Antilles in 1838. Cardoso [1975:38-39] lists the first importation of machinery as 1841-42.

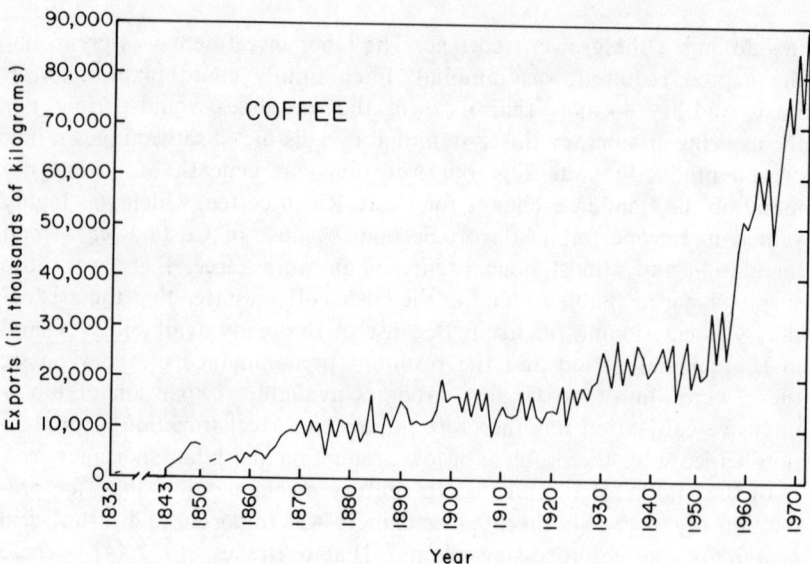

Figure 2. Coffee exports, 1832–1970
Sources: Dirección General de Estadística y Censos, 1941:14; Salas Marrero and Barahona Israel, 1973:533; Monge Alfaro, 1966:203; Vega Carballo, 1973:118.

Rica states that the labor supply was insufficient to meet the demand for work [Dunlop, 1847:116].

Foreign credit served to further reduce the labor shortage problem. Since Costa Rican coffee was so well received on the London exchange, buyers there were anxious to guarantee themselves a continuous supply of it. To do so, they would pay the beneficio owners an advance for their crop, so as to guarantee delivery the following year. Part of this credit was, in turn, offered to the producers in the form of *adelantos*, or partial payments in advance for the unripe berries. The adelantos were then used by the producers as a means of attracting labor during the harvest season. Since, however, the majority of peasants at this time were landed, few were available for picking. In order to encourage more people to enter the labor force of pickers, extraordinarily high wages were offered. According to Dunlop [1970:116], the *peón* was paid approximately one shilling a day, or seventy-five dollars a year. The selling price of coffee in San José at that time was some five dollars a quintal, or twenty shillings, half of which went to pay production costs.[3] With a profit the

[3] Dunlop's report gives the five-dollar price for the year 1846, rather than 1844, the year the author was actually in San José. Since, however, the book was written in Guatemala in

equivalent of ten shillings a quintal, the small producer would have had to produce thirty quintales a year in order to break even with the wage earner. This was no small quantity of coffee for one individual to produce, since it would have required maintaining under cultivation some five hectares of coffee fields[4] and, consequently, would not have been possible without the aid of unpaid family labor. These same family members could just as well have been working on the hacienda for the comfortable wage of seventy-five dollars a year.

In all likelihood, few adult coffee farmers at this time were induced by high wages to leave their parcels and move onto the hacienda, since the attachment to the homestead was probably too great. Most likely only those with large debts hanging over them took this course of action. It is quite likely, however, that many of the children of these smallholders left the family plot to work on the hacienda, while either retaining their small piece of inherited land for subsistence crop production or selling the plot altogether for a dowry.

Work on the hacienda did, of course, have its distinct advantages. First, it was secure. The peón was assured that every Saturday he would receive his wage and with that cash he could buy his weekly supply of food.[5] Second, it was worry-free. The small producer, in contrast, had a never-ending list of problems to ponder. Would the crop be a good one? Would disease strike? Would there be heavy rains during the harvest that would cause a loss of cherries? Would the world price of coffee go down? Would the oxen be healthy enough to haul in the crop? Would the bridge leading to the beneficio wash out? Would the machines at the beneficio break down and leave his unprocessed crop to rot? Worries such as these constantly plagued the smallholder. A final and perhaps

---

the two years subsequent to his trip to Costa Rica, the author may have been citing the correct price for that year as told to him by recent arrivals from San José [Dunlop, 1970:105-6].

[4]There are no estimates of yield per hectare for this period, but the Ministerio de Agricultura y Ganadería [1973:11] estimates that in 1950, the year before any concerted government program of technical assistance to coffee growers began, production averaged seven quintales per hectare. It can be assumed that yields were even lower a century earlier, when no technical improvements in seed, fertilizer, spacing, shade, etc., had been introduced. However, because soils were in their virgin state in many parts of the meseta in the last century, it is possible that yields in new farms were considerably higher than this, at least for the first few years of production [Cardoso, 1975:36].

[5]Unfortunately the peón was not accustomed to receiving cash and often spent it on alcohol. Thus, a tradition of very heavy Saturday night drinking has grown up around the haciendas in Costa Rica, and alcohol consumption per capita is said to be among the highest in Latin America [Centro de Estudios sobre Alcoholismo, 1973].

most important reason why many sons of smallholders chose hacienda labor was the fact that the high wages paid on the plantation meant that they could improve their life-style at least marginally. Remaining on the family plot offered no possibility of such an improvement. The wages became an even greater incentive in later years. It is reported that in 1853 wages rose to two shillings a day, up to three shillings in 1868, and to six shillings in 1872 [Vega Carballo, 1973:94].[6]

Problems of Capitalist Agriculture

Decline in Food Production

When coffee was first introduced, Costa Rica was still using the cacao bean as the medium of exchange. Although the aristocracy had managed to accumulate small amounts of capital from the cacao and tobacco trade,[7] most buying and selling was conducted under the barter system. With the introduction of coffee, however, the economy became monetarized. The subsistence peasant was confronted with an economy increasingly based upon cash. In order to obtain needed supplies, cash was now required for food purchases and other business transactions; therefore the peasant had to plant coffee. As a result, however, the limited supply of family labor had to be diverted from subsistence crop production to coffee production. Consequently, food supplies began to diminish in an ever-downward spiral as acreage once devoted to food production was turned over to coffee plantings [Monge Alfaro, 1966:204].

Throughout the colonial period Costa Rica had been self-sufficient in the production of wheat, so that bread, not tortillas, had been the traditional carbohydrate [Meléndez, 1966:66]. By 1854, however, most of the flour was being imported from Chile, and later on from California. By 1884 only 145,541 liters of wheat were being produced; the figure dropped to 27,871 in 1888, and to zero in 1889 [Oficina Nacional de Estadisticas, 1912:107]. The second national agricultural census, compiled in 1905, does not even list wheat as being grown in the Republic [Departamento Nacional de Estadística, 1905]. Only when the world price of the grain went very high (as it did in the period 1880-90 and

[6]Hall [1976:57-58] believes that there is no satisfactory explanation for the fact that many peasants chose work on the plantation rather than setting up their own farms on public domain land. I believe the reasons expressed in the above paragraph explain it quite well.

[7]Arias Sánchez [1971:61] reports families with as much as five thousand pesos in colonial days.

during World War I) did Costa Rica briefly return to wheat production, if only on a small scale. Today, no wheat at all is produced in the country, and a loaf of bread costs about 20 percent of an agricultural laborer's daily minimum wage. An economist might argue that this system of substituting coffee for primary foodstuffs is a good one, since it moves the world economy in the direction of optimal productivity and a more rational international division of labor. The peasant, however, found his income insufficient to permit him to purchase the food supplies he once produced himself. As production of food dropped off, prices began to rise. The resulting inflation directly affected the peasant, since the lion's share of his earnings were spent in food purchases, whereas the richer classes spent a proportionately lesser amount of the family budget on such items.

Proletarianization

The system of high wages, coming as a direct result of the mechanization of coffee production and the availability of foreign credit, was eventually responsible for a massive proletarianization of the Costa Rican peasantry. Although there are no census figures for the period preceding the introduction of coffee that indicate occupational categories, all of the accounts point to the predominance of the smallholder (see chapter 1). Fifty-six years after the introduction of coffee, however, a census was taken which provides a reasonable indication of the occupational breakdown at that time [Costa Rica, 1868]. Out of a population of 120,499, 53 percent made up the economically active sector (i.e., listed as having an occupation). Of these, 46 percent were employed in agriculture. Thus it can be seen that at this early date more than half of the population was no longer living directly off the land. Of those employed in agriculture, 49 percent are listed as wage laborers (*jornaleros* and *chacareros*). By 1864, nearly half the peasants were no longer yeomen.[8] Nearly twenty years later, the 1883 census figures reveal 71 percent of the agricultural population were landless laborers [Costa Rica, 1885]. It was during this period that coffee production increased five-fold, the fastest increase in Costa Rica's history.

Concentration of Land

Three factors conspired to deprive peasants of their land. The first of these, labor scarcity and the resulting high prices of labor, have already

[8]It is not possible to determine whether some of those listed as wage laborers actually owned a small piece of land; some probably did. This, however, is not too relevant, for if the individual, in responding to the census-taker's question regarding occupation, considered himself to be mainly a wage laborer rather than a small farmer, it meant that his main source of income probably was derived from the sale of his labor.

been discussed. The other factors, high land prices and mortgage foreclosures, will be discussed here.

In colonial days land had little value; it had not really been considered a commodity to be bought and sold, and practically had been given away [Cardoso, 1973:27; Hall, 1976:55]. The profits gained in the sale of coffee completely changed this situation, so that land soon came to be viewed as an all-important factor of production.

The amount of land suitable for coffee cultivation represented only a small percentage of the total land area. In Costa Rica the vast bulk of ideal coffee land consists of those areas enclosed by the mountains of the meseta central, for coffee will not grow well at either very low or very high altitudes (below 800 meters or above 1,500 meters). Consequently, land prices in the valley soared. Stone [1969:195] has pointed out that relative to Guatemala, Costa Rican land prices were high. He found that in 1850 an acre of good land on the meseta central was selling for the equivalent of eighty-eight dollars, whereas in 1877, in Guatemala, a comparable piece of land sold for seventeen dollars. It is estimated that meseta land prices rose twenty to thirty times between 1820 and 1850 [Cardoso, 1973:28].

As a result of these high prices there was a strong incentive for the peasant to sell his land. This was particularly true of young men, who had to choose between earning a good wage on the plantation and eking out a living on a small inherited plot. It should be recalled, in this regard, that land in Costa Rica is divided up among *all* the sons and daughters [Rawson, 1975:163-72]. Consequently, after even a single generation, the size of the parcel is likely to become quite small and uneconomical to farm.

It will be recalled that the beneficios advanced to the small producers adelantos on the forthcoming crop. According to several writers [Facio, 1972:44; Stone, 1969:183-84; Vega Carballo, 1972:33; Cerdas Cruz, 1972:62], it was the failure to pay back these loans that caused many producers to lose their land. The alleged reason for this is that the land was always offered as collateral for the loan, each borrower being required to sign a *prenda* (pledge) in which it was clearly stated, "It is a condition [of the agreement] that the creditor can collect the entire debt before the term of the contract and make effective the guarantees if the debtor fails to fulfill the obligations relative to the delivery of the coffee in total or in part" [Certificado de Prenda, n.d.]. If the producer defaulted in *any* aspect, he could unceremoniously lose his property. It is not likely, however, that the adelanto was the cause of very many defaults. What the above-named writers fail to take into consideration is that the adelanto never covered more than 40 percent of the value of the harvest, since the intended purpose of the advance was to provide money only for picking and the care of the *cafetal*. The producer who had a bad year and turned in a crop 20 percent to 30 percent less than expected would still have sufficient coffee to cover the IOU. It would have been highly unusual for the yield to be so bad that over 60 percent of the crop was lost, and even then, it is not clear that the beneficio would always have demanded payment. This must have happened in some cases, but the failure to pay adelantos was probably not the primary cause for producers to lose their land.

The fact that a substantial number of peasants did in fact lose their land cannot be attributed to the adelanto; what can be blamed is the inability of the peasants to pay their mortgage. It is common practice in Costa Rica to mortgage property for relatively short term loans. This practice has developed as a direct result of the introduction of agrarian capitalism. Before coffee's introduction, it will be recalled, the economy operated on a barter system. With the advent of coffee, a need was created for cash. Since the profits of the smallholders on the sale of their coffee were not large, many owners found themselves in need of loans in order to cover debts at the local general store or to make an improvement on the farm, marry off a daughter, buy a new stove, etc. The only source of credit was the beneficio, since there were no permanent banks in the country until 1863. The beneficios were, in effect, rural banks.[9] The foreclosing of mortgages was probably quite common throughout the nineteenth century and became very frequent in times of low coffee prices [Saenz Ulloa, 1973:6; Saenz P., 1969:27-28]. In 1892, for example, a year after two successive drops in coffee exports, some 11.1 percent of all registered property changed hands, although it is not known what proportion of these transfers resulted from foreclosures.

There is evidence which substantiates the impact on land concentration of the three factors just discussed. A study of land sales in Costa Rica [de Andrade, 1966:138] demonstrates how dramatically coffee converted land into a factor of production. As shown in table 2, throughout the entire colonial period, land purchases never amounted to more than 139 in a ten-year period (from 2 to 9 per 1,000 population), with the mean price of the land coming to 280 reales. By the period 1830-39, there were 608 purchases (14 per 1,000 population), at an average price

[9]The importance of the banking function for the beneficio owners was evidenced during the administration of Juan Rafael Mora, leader of the battle against the adventurer William Walker [Guier, 1971]. Following the signing of a contract with an Argentine, Crisanto Medina, to open the first bank [Núñez M., 1971:126], a coup d'etat was arranged by the beneficio owners, who, fearing the loss of their control over the banking function, had Mora thrown out of office in 1859, and two years later, shot [Facio Brenes, 1972:46; Fernández G., 1967:110-12; Alvarez, 1954:5; Araya Pochet, 1971:81].

of 368 reales, and by the period 1840-49 this figure had more than doubled to 1,311 (16 per 1,000 population), at an average of 3,135 reales!

These data also reveal that the land was being bought up by a few individuals, which meant that considerable areas were being concentrated in their hands. Moretzsohn de Andrade [1966:139] examines the names of the 3,387 individuals who purchased land in the period represented in table 2, and finds that there were 62 individuals who bought five or more properties and who sold less than 50 percent of the total value of their purchases. These individuals he denominates "monopolists" (*acaparadores*). It can be seen in table 2 that from 30 to 40 percent of the value of all land purchases made in the period after the introduction of coffee were made by these individuals who comprised only *1.8 percent of all the purchasers of land*.[10] Unfortunately no hard data are available for comparing the overall concentration of land before and after the cof-

Table 2. Land Purchases, 1700-1849

	Total Purchases			Percent of Purchases Made by Monopolists	
Year	Number	Value (reales)	Per person	Number	Value (reales)
1700-09	30	15,987	.008	0	0
1710-19	32	16,639	.009	0	0
1720-29	54	15,636	.009	1.8	2.2
1730-39	30	10,310	.005	3.3	9.6
1740-49	30	12,869	.003	3.3	10.8
1750-59	28	8,766	.002	7.1	7.9
1760-69	36	6,822	.003	0	0
1770-79	80	15,626	.006	2.5	18.5
1780-89	105	16,238	.004	0.9	0.3
1790-99	57	8,387	.002	10.5	6.1
1800-09	129	56,377	.003	24.0	31.3
1810-19	139	26,494	.003	17.0	19.9
1820-29	241	90,136	.005	20.7	41.4
1830-39	608	222,967	.014	18.7	30.8
1840-49	1,311	974,876	.016	16.7	30.9

Source: de Andrade, 1966: 138.

[10] In the decade 1770-79, 18.5 percent of the land was bought by the monopolists, but de Andrade [1966:139, n.1] points out that this was a result of the purchase of two large haciendas by one single individual. Hall [1976: 83-86] disputes de Andrade's contention that land became concentrated during the expansion of coffee production. She uses the

fee boom. We do know, however, that as coffee production increased, the number of haciendas increased. Hence between 1883 and 1892, a period of major expansion in coffee production, they increased by 20 percent [Costa Rica, 1885, 1893]. The concentration of land which began during the coffee boom has continued up through the 1960s and 1970s, as is documented in chapter 6.

Out-migration and Spontaneous Colonization

If the Zapatista uprising in Mexico is a story "about country people who did not want to move and therefore got into a revolution" [Womack, 1968:ix], then the story of the Costa Rican peasantry is about country people who did move and thereby avoided one. Some peasants, caught between the push and pull of the advancing capitalist economy, sold out and moved onto the hacienda. Others, refusing to accept the proletarian way of life, moved away in search of new lands where they could continue their yeomanly existence.

Several factors induced the peasant to search for new lands. The concentration of land in the hands of the aristocracy and the concomitant loss of land by the peasantry have already been discussed. Monitarization of the economy, mentioned earlier, encouraged some peasants to seek a way to return to their precapitalist existence, free from rising prices and never-ending debts in the general store. To do this they would have to find a place where there was enough farm land available for them to be able to make themselves self-sufficient once again. Finally, a population explosion put pressure on the family farm, pressure which could only be alleviated by out-migration.

The annual population growth rate in 1751 was .5 percent. By 1824 the rate had risen to 1.1 percent annually, and went even higher, to 1.6 percent in 1836, 2.5 percent in 1844, and 2.7 percent in 1875. By the year 1892, the rate reached an all-time high for the nineteenth century of 3.7 percent annually [Dirección General de Estadística y Censos, 1977:11]. The population explosion was in large measure a result of the lowered death rates and longer life expectancy attained during the pe-

---

1935 coffee census to do this, along with other data. The difficulty with the Hall analysis is that it mistakenly assumes that because many peasants did own land and because there were no haciendas which approached in size those found in Mexico, Peru, etc., the land remained equitably distributed. The Gini index data presented below demonstrate that her analysis is faulty. The many peasants who own land own tiny amounts of it, whereas the bulk of the land area is concentrated in a few hands. Given Costa Rica's tiny size compared to other Latin American countries, it is clear why few, if any, of the haciendas in Costa Rica achieved the size of those found elsewhere. Further discussion is found in Cardoso [1973:28-30].

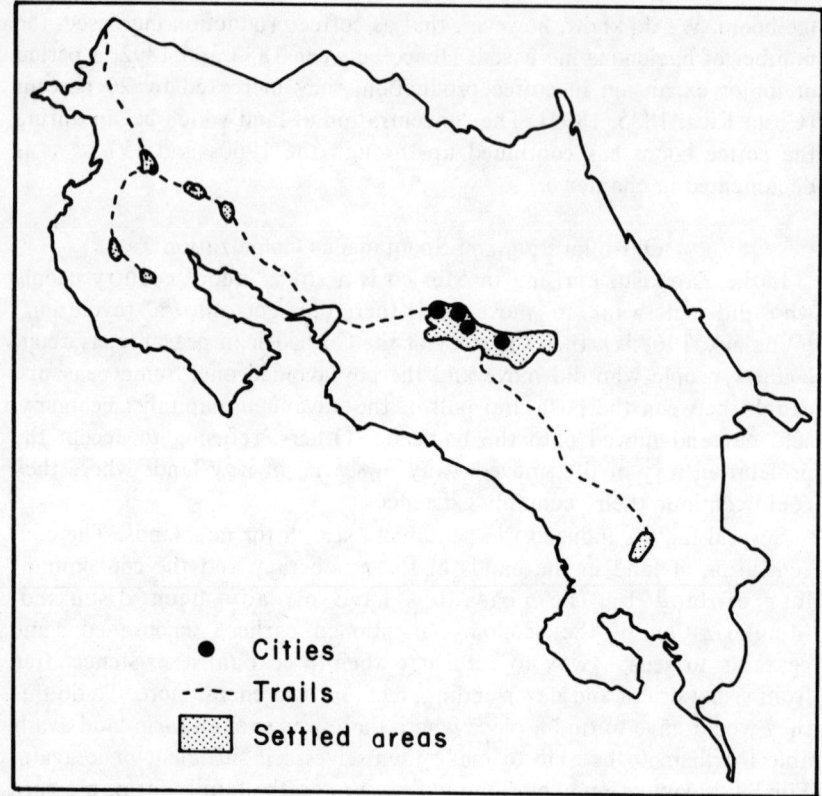

Figure 3. Population distribution, 1824
Adapted from Nunley, 1960:19

riod.[11] As mentioned above, that the newly found wealth of the country attracted immigrants, among them doctors, and with the doctors came medicines and improved public health care facilities. A study conducted in 1959 in one *cantón* indicated that this pressure persisted into the middle of the twentieth century [Montoya and Reuss, 1960:10]. It was found that in 79 percent of the cases, the father's farm had been divided up among five or more heirs, and that in 38 percent of the cases the division was among eight or more heirs.

The process of spontaneous colonization began slowly in the middle of the nineteenth century, shortly after the initiation of coffee exportation. Up until that time, the population had still been heavily concentrated on the meseta central (see figure 3). During the period 1850 to 1900, how-

[11] Fabian Dobles [1970:16-17] eloquently describes the impact of this population pressure and subsequent peasant migration in his novel *El sitio de las abras*, which is set in the year 1875.

Coffee and the Decline of the Yeoman

ever, the colonists made their first large-scale moves off the meseta and onto the Pacific lowlands to cultivate bananas (see chapter 3), onto the Guanacaste peninsula to herd cattle, and onto the highland regions of the north and south to continue to grow coffee (see figure 4). The effect of these early migrations, however, was not great in terms of changing the population distribution of the country; in 1864, 84.5 percent of the populace lived on the meseta central; by 1892 this figure had dropped by only 4 percent, to 80.1 percent [Nunley, 1960].

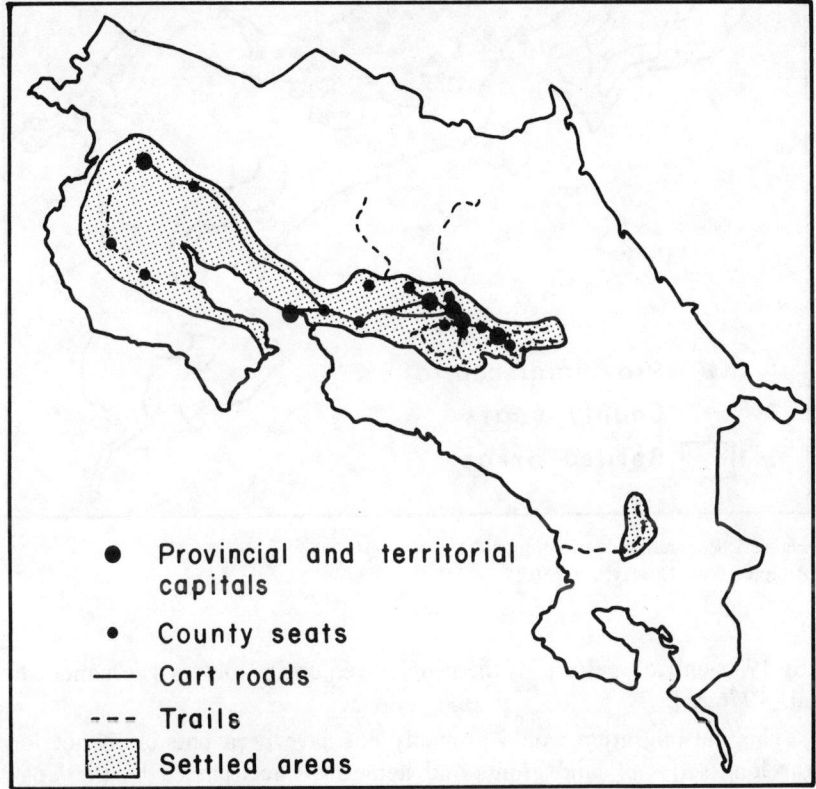

Figure 4. Population distribution, 1864
Adapted from Nunley, 1960:23

The more active movement off the meseta occurred in the period after the turn of the century. By 1927 the population of the meseta had fallen to 75.3 percent of the total population. Thus, one-fourth of the people no longer lived within its confines (see figure 5) [Nunley, 1960]. The period from 1927 to mid century has seen the most drastic shifts in population.

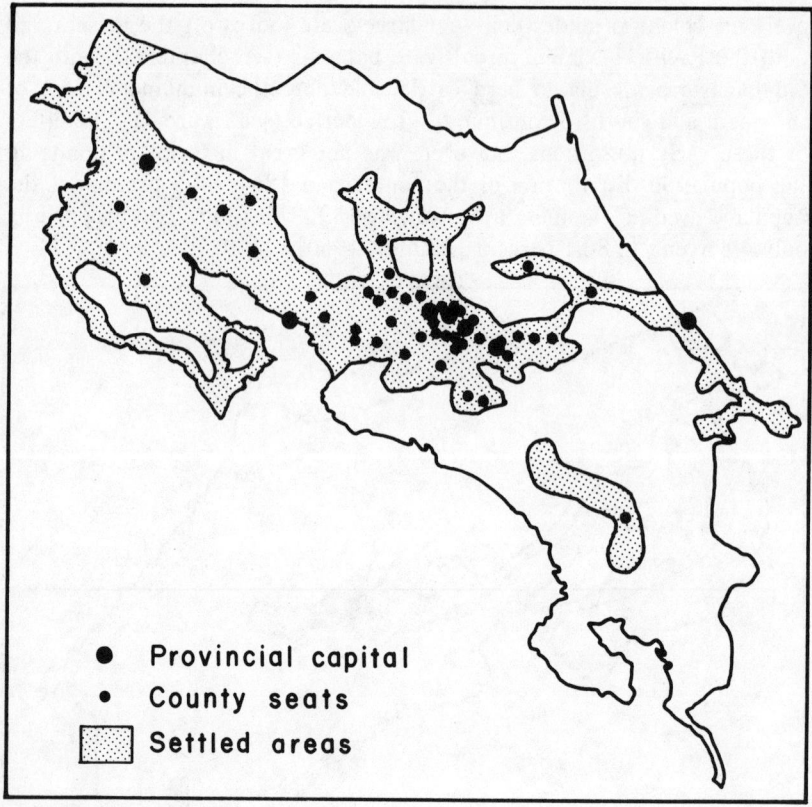

Figure 5. Population distribution, 1927
Adapted from Nunley, 1960:30

By 1973 only 57 percent of the people lived on the meseta [Fernández et al., 1976:81].

This out-migration would probably not have been possible if not for the long series of land grants and homestead acts passed by the Congress; these grants and acts encouraged those who wanted land to go out and take it. Just as the homestead acts in the United States opened up new lands for those with insufficient "elbow room" in the East, so did the Leyes de Terrenos Baldíos and Leyes de Cabezas de Familia serve the Costa Rican peasant. The first of these laws was passed in 1840, when coffee already was beginning to take a solid grip on the economy. Thus, the Decreto-Ley no. 26 of October 16, 1840, came on the heels of the laws mentioned earlier which distributed land in the area of the meseta central. In the 1840 law, land in the area of Matina, Térraba and

Sarapiquí were given away to those willing to settle there [Soley Güell, 1947:167]. Colonization in the area of Turrialba, today heavily dominated by large plantations, came as a result of the decree issued in 1841. This law gave the homesteader all the land he could cultivate, plus two times that amount if he cultivated it for ten consecutive years. In 1843, more land was given away in the Turrialba area, and in the following year San Ramón was the target. Similar decrees were issued nearly every year from 1850 to 1859.

Another stimulus for colonization came when the government, both central and municipal, used state lands for the payment of public debts owed to large coffee growers. For example, loans made to the government during its struggle to defend itself against a foreign invasion in 1856-57[12] were amortized with state land. In a similar manner, the cost of a road-building project to Limón was covered by land grants to the bondholders in 1861 [Salazar Navarrete, 1962:76-77].

The grants of land to the aristocracy opened new territories to the peasant, who, riding on the coattails of the hacendado, carved out a small piece of jungle bordering on the hacienda and called it his own. The peasant took the land, since he felt he had a right to it. The 1841 legal code stipulated, as had colonial law, that land could be acquired through a form of squatter's rights (*prescripción adquisitiva* or *prescripción positiva*), and the code of 1886 continued this procedure, the major modification being that the land so acquired had to be inscribed in the newly created Land Registry [Clark, 1971:23-25]. Registering land, however, was no easy task. First, the individual had to have occupied the land for ten years. Second, he had to have a survey plot made of the property, which required the hiring of a civil engineer and the paying of his transportation, room, and board. Few engineers, it should be noted, found it worth their time to make the long, hard trip out to some remote spot simply to survey a small piece of land. Third, the individual had to hire a lawyer to prepare the necessary legal documents. Lawyers, too, were hard to come by in the countryside. Fourth, the neighbors whose land bordered on the property in question would have to travel to the county seat, at the expense of the interested party, and testify in his behalf. Fifth, the interested party would have to have published an official announcement (in the *Gaceta Oficial*), on three separate occasions, of his intention to title the property. Finally, the local judge would have to instruct a representative to make a visual inspection of the property,

---

[12]Costa Rica was invaded by William Walker, a United States adventurer, who sought to incorporate the Central American Republics as slave states in a confederation with the American South. Walker's plan was eventually foiled, but the episode caused the rise of nationalistic sentiments in Costa Rica [Guier, 1971].

again at the solicitant's expense [Hill et al., 1964:46]. In theory, it is possible to complete this entire process in three or four months, but in reality, the average time it takes is close to four years, and it is not uncommon to encounter cases that have gone on for more than ten years. Thus, in 1970, in one judicial district alone, some two hundred land-titling applications that had been initiated in 1950 were still pending twenty years later [Saenz P. and Foster Knight, 1972:154]. A study of titling costs in one rural area indicates that the total can amount to a substantial fraction of the entire value of the property.

As a result of this complex, time-consuming, and costly procedure, few peasants were able to obtain title to their land, and thus never obtained full legal rights. This fact came to haunt the countryside, making land disputes extremely common, creating problems of economic insecurity, and facilitating squatting.

In the twentieth century, land give-aways continued under the various homestead acts. In 1909 a law was passed giving up to a maximum of fifty hectares of national land to heads of families. This law was followed by another in 1924, which contained similar provisions. Two more homestead acts were passed, one in 1934 and the other in 1939, each designed with essentially the same purposes in mind as the previous laws [Clark, 1971:28-34]. Although these laws were designed to relieve the unemployment problem which had been created by the stagnation of the coffee industry, many large landholders took advantage of them to grab more land.

Perhaps the biggest land give-away of all resulted from a law passed in 1942 (Ley de Ocupantes en Precario). This law was designed to provide relief to landholders on the meseta central whose land had been squatted on. Under this law the government would purchase lands squatted on and, in return, would give the damaged party land of equal value. Land on the tiny meseta, as has already been pointed out, was very expensive in the eighteenth century and became even more so in the twentieth, whereas the frontier regions had very little value. Consequently, many hacendados used this law to exchange small pieces of territory on the meseta for huge estates in the outlying areas. It is reported that the hacendados even hired squatters to invade their property so that they could then file a claim for the exchange lands [Clark, 1971:32].

Concentration of Production

In 1887 there were 256 beneficios in Costa Rica, or one for every 12.7 kilometers [de Andrade, 1966:143].[13] By 1940 this figure had dropped to

---

[13]This figure is based upon the calculation that the meseta central covers 3,246 square kilometers [Dirección General de Estadística y Censos, 1973a:1].

221 [Revista del Instituto de la Defensa de Café, 1940: 338-44], was down to 120 by 1966-67 [Oficina del Café, 1972:15], and by 1972 was reduced to 114 beneficios [Oficina del Café, 1973b]. Since the land area on which coffee is being planted today greatly exceeds that of 1887, each beneficio now services a considerably wider area than it once did. This fact becomes dramatically evident when it is noted that in 1973 there was one beneficio for every 2,252 square kilometers,[14] compared with one for every 12.7 square kilometers in 1887. The concentration of beneficios is even greater than these figures reveal. The figure of 114 beneficios is misleading, since it gives the impression that there are 114 separate firms. Actually, many of these beneficios are owned by the same families, and interlocking directorates are quite common. A comparison of the list of beneficios [Oficina del Café, 1973b] and the list of names of the individuals authorized to sign legal documents in the Oficina del Café (National Coffee Office) reveals that a number of names appear for more than one beneficio. By this process it is possible to reduce the number of independent beneficios by 21, leaving only 93.[15] If cousins and other relatives were counted, even more beneficios could be struck from the list, but no attempt was made to trace family ties. Unfortunately the list does not provide the full membership of the boards of directors of the beneficios, so that other multiple ownerships may have escaped detection.

What was the cause of this dramatic decline in the number of beneficios? To answer this question it must be recalled that coffee transportation requires good roads, and while the road network did undergo major improvements in the eighteenth century, it was still in a rather rudimentary state by the turn of the century. Nevertheless, the roads were adequate for the plodding oxen drawing their heavily laden carts to the local beneficio. Moreover, the distances were never more than a few kilometers between the beneficio and the furthest fields. It is, of course, no coincidence that the beneficios were so closely spaced, since if the distances between them had been greater the coffee would have begun to ferment before it reached the plant. The age of the automobile was to change all this.

Trucks made it possible for the beneficio owner to set up what are called *recibidores*, or substations, over a wide geographical area. These

[14]This figure is obtained by dividing the area of each cantón that produces at least .1 percent of the nation's crop, by the number of beneficios. This, of course, is only a rough estimate, since coffee tends to be concentrated in certain areas of the cantón and not in others.

[15]Considered to be "repeaters" are those who have the same first name and two last names, or those who merely have the same two last names (i.e., brothers or sisters).

wooden, box-like structures are built overhanging the edge of a little hill and have a chute pointing to the road below (see plate 3). The oxcarts are still in charge of hauling the coffee from the farm, but they only bring it as far as the recibidor, where they pull the load up the hill and dump the coffee onto the downward sloping floor of the box. Several times a day a truck comes along and the stored up coffee in the recibidor is emptied into it for carting to the beneficio, which may be located as far as thirty to forty kilometers away [Barrenechea Consuegra, 1956:21-22].

At first, the system of recibidores initiated a phase of competition between beneficios which proved advantageous to the small producer. With several recibidores in his area he could choose among beneficios, an option which he had not had when his choice had been dictated solely by the proximity of the beneficio. The choice could now be made on the basis of the terms offered by each beneficio. Consequently, the richer beneficios, in order to attract customers, increased the size of the advances (adelantos) and sometimes even raised the purchase price.

This felicitous situation did not last long, however, since the larger, better-financed beneficios were able to out-compete the smaller ones in their immediate area, and could thereby drive them out of business. Until World War II, however, many smaller beneficios did manage to survive, because of the nature of the world market up to that time. Up until the war most Costa Rican coffee went to the European markets, particularly England and Germany. These markets demanded a very high grade of coffee, quality being determined as much by the appearance of the bean as by its flavor in the cup; nearly all European coffee was marketed to the consumer unground, the grinding taking place only after the consumer had selected the beans he wished to purchase. In response to this market, each beneficio established, back in the nineteenth century, brand names for the coffee it produced, so that the importer could request a particular quality of coffee by its brand name. This system resulted in a confusing array of over three hundred brand names for Costa Rica alone [Jiménez Castro, 1971:213-14]; but it was well suited to the European market, since purchases were made in relatively small quantities of a few hundred sacks and buyers were able to select their favorite brand. The brands corresponded to the coffee produced in a specific part of the country; since each area differed in altitude and rainfall, it produced a slightly different quality of bean and therefore a different quality of brand. Thus, a beneficio was restrained from establishing recibidores over a very wide area by its own unwillingness to process a mixture of grades of coffee coming from different areas, since this would have resulted in the mixing of the less-costly brands with the more-expensive ones. Such mixtures received low prices in Europe. The nature of the market, therefore, kept the beneficio from casting too wide a net of recibidores.

This was all to change, however, with World War II. From the onset of the war, the European markets were closed completely to the Costa Rican coffee trade, and for that matter, to nearly all coffee produced in the hemisphere (see table 3). In order to stave off a severe economic crisis in Latin America (and also to help guarantee the loyalty of its allies), the United States agreed, on November 28, 1940, to purchase the bulk of Latin American coffee. In so doing, the United states set a single price for all the coffee coming from each individual country, refusing to distinguish among brands. The reasons for this are two-fold and readily understandable. First, the pressures of the war required as much administrative streamlining as possible for a complex operation such as this; it thus was not feasible to establish a coffee exchange in which each brand of coffee would be evaluated and priced separately. Second, and perhaps more important, the North American consumer had traditionally been used to buying coffee in its ground state, so that the appearance of the bean was an irrelevant factor in pricing. The coffee consumed in the United States, therefore, had traditionally been whatever was leftover after the European markets were satisfied. In effect, the North American consumer had long been accustomed to a fairly low-grade product [Montealegre R., 1948:69-70].

Table 3. Coffee Exports, 1940-50 (in kilograms)

Year	England	All Europe	U.S.A.	Others	Total
1940	8,568,377	10,966,087	6,876,056	336,894	18,704,132
1941	0	984,458	16,189,438	1,640,279	21,504,002
1942	2,773	951,948	14,266,255	637,311	20,672,426
1943	820	667,675	18,355,244	2,717,723	24,214,463
1944	0	649,184	14,333,938	787,121	18,778,398
1945	70	876,149	19,179,229	604,705	21,842,894
1950	24,500	6,102,260	11,962,309	758,836	19,055,471

Source: Alvarez, 1954: 14-15.

This unified price structure permitted the beneficios to mix all of their coffee together without suffering any loss of income. Now coffee from the lower, less-favorable areas could be mixed with the quality coffee coming from higher zones. As a result, the recibidores were spread over a much wider area. Inevitably, competition forced out of business the smaller, less-efficient beneficios and left the producer once again facing a monopolized market. Once the beneficio owners no longer had to worry much about competition, they could, and did, lower the prices they paid to the producers. Thus the advantage to the smallholding peasant of using the beneficio of his choice was lost during World War II.

Government Intervention

The introduction of the recibidor system and the subsequent reduction in the number of beneficios affected many larger growers as well. As a result, the peasant was not completely alone in his struggle, for the larger producers, having been forced to close down their beneficios as a result of competition from the giants, found themselves being exploited in the same way that they had once exploited the peasants. However, as a group these larger producers could exercise some pressure on the government, and began to do so as early as 1930. In that year they established the Asociación Nacional de Productores de Café, whose stated purpose was to pressure for government intervention in the relationship between producer and exporter [Barrenechea Consuegra, 1956:6]. They achieved success in 1933 when, in the depths of the economic depression, the government for the first time decided to intervene in the coffee industry, thus ending its century-old policy of laissez-faire. The Junta de Liquidaciones de Café (Settlement Board) was established, composed of one representative from the government, one from the beneficio owners, and one from the producers. The task of this junta was to set the price that each beneficio was to pay the producer; it based its calculations on the quality of the coffee and set a maximum profit for the beneficio at 12 percent [Barrenechea Consuegra, 1956:6]. At the same time, the Instituto Nacional de Defensa del Café was established, an organization designed to promote the production and sale of Costa Rican coffee.

Never before had the coffee barons been faced with government intervention in their private business affairs. Clearly, 1933 marks the date after which the power of the coffee interests no longer could be exercised with impunity. The depression forced the government to take some control over the most productive sector of the economy. An indication of the decline in power of the coffee aristocracy came in 1935 when a minimum wage law was established for coffee workers (Ley no. 157, of August 21, 1935) setting the wage at twenty-five *céntimos* an hour, and guaranteeing a minimum of six hours work a day.

Despite these infringements on their power, the coffee barons managed to retain a large measure of control over the coffee industry. In the case of the Junta de Liquidaciones, all they needed for control was two out of the three votes, and since two representatives from the coffee industry were elected by the Instituto Nacional de Defensa del Café, which in turn was dominated by the largest coffee interests, control in the Junta de Liquidaciones was easy to establish. The minimum wage laws were even easier to evade since there was inadequate enforcement machinery. Consequently, the situation for the small growers continued to become more and more desperate as the number of beneficios shrank and prices dropped. With the coming of the war and the even sharper reduction in the number of beneficios, the situation reached the limits of tolerance. Something had to be done.

The establishment of the first Costa Rican coffee cooperative in the town of Grecia, in 1943, was the growers' response to this desperate situation. Here again the larger, non-beneficio-owning producers proved to be an all-important ally of the peasants. In Grecia, at this time, the major sugar-refinery and coffee beneficio were in the hands of a German family [Facio, 1943:232]. With the outbreak of the war, the United States State Department ordered the confiscation of all Axis-power property in Costa Rica. Consequently, the German interests in Grecia were taken over by the government and later turned over to Costa Ricans in the form of a cooperative, appropriately named Victoria.

In the mid 1970s there were a total of thirty-two coffee cooperatives whose membership was over 10,000, and all but two of them were organized into a federation (Federación de Cooperativas de Caficultores, R.L.) [Víquez and López Guzmán, 1971]. Theoretically, the cooperative made it possible for the small producer to get a fair price for his crop. In some cases, however, several of these cooperatives were in deep financial trouble. In such cases peasants found that the price they received per *fanega* was even lower than that which they were getting when the beneficio had been in private hands. This low pricing would occur whenever the previous owner of the beneficio was deeply in debt to the Banco Nacional, the major source of coffee credit in Costa Rica. When it became clear that the owner would never be able to pay back the debt, the bank would foreclose on the property and offer it to the local producers in the form of a cooperative. The producers would then be told by the bank that this was their chance to end their years of exploitation. What would not always be made clear, however, was the magnitude of the debt which was being transferred to their shoulders. Since up until the early 1970s the national office of cooperatives was a department of the Banco Nacional, it clearly was not in the Bank's interest to emphasize to producers the difficulty that they might face in trying to pay off the debt of the previous owner. As soon as the cooperative got under way, however, the producers would find that all of their newly found profit was needed to pay the debt to the Bank. In one case with which I am familiar, the debt is now so large that the interest on it grows faster than the producers' annual payments are able to cover.[16] Consequently, the total grows larger each year, placing the producers deeper and deeper into debt. On the whole, however, the cooperative movement has been of great benefit to many small producers since it has finally been able to establish some equity in the relationship between producer and beneficio. There are some coffee cooperatives which are highly successful and have served to convert poverty-stricken producers into relatively prosperous ones [Centro de Estudios Democráticos de América Latina, 1971].

Credit Dependency

Costa Rica traded its colonial political dependence on Spain for economic dependence on the world coffee market [Seligson, 1977a:211-20]. Before the days of capitalist agriculture, Costa Rica had tenuous ties with the international economy, and the ups and downs of the latter had little impact on her peasantry. Once the country, and consequently the peasant, became linked to the world economic system, this isolation was destroyed. It was once said about Brazil that when New York sneezes, Brazil catches a cold. The same can be said about Costa Rica in the nineteenth century, but in this case it was Europe whose sneezing was a matter of concern. Thus, the social upheavals in France in 1848 and the depressions of 1873, 1882, 1900, and 1929, all had severe economic consequences for this Central American country [Facio, 1972:49]. High prices at the *pulperîa* (general store) prevented the peasant from accumulating any significant savings. When the crises in Europe forced down the price of coffee, what little savings the peasant had were wiped out as he dug deeper into his pockets to pay for the food he was no longer growing himself and for the imported agricultural implements he needed to work his crops.

It will be recalled that before World War II, credit for coffee production was exclusively in British hands. Each year the London coffee importers financed the new crop in order to guarantee delivery of Costa Rica's high quality coffee. Since the collateral for the credit was the coffee itself, there was very little risk involved in the transaction; nevertheless, the interest on these short-term loans proved quite profitable for the London firms. Thus, on top of the already substantial profit margins they were earning, the importers made an additional sum by extending low-risk loans to finance the crop. For Costa Rica, this meant an additional loss of profit and, hence, a loss of capital that otherwise would have been used for domestic development. The mentality of de-

[16]The details of this case are recounted in an oral history of a Costa Rican peasant [Berk-Seligson and Seligson, 1978].

pendency was so deeply entrenched in Costa Rican circles, however, that the thought of domestic financing seemed ludicrous. The events of World War II were to prove that the bankers were operating under a delusion.

The first weak attempts of the national banking system to play some role in Costa Rica's most profitable business did not come until 1932 when, due to the scarcity of capital on the world market, the Banco Internacional (today the Banco Nacional de Costa Rica) provided funds for the construction of beneficios in areas where there were none. Coffee planting had expanded, owing to outward migration, and further expansion into new zones was being hamstrung by the lack of processing facilities. Despite the fact that roads had been improved and trucks had expanded the radius from which a beneficio could receive its coffee, the fragile nature of the harvested cherries placed limits on that expansion.

Investing in beneficios, however, was not akin to financing the crop itself. The difficulty which Costa Rica was having in obtaining credit in London during the depths of the economic depression finally made it necessary for the Costa Rican government to think seriously, for the first time, about domestic financing. In 1933 a law was finally passed providing for two million colones of credit for coffee production, yet the country was so unsure about its ability to finance this small sum, one twenty-fourth of the total value of the crop of that year, that in 1934 this law was rescinded and replaced by another which reduced the financing by half [Facio, 1972:42].

By 1940 Costa Rica found that the London credit markets had completely dried up, so that emergency measures had to be taken. In that year a law was passed which, among other things, provided for domestic financing of coffee. As a result of this law, the 1940-41 crop was financed in its entirety by the national banking system [Alvarez, 1954:21]. This law meant that the banks were able to expand their financing from approximately 250,000 dollars a year in the prewar years, to over 7 million dollars in 1942-43 [Oficina del Café, 1973:23]. The fact that such a drastic change took place so easily demonstrates that Costa Rica's previous dependence on foreign financing for its coffee was based on the economic myth that it could not emit colones unless it had the prior backing of hard foreign currency (for example, pounds sterling). It had been believed that violent inflation would result from issuing colones without such backing. There was, of course, some validity to this reasoning, and the fact that the war cut Costa Rica off from most foreign imports meant that the unbacked colones issued in 1940-41 could not be used for large foreign imports.[17] Nevertheless, the measure could have

[17] I would like to thank Lic. Eduardo Lizano Fait, professor of economics at the Universidad de Costa Rica, for making this point during a personal interview [1973].

been taken many years earlier if the country had been willing to implement import restrictions. Apparently, however, this notion had never been seriously entertained.

The Concentration of Exporters

Changes in the world market have had a great impact on the structure of the export business, permitting the exporter to concentrate his power more tightly than ever before. Even in the early years of coffee production, exportation was dominated by a small group of individuals. It has been reported that in 1850 only 16 beneficios dominated 85 percent of the exports; 16 percent of the exports for that year came from one single beneficio, owned by Juan Rafael Mora, then president of Costa Rica [Hall, 1976:51].

In 1933-34, the year that the Junta de Liquidaciones was established and consequently the first year for which solid data are available, there were 194 exporters operating in Costa Rica. By 1941, the first year of Costa Rica's entry into the War, this figure had shrunk to 81, and by 1945 it stood at only 13. The reason for this change, as already hinted at above, was the war. It will be recalled that because of the hostilities in Europe, it was impossible for Costa Rica to ship any substantial quantity of her coffee there. Instead, nearly all Costa Rican coffee was sold to the United States (see table 3). As a consequence, export houses which had long-established ties in Europe but no links to the U.S. market found themselves out of business. What occurred at this point was a general consolidation of the export houses into a few giant operations with firm links to the U.S. market. For example, one new firm, called The Costa Rica Coffee House, unknown in the 1930s, exported nearly one-third of all Costa Rican coffee in 1944-45, making it far and away the largest exporter.

One would expect that with the war over, there would have been a reestablishment of the old European-oriented firms, since Costa Rica once again shifted a large share of its exports back to the lucrative European market. Surprisingly, in 1973 there were only 24 export houses in existence, even though about 75 percent of Costa Rican coffee fills European cups [Oficina del Café, 1973c:25]. This small number demonstrates that, even though the export market has returned to its prewar structure, most of the firms which once did business with Europe have not been revived. Of the 24 export houses which existed in 1975, at least 4 had easily identifiable interlocking directorates. Thus, at most, coffee exports are in the hands of 19 private firms plus the federation of cooperatives (which is responsible for approximately one-eighth of total exports), for a total of 20.

It is difficult to understand precisely why the export market is restricted to so few houses. When asked why they no longer export, beneficio owners state that it is simply too complicated a business. One suspects, however, that there must be more to it than that, since complications have never kept eager entrepreneurs from earning a profit. This is particularly true in the case of an export business which is so highly profitable. According to the law enacted in 1965 [Jiménez Castro, 1971:83-134], the exporter is allowed a net profit of 2.5 percent [Jiménez Castro, 1971:110]. This percentage would amount to 1,843,246 dollars or an average of 92,162 dollars per exporter (counting 20) in 1971-72. It is generally known that this 2.5 percent limit is frequently exceeded, since it is impossible to learn exactly what price the importer actually paid the exporter. The contracts themselves are strictly confidential according to law [Jiménez Castro, 1971:103], and subject to review only by the Oficina del Café.

An examination of the composition of the board of the Oficina del Café reveals why its supervision of exporters' profits might be lax. The board is composed of six members, one representative each from the government, the beneficio owners, the local roasters (*torrefactores*), and the exporters, and two from the producers [Jiménez Castro, 1971:121-22]. Since there is no stipulation to the contrary, nothing prevents the member representing the producers from simultaneously being a beneficio owner, roaster, and exporter. Since many of the economically strongest coffee barons have operations in all sectors of the coffee business, the "representative" nature of the Oficina del Café is really a facade. The peasant producer, of course, plays no role at all. In the 1961 law [Jiménez Castro, 1971:61] there was a provision that at least one member of the then six-man board be a representative of the Federation of Cooperatives, but that position was eliminated in a 1965 reform. One might surmise that the representative of the cooperatives turned out to have interests quite incompatible with those of the other members of the board and that therefore he had to be eliminated. The only other troublesome element on the board was the representative of the government, and although (for political reasons) he could not be removed, as had been the representative of the cooperative sector, the 1965 revision made the government representative an ex-officio member. The Oficina del Café, designed to regulate the relationship between producer, beneficio owner, and exporter, behaves as most regulatory agencies in the United States do [Edelman, 1964]; that is, the regulated end up doing the regulating.

The law on exports [Jiménez Castro, 1971:100-101] further helps explain the limitation on the number of exporters. The law specifies that all exporters must post a bond of between 5,000 dollars and 20,000 dollars with the Oficina del Café, to protect the beneficio owner, who turns his coffee over to the exporter and then awaits payment until the exporter himself is paid, and also to protect the government (which permits exportation before taxes are paid). Those who post the bond of 5,000 dollars may export up to twenty times that amount of coffee, and those who post the maximum bond of 20,000 dollars may export an unlimited amount of coffee. It is apparent that the bond is far too small to protect the beneficio owners adequately. At the same time, however, it does serve to prevent small exporters (that is, potential competition) from getting into the business, since it requires a deposit of a fair amount of cash, by Costa Rican standards. In addition, the fact that there is no upper limit for the largest exporters gives this group a further advantage.

Urbanization and the Struggle over Taxation

In the preceding section it was demonstrated that the coffee aristocracy, made up of the beneficio owners and exporters, underwent a consolidation of its ranks in the twentieth century by driving out the weaker competitors. In so doing it increased the pressure of its stranglehold on the peasant and left him less and less room in which to maneuver with each passing decade. But just as the peasant has been squeezed in this century, so too has the coffee aristocracy itself, which finds that its once dominant economic and political position is being eroded by the increasingly pluralistic nature of Costa Rican society, a society to which it has not successfully adjusted.

Oddly enough, agrarian capitalism, which had served the colonial aristocracy so well by providing it with the economic basis for underwriting its political and social power, ultimately proved to undermine some of that power. It will be recalled that the colony was impoverished, perhaps the poorest in all of Latin America. For this reason, few who left Spain for the New World selected Costa Rica as their destination. The 113 Spanish settlers (no more than forty families) listed as making up the total population of the colony in 1569, contained the tiny nucleus of the Costa Rican aristocracy. These people, isolated from all outside contact, intermarried quite frequently and consequently produced a very tightly knit line of descendants. Throughout the colonial period this small group, living mainly in and around the town of Cartago, held the reins of power in the colonial administration. Royal commissions were given to them by default, since they were the only aristocrats in the colony and no new members of their caste were willing to go there.

With the coming of independence, this same group took control over the new government. And control it they did. Few democratic systems in the world have had power so tightly concentrated in the hands of so few.

Coffee and the Decline of the Yeoman 43

A recent study [Stone,1971a;1971b;1975] has shown that 33 of the 44 people who have served as president of the country from 1821 until 1970 were descendants of three of the original settlers, and that 350 of the 1,300 representatives who have served in the legislative assembly during this period were descendants of four of these families. One single family, that of the conqueror Juan Vázquez de Coronado, has produced 18 presidents and 230 *diputados*! Stone [1969] has also discovered that it was these same individuals who became the coffee barons. Since it was this group which had been at the forefront of the search for a source of wealth for the colony, it is not at all surprising that when coffee was hit upon, they played a dominant role in its exploitation. The picture that emerges of the nineteenth century is that of a society in which political, social, and economic power were coterminous.

This situation remained essentially unaltered throughout the nineteenth century, although by the end of that century signs of change could be noted. Coffee injected an enormous amount of capital into the system and, as a consequence, the simple two-class system of aristocracy and yeomanry began to become more differentiated. As was pointed out earlier, agrarian capitalism was the prism through which this fused society passed during the last century. What emerged was a society with an entirely new, pluralistic social structure. The differentiation of the peasantry into landed and landless has already been discussed and will be elaborated upon further in chapter 4. The rise of the middle class, a new element in the Costa Rican social equation, was to place new burdens on the wealth produced by coffee.

Before the introduction of coffee there were no urban centers in Costa Rica. In fact, the census data of 1700 report only one town, Cartago, as having a population of over 2,000 [Nunley, 1960:49]. One hundred and sixty-four years later, that same town had grown by only some 600 residents. At that time, in 1864, the largest town in Costa Rica, San José, reported a population of 5,533 people. Of the 120,499 residents of the country, 81 percent were living in rural areas [Costa Rica, 1868]. It can be seen that in 1864 Costa Rica was still a highly rural country. Its provinciality is attested to by the fact that there were only three bankers and seven doctors in the entire country at this time [Costa Rica, 1868:86-87].

The concentration of people in towns occurred only with the entrenchment of coffee as the mainstay of the economy. As the plantations expanded and small farmers were squeezed out, many moved to the cities, where they took up jobs in the secondary and tertiary sectors. The towns grew, but the growth was spectacular neither in its rapidity nor in its magnitude [Gibson,1970:135-48]. Yet the development of what may be called quasi-urban areas saw the creation of a small urban middle class composed of merchants, laborers, and government employees. The merchant sector received its impetus from the import/export business that was generated by coffee. New items were brought to the country by the never-ending stream of ships docking at Puntarenas. An urban labor force developed as a response to the demands created in the population centers. A small group of government employees, mainly bookkeepers and minor functionaries, was created when the government began to exercise a few limited state functions related to the control of the import/export business (tariff collection, for instance). In 1883 we find, out of a total population of 182,073, a merchant "class" composed of 652 wholesalers and retailers; a working "class" composed of 70 bakers, 358 shoemakers, and 419 carpenters; and a bureaucracy composed of 786 public employees [Costa Rica, 1885:70-90]. Physicians increased from 7 in 1868 to 35 in 1883. The peasants, however, continued to predominate. As late as 1950, only 34 percent of the population lived in urban areas, but by 1973 this figure had risen to 42 percent [Fernández et al., 1976:84]. The pace of urban growth, which during the period 1864-1927 equaled that of rural growth (2.2 percent), far exceeded it in the period 1927-50 (4.9 percent compared to 1.4 percent).

We see, therefore, that with the coming of agrarian capitalism the towns began to grow, and with them came the development of new social groups. These groups, whose interests were often not congruent with those of the coffee aristocracy, began to demand a say in the government. At first these demands were so weak that they could be successfully ignored by the coffee interests. Furthermore, up to the end of the last century coffee continued to act as the motor of the country's economic growth, and therefore harsh criticism of the oligarchy was perceived as inappropriate. This growth, however, was dependent upon forces external to the Costa Rican system, namely, the world market. As long as that market stayed firm, Costa Rica continued to prosper. Whenever world economic crises produced sudden drops in foreign exchange earnings, that prosperity was seriously eroded. Thus when in 1882, 1900, and 1914 the world price of coffee declined, Costa Rica experienced major unemployment. The small but growing middle class in the cities was hurt badly by the slumps, since its economic position depended on the circulation of capital earned from the sale of coffee. This group now began to have a legitimate basis for its complaints against the coffee oligarchy.

The only sure way that the city dweller could isolate himself from crises was to obtain a government job, which meant, above all, security, a commodity desperately desired by the nascent middle class. The coffee aristocracy running the government had always sought to keep government small, however. Expansion of government not only contradicted the classic liberal philosophy of laissez-faire, which they professed, but also meant that they themselves would have to bear most of the costs of government growth, since they were the only ones with incomes large enough to be taxed. Thus throughout the nineteenth century, when the aristocracy held a firm grip on the political system, budgets were kept to an absolute minimum. Expenditures of the central government, which stood at 24,000 colones in 1826, rose to 1,620,000 colones forty-nine years later in 1875. That is, expenditures went from approximately 1.7 colones per capita to 13.5 per capita. This increase was possible entirely because of the income earned through customs duty, not because of direct taxation of the coffee industry. The first tax on coffee did not appear until 1841, when the symbolic charge of one real per quintal was levied. Even though in 1855 this was raised to two reales, the tax was still a minor one. It was not until thirty-five years later that another tax was finally voted on coffee and this was a tax of twenty céntimos a quintal [Oficina del Café, 1954:15] to pay for the construction of the national theater, a long-desired addition to the aristocracy's cultural life. The theater was not designed to provide entertainment for the masses but was a very exclusive affair.[18] The aristocracy, therefore, was merely taxing itself to provide for its own cultural needs.

The first radical departure from this hands-off policy was made in 1893, when because of a severe balance of payments crisis created by world coffee prices, the legislative assembly voted a tax of six shillings per quintal in order to help pay the interest on the foreign debt. What is significant about this tax is the reasoning that was used to implement it. Article 4 of the law states the following: "Notwithstanding the desires of the Government to protect the agriculture of the country in order that it achieve its greatest development, in the present circumstances it is necessary to ask of it the resources that the Nation needs" [Oficina del Café, 1954:20]. For the first time, profits in the coffee industry were recognized as an acceptable target of state taxation to help bail out the nation in times of need. It should be added, however, that the proceeds from this tax were destined exclusively for the payment of interest on the for-

---

[18]This fact is clearly indicated by the layout of the building, which has two entrances. The orchestra and lower-tier seats are entered by way of the front entrance of the theater, which leads into an ornate marble, red-velvet-carpeted lobby. The upper balcony seats, in contrast, are reached through an obscure alley entrance which leads to a dimly lit staircase. There is not even a pretense of a lobby. Furthermore, in glaring contrast to the plush, velvet-upholstered seats below, the balcony seats are simply long wooden benches. It was not until the mid 1970s that plans were made for a "popular theater," to be located ten blocks from the national theater. That theater was finally opened in 1978.

eign debt and, therefore, could not be used for social programs or for the expansion of the state bureaucracy. Moreover, only eight months later, the tax was cut by one-third, "with the goal of improving in whatever way possible the condition of the exporters . . ." [Oficina del Café, 1954:20]. Nevertheless, the 1893 law opened the way toward increasing taxation. In 1898, the state set up its own official coffee-classifying agent, who was to decide which coffee would have to pay the export tax (the low-quality, low-profit coffee called *terceras* was specifically exempted under that law). The establishment of this agency was crucial, since it meant that the government now had the right to challenge the exporters' classification. From this point on, the government established its role in the previously untouchable area of exporting.

As a reaction to government intervention in the coffee business, a law was passed in 1914 prohibiting the imposition of any new taxes on coffee for the next twenty years, but in that same year, almost as an indicator of the aristocracy's growing impotence, the law was repealed. As a result of international marketing problems caused by World War I, a new tax of 2.30 dollars was imposed for each quintal of coffee exported. This tax was lowered in 1917 to 1.50 dollars. In 1937 an 8 percent ad valorum tax with a 1.50 dollar upper limit was established [Oficina del Café, 1954:24-25]. The most stunning blow of all hit the landed aristocracy in 1939 when the first land tax in Costa Rican history was imposed. Although the rate was low, what was particularly hard for the aristocracy to bear about this tax was its progressive nature, since the more valuable the property, the higher the tax rate. Moreover, there was a special surcharge levied against uncultivated land which specifically penalized those hacendados who were not making full use of their estates [Oficina del Café, 1954; Kalnins, 1972:7]. Owing to difficulties in administering it and a general unwillingness to pay it, however, it was never collected.

Thus between 1890 and the first decades of the twentieth century, the coffee industry lost its immunity to taxation. It is quite clear that this could not have happened if it had still controlled the political system as completely as it had during the first century of the coffee boom. Evidence of the loss of control is provided by Stone [1971a:115], who demonstrates that after 1900, the proportion of diputados in the legislative assembly who came from the elite families began to decline. The once-unified and omnipotent aristocracy was now beginning to break up and lose its control over the political system. New power bases were developing in urban areas with sufficient power to elect their own representatives to the assembly; once elected, these representatives would begin to tax the only major source of wealth: the coffee industry. In

1910 Ricardo Jiménez Oreamuno was elected president. Although he was a member of the coffee aristocracy, he was the first president to actively seek the support of the rural areas. Moreover, after his election Jiménez eliminated the electoral college system and substituted the direct election of the president. Thus began a revolution of popular participation which was to weaken further the grip of the aristocracy [Rodríguez Vega, 1974:97-121; Chacón Pacheco, 1975:164-69]. By 1927 San José had grown to over fifty thousand and the number of diputados in the legislative assembly stood at fifty-two, thirty-two more than in the previous century.

By the first quarter of the twentieth century Costa Rica was finally emerging into the modern world. In the course of a few short years her isolation from the once-irrelevant ideologies of popular participation and socially responsive government dissolved. The world economic depression of the thirties only accelerated this process. The Communist Party, founded in 1931, cultivated supporters in the banana regions, as is shown in the next chapter [Herrera García et al., 1971:33]. The populist leader Dr. Rafael Angel Calderón Guardia, elected president in 1940, established the social security system, the labor code, and social guarantees (eight-hour work day, right to unionize, minimum wage, etc.) [Creedman, 1971]. Also in 1940 the Centro Para el Estudio de Problemas Nacionales, the student group which was to lay the ideological foundations for the Revolution of 1948, was founded [Aguilar Bulgarelli, 1969:56; Bell, 1971:14-15, 34-38]. That revolution was to alter fundamentally the nature of Costa Rican politics, initiating a system primarily tailored to meet the needs of an ever-growing middle class by expanding tremendously the size of the government bureaucracy. Between 1960 and 1975 the number of public employees increased from 32,000 to 100,000, an annual rate of 7.9 percent compared to an increase in the economically active population of only 3.5 per cent annually [Arias Sánchez, 1976:244]. In the new political system the coffee aristocracy saw its economic power declining. While in the last century coffee made up 60 percent to 90 percent of foreign exchange earnings [Facio, 1972:48], in the 1970s those earnings have dropped to around 25 percent [Dirección General de Estadística y Censos, 1972], as other agricultural exports (such as bananas, cattle, and sugar) have increased in importance. Beginning in 1963, with Costa Rica's entrance into the Central American Common Market, a new industrial sector was created which further reduced the importance of coffee. Interestingly enough, Stone [1973] has found that the coffee aristocracy played an almost insignificant role in this industrialization, indicating that it was incapable of making the transition from coffee to newer, more profitable forms of investment.

Summary

Three central facts emerge from the previous discussion: first, by the 1970s the coffee aristocracy, which had once comprised the unchallenged social, economic, and political leadership of the country, was eclipsed by a new coalition of political and economic interests catering primarily to the needs of a growing middle class. Second, despite its decline in power in the national political scene, the coffee aristocracy managed to tighten its already firm control over the coffee industry and, by dint of that control, to retain a firm grip on a large sector of the Costa Rican peasantry. Third, even though year by year, increasing numbers of Costa Ricans have been incorporated into the economically comfortable middle class with its "cradle to grave" social security system and guaranteed job security in the bloated bureaucracy, the peasantry continues to move irreversibly downward. The fitting together of these three factors provides us with a critical key to understanding the development of modern Costa Rica. That key is the realization that it is the peasantry which bore the cost of economic development in the past and continues to do so in the present. Therefore, it is on the peasants' back that the coffee aristocracy and the growing middle class ride.

Economic development relies upon the generation of an investable capital surplus [Malloy, 1971:24]. Since the introduction of agrarian capitalism in Costa Rica in the beginning of the last century, coffee has produced this surplus and therefore the economy has had the potential for growth. However, the accumulation of such a surplus in economically dependent countries is exceedingly difficult, because much of that surplus is skimmed off and transferred to the industrial nations [Johnson, 1972]. To the extent that there has been economic development in Costa Rica, it has been a product of the ability of the elites to extract an even greater surplus from the underlying peasantry, while at the same time restricting the peasantry from partaking of the benefits of that developed society. The banana industry, which developed at the turn of the century, offered the nation a potential source of wealth which, if it had been properly chanelled, would have greatly assisted economic growth. As we shall see in the following chapter, the coffee aristocracy refused to take advantage of this potential and allowed the gargantuan profits brought by banana exports to slip through its fingers. The peasantry, on the other hand, found at least temporary salvation on the steamy banana plantations. Let us now turn to this next development in agrarian capitalism.

3 Bananas and the Rise of the Rural Proletarian

Bananas are a historical by-product of the coffee industry in Costa Rica. In this chapter it will be shown how the coffee industry led to the banana industry, and more important, what effect bananas have had on the economy and on the peasantry. As far as the economy is concerned, a century of large-scale, highly profitable banana cultivation has had little impact on capital accumulation and, hence, on economic development. With reference to the peasantry, two themes will be developed. First, it will be shown how the banana industry gave relief to a moribund, coffee-based economy by providing an escape valve for labor no longer needed there. Second, it will be shown how the banana workers proved to be the sector of the peasantry most susceptible to unionization.

Coffee Gets Its Railroad

Since it was an export crop, it would have been ideal if coffee could have been grown along the Atlantic coast; such an arrangement would have made transportation costs to the port and shipping expenses to Europe as low as possible. Unfortunately, coffee is a highland crop and will not grow well in the steamy coastal lowlands. As production increased, the problem of shipping tons of coffee from the highlands down to the coast became more and more acute. Moreover, since the route to the Atlantic port was so hazardous, all coffee was carted to the more distant Pacific port of Puntarenas, and from there shipped to Europe via a circuitous trip around Cape Horn. It is reported that the sea voyage took between 130 and 140 days, and cost some five pounds sterling per quintal, whereas a trip from the Pacific port of Limón cut the time by almost three months, and brought the price down to two pounds [González Flores, 1933:22-23; Nunley, 1960:25]. Clearly, a route to the Atlantic was needed, and since this was the heyday of the iron horse, a railroad was the method of transportation chosen.

Constructing a rail system from the meseta to the Atlantic port was no easy task. The jungle which separated the two was one of the densest in the world, owing to rainfall that exceeded fifteen feet a year. In addition, malaria, yellow fever, and dysentary were commonplace. Thus the area was extremely unattractive for laborers accustomed to the salubrious climate of the meseta. As a consequence, Costa Rica at first abandoned the idea of an Atlantic railroad and attempted to construct a railroad to the Pacific port, despite the higher maritime transportation costs. In 1854, Juan Rafael Mora Porras, president of Costa Rica at the time, decreed that Joaquín Jiménez had the exclusive right to use "carros de cuatro ruedas" on a route to the Pacific. In that same year the Congress authorized the construction of a wooden or iron railroad to the port, and in 1857 the first nine miles were finished between Puntarenas and Barranca. This small stretch of track was to be the first railroad in Central America and also earned the dubious distinction of being the first failure. It was not designed for the iron horse, but for animal power: it was baptized the "Burrocar." But the poor burro was able to manage no more than two miles an hour with the car empty. Attention was once again focused on the Atlantic port [Garrido Guerrero, 1968:4-5].

Costa Rica secured the services of the German engineer Francisco Kurtze, who succeeded in mapping out the first Atlantic to Pacific railroad route; his plan was so well designed that, with only minor modifications, it is the route over which the present coast-to-coast railroads still travel. In 1866, President Castro Madríz authorized Kurtze to negotiate with a New York concern to finance the construction of a railroad to the Atlantic. Kurtze, however, had no success in the endeavor. He negotiated a contract with John C. Fremont and his associates in 1866, but it eventually became obvious that Fremont was not going to build the railroad, and the contract was terminated in February, 1868 [Macune, Jr., 1963:16-18]. In 1869 a contract was signed with Edward Reilly for an interoceanic railroad, but this too proved fruitless. The following year, after a military coup, General Tomás Guardia Gutiérrez took power and promised Costa Ricans that he would build the railroad, in his words, to bring the country to the "*tierra prometida.*" Thus, in 1871, Guardia arranged the first railroad construction loan from a European firm.

A total lack of experience in matters of international finance on Costa Rica's part meant that the Guardia loan, and several that followed, were failures. The first loan, for example, was for 1 million pounds sterling, but only 450,000 of the total actually reached Costa Rica. The lenders retained 200,000 pounds as their commission for floating the bonds, even though there was almost no risk involved for them in the proposition [González Víquez, 1914:187-232; Soley Güell, 1940:56 Macune, Jr., 1963:34-36]. Since the net amount obtained by the loan was far too little to finance the construction of the massive project (the initial estimate was 1.6 million pounds), a new loan for the sum of 2.4-million pounds was made through a group of French and British financiers, but this loan turned out to be even more disadvantageous to Costa Rica than the previous one, since only 900,000 pounds of the total actually ended up in Costa Rican hands. This time, however, the borrowers were not going to be fooled (or so they thought): they hired a law firm to sue the lenders. The case was drawn out over six full years and in the end, after paying 400,000 pounds in lawyers fees, Costa Rica lost. Thus, the total gain on this 2.4 million pound loan was a trifling 500,000 pounds. With the two loans combined, Costa Rica had obtained 1.3 million pounds (out of 3.4 million), or a bit less than 7 million dollars. To this was added 15 million dollars from her own budget during the period 1870 to 1882. This was an enormous sum for the small country, representing nearly half of its entire state income for this period [Soley Güell, 1940:57]. But railroad fever was high, and the money lenders in London seemed to be quite aware that Costa Rica was ready to pay almost any price.

While the loans were being secured, Guardia turned his attention to the question of the construction itself. He sent his Minister of Public Works to Lima, Peru to negotiate with Henry Meiggs, the famed railroad builder of the Andes [Kepner, Jr., 1936:37; Soley Güell, 1940:57]. A contract was signed in 1871 for 1.6 million pounds sterling and the project was ready to begin. First, however, Guardia received an 800,000 dollar kickback from Meiggs—a fact which he was later to admit openly, stating that it was not a kickback but "an act of pure generosity" on the part of Meiggs [Stewart, 1964:11-12]. Despite the kickback, Meiggs himself had no intention of building the railroad, since he was so heavily committed in Peru. He signed the contract only to lend prestige to it (and earn a fat commission), and the very same day turned it over to his nephew, Henry Meiggs Keith.

The first rails were laid in late 1871. From an engineering standpoint, it would have made sense to begin the railroad at the port and move upland, using the already constructed lengths of track to haul supplies to the most forward point. For political reasons, however, this could not be done. An enormous amount of public distrust had already built up in San José over the railroad. It should be remembered that up to that time nobody had ever seen an iron horse, but everyone had heard of the enormous debts that the public treasury was incurring. Thus, in order to win public confidence, the first locomotive was actually hauled by oxcart from Puntarenas to Alajuela (a trip that lasted three months) where it made its first run [Kepner,Jr., 1936:38; Stewart, 1964:22-24; Zúñiga Huete, 1928:76]. With that show over, the serious and difficult job of hacking a railroad line through the forbidding Atlantic jungle began. The work was painfully slow, as mud slides produced by the incredibly heavy rains washed out sections of the newly completed roadbed. Rivers were forded, bridges built, and then floods would wash away months of work. The three years planned for building the railroad were extended to five, then to ten, and finally to nineteen years.

Minor C. Keith, brother of Henry Meiggs Keith, had been placed in charge of the railroad company stores in Costa Rica. The young Keith turned out to be an able railroad builder, and more important, a very astute businessman. In 1884 he persuaded the government to sign the now infamous Soto-Keith contract. Under the terms of this agreement, Keith absorbed the English debt and promised to finish within three years the remaining 52 miles of the railroad's 142 miles. In return, Keith was granted a 99-year lease on the railroad, 800,000 acres in state lands in any part of the country (almost 8 percent of the entire area of Costa Rica), exemption from taxes on the land for twenty years, and exemptions from import duty on all construction materials used to build and maintain the railbed, cars, and engines [Archivo Nacional, 1884].

The Soto-Keith contract eventually became the mainstay of the banana monopoly. In 1886, under the terms of the contract, Keith organized the Costa Rica Railway Co., Ltd., which took charge of completing the line and then, when it was completed, of administering its operations [Zúñiga Huete, 1928:77]. The government of Costa Rica at first retained control of one-third of the shares of this company. This control was lost, however, in 1899, when the government found itself unable to repay a loan contracted with Barring Brothers. Keith came to the government's rescue, lending it 75,000 dollars; he accepted the government-held shares of the railway as collateral. Unfortunately, before the Keith loan came due, he sold his shares to a third party and, in this way, Costa Rica lost all control of the railway [Woodbridge, 1961:273].

After nearly half a century of hopes, nineteen years of construction work, and a loss of lives which is estimated at 4,000 for the first twenty miles alone, the railroad was finally completed in 1890 [Stewart, 1964:43]. It was a great day for Costa Rica. Fast, low-cost transportation to Europe was finally available. Now coffee could reach the London exchanges in a matter of weeks instead of months.

After a few decades the victory of the railroad took on a hollow ring. First of all, the Panama Canal was opened in 1914, so the trip around the Horn was no longer necessary.[1] Second, the rates charged by Keith on his railroad were a good deal higher than had been anticipated, so that the savings in transportation from San José to the port were negligible. Third, owing to the high rainfall in the Atlantic side, many bags of coffee were ruined either on the train or in the warehouses of Limón [Hall, 1976:67-68]. All this aside, Costa Rica now had its railroad and therefore considered itself a modern nation, for in those days having a railroad was equated with modernity. But the most important impact that the railroad had on Costa Rica was not even vaguely perceived in 1890; it indirectly provided a reservoir of employment for the mass of landless peasants who had lost their lands to the expanding coffee haciendas. Thus, considered from this point of view, the railroad turned out to be a boon for the coffee industry after all, by saving it and the society which it supported from the destabilizing impact of massive unemployment. Exactly how this came about will be discussed below.

The Railroad Transports Yellow Gold

Minor Keith, as has been mentioned, was an excellent businessman—one who did not miss an opportunity for profit. Keith reasoned that until the last link of the railroad between the meseta and the port was completed, very little, if any, coffee would be shipped. Lack of shipments meant that his line would not earn a single penny until its completion, unless, of course, he could transport some other commodity produced in the region where the track had already been laid. Bananas proved to be the answer.

Bananas had been exported from Jamaica as early as 1870. The demand in foreign markets for the novel tropical fruit far exceeded supply, and the price per bunch was consequently quite high. Observing this, Keith began to plant the fruit, introducing a variety called "Gros Michel" that was superior in quality to the type then being grown on the meseta.

In 1879, the year that he obtained his railroad contracts, Keith exported his first bunches of Costa Rican bananas. He then organized the Tropical Trading and Transport Company, one of a score of companies operating in the banana business at that time [Kepner, Jr., 1936:36-39;

[1] Hall [1976:69] reports, however, that few exporters used the canal route.

Garrido Guerrero, 1968:9; Stewart, 1964:144-48]. Keith went into heavy debt to finance his banana operations. Unfortunately for him, his distributors in New Orleans went bankrupt, and he lost some 1.5 million dollars. He then approached the successful Boston Fruit Company, banana exporters in the Caribbean, and arranged to have it distribute his fruit; the two concerns merged operations in 1899, and the United Fruit Company was born [Garrido Guerrero, 1968:9-10]. The operation was successful, and banana exports skyrocketed (see figure 6). The profits from the bananas far exceeded those earned from the railway; coffee freight paled into insignificance in comparison with the huge quantities of bananas being exported. In a matter of a few years the United Fruit Company dominated banana production in Colombia, Panama, Honduras, and Guatemala, as well as in Costa Rica.

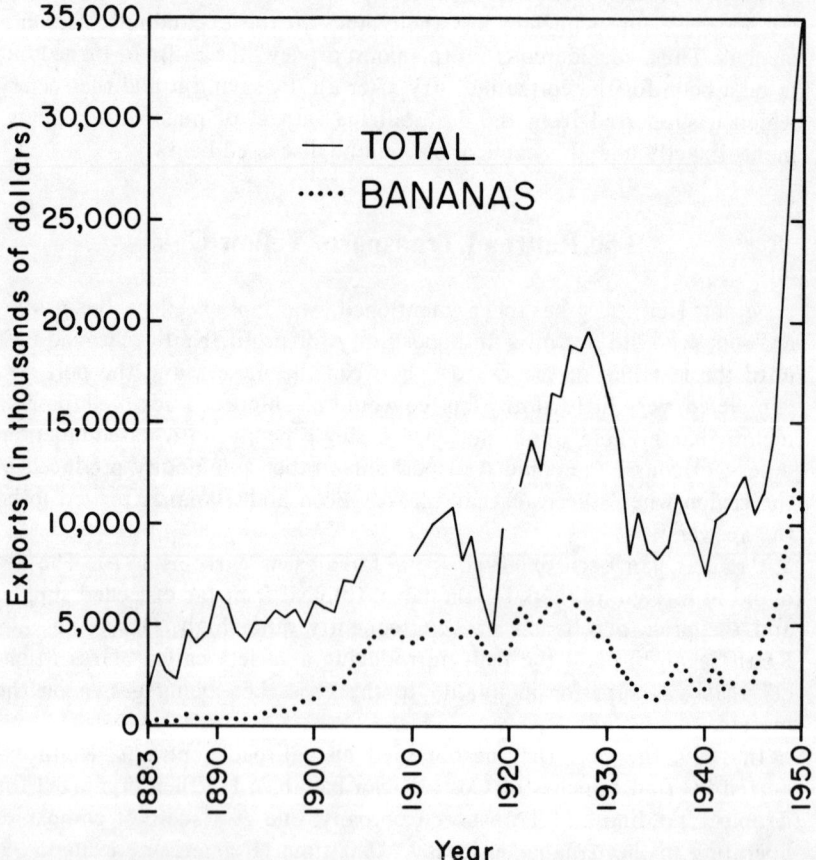

Figure 6. Banana production
Sources: Facio, 1972:55; May and Plaza, 1958; Dirección General de Estadística y Censos, 1973b.

Keith was not the only producer of bananas in the area, however; several Costa Ricans were attempting to establish themselves as producers. As early as 1884, 305 small banana farms existed in the region [Hernández, 1975:188]. The small producers, of course, owned neither a railroad nor a fleet of banana boats and consequently had to sell all their fruit to Keith, who either owned or controlled (through leasing arrangements) both of these means of transport. Using monopolistic practices made famous by John D. Rockefeller and Andrew Carnegie in the United States, Keith developed a system of differential railroad rates and services for the bananas which he himself grew. For example, Keith's bananas were charged thirteen cents for transportation, whereas all other producers had to pay twenty cents. In addition, the trains would stop at any point along the line to pick up Keith's bananas, a privilege extended to no other producer. This did not sit well with the local growers. They protested to the Costa Rican government and to the Costa Rica Railway Company, which was administered by Keith and leased to the London stockholders. As a consequence, by the close of the nineteenth century Keith found himself in conflict with the growers, the government of Costa Rica, and the board of directors of the Railway. They all objected to the preferential treatment given to his bananas [Stewart, 1964:152].

Keith was undaunted by this three-pronged attack. Rather than capitulate to the protests, he sought instead to increase his control over the banana business by establishing his own rail line in the plantation areas. In 1900 he organized a new railroad corporation, the Northern, designed to compete with the Costa Rica Railway for local banana freight. In 1901 the Northern Railroad took over two government contracts from Tropical Trading and Transport Co., another Keith operation [Stewart:135-43]. These were the Vargas-Schutt contract of 1892, for the construction and operation of a feeder railway between the port of Limón and Río Banano, a few miles to the south, and the Pacheco-Hoadley contract of 1894, for the construction of a branch railroad from Matina to Río Banano. At this time Keith did not have permission to cross the lines of the Costa Rica Railway; nor did he have permission to build a wharf at the terminus of the rail line, permission which the other railway did have. As a result, popular sentiment was so hostile toward the Costa Rica Railway Co. that the Northern was viewed as healthy competition. Small producers in particuar viewed the development of a competing rail line with considerable favor, hoping that they would be given lower freight rates and better service. In 1902 the Pacheco-Pacheco contract was signed, granting to the newly formed Northern Railroad the concessions it needed to compete with the Costa Rica Railway Co. [Woodbridge, 1961:275; Stewart, 1964:136-37, 153].

Keith began shipping all of his bananas on his new railroad, charging himself whatever he pleased for the freight. Once the Costa Rica Railway lost its largest customer, it was only a matter of time before it was forced to sell out to Keith, and in 1905 the deal was made. The Costa Rica Railway sold its lease for the unexpired portion of the 99-year contract to the Northern. Keith now had exclusive control over the banana transportation system. The government of Costa Rica protested; the 99-year lease signed with Keith in 1884 specifically stated that the right to the railroad was not transferable. The government refused to recognize the legality of the transfer, but it was a *fait acompli*, and nothing was done to change it [Molina, Rivera and Lyra, 1934; Kepner, 1935:50]. Hence by 1905 Keith totally controlled the banana industry in Costa Rica.

A full-blown history of the banana monopoly, though a fascinating subject, would take us too far afield from our central interests. What is germaine for us, however, is a comparison of the banana industry and the coffee industry, analyzed from the point of view of agrarian capitalism. What follows is just such a comparison.

Coffee versus Bananas: A Comparison of Forms of Agrarian Capitalism

The fundamental difference between the forms of agrarian capitalism represented by the coffee and banana industries in Costa Rica lies in the role that the industrialized nations have played in relation to them. As the Costa Rican economist Rodrigo Facio [1972:90] has explained, foreign capital invested in coffee cultivation stimulated the national economy. The foreign capital used by the banana industry, on the other hand, was used for the creation of enclave economies that were independent of the national economy. It will be recalled that British capital was introduced into the coffee industry at an early stage of the latter's development in the form of short-term loans to finance the following year's coffee crop. Later, this role was expanded to the financing of beneficio construction. For the most part, however, the owners of the coffee plantations and beneficios remained Costa Rican; the London firms played no role in the production process. The London investors were not prohibited from growing and processing coffee, and there were absolutely no restrictions placed by the Costa Rican government on such involvement; indeed, many foreigners—particularly Germans—did come to Costa Rica to start coffee plantations. However, on the whole, the London firms found the risks too high and the profit too low to warrant their involvement. British capital, then, simply served to stimulate greater production and left ownership of the means of production in the hands of Costa Ricans.

The banana industry presented a very different picture: it was a classic example of what has come to be known in the literature on dependency as an "enclave economy" [Johnson, 1972:80-88; Frank, 1972:377]. The means of production were almost totally in the hands of the United Fruit Company: the plantations, roads, railroads, docks, and ships were either owned by, or on 99-year lease to, the Company. Plantations which were not owned by the Company were effectively controlled by it through its monopoly on transportation and exportation.

Defenders of United Fruit do not tire of pointing out that had it not been for Keith and those who followed him, large-scale banana production would probably not have been undertaken in Costa Rica until many years later, if at all [Adams, 1914: 163-93; Wilson, 1947:51-68; May and Plaza, 1958: 19-23]. Before the construction of the railroad, the Atlantic lowland was almost totally uninhabited, and few Costa Ricans entertained the notion of trying to farm in its forbidding jungles. A further deterrent to farming in the region was the impossibility of obtaining sufficient capital to make the establishment of a plantation successful. Banana production is a very complex operation: the crop must be harvested at the precise moment of optimum ripeness and then rushed to port for rapid shipment to market in specially constructed refrigerated ships. For production of this nature capital was needed in quantities far beyond the resources possessed by Costa Ricans in the last century. Coffee, too, has its complexities and capital requirements; but once the crop is in the beneficio, months and even years can pass before it is consumed, with no appreciable damage done to the bean if it is stored correctly.

Supporters of the banana enclaves are also correct when they point out that within the banana monopoly there was room for Costa Ricans to own and operate their own banana farms. The Company encouraged this practice, since in this way it was assured of sufficient production to fill the never-ending stream of banana boats tying up at Limón Harbor; furthermore, by encouraging local banana production, it did not have to invest more of its capital or be faced with excess production in times of a bad market. The United Fruit Company made contracts with the local growers for the purchase of the fruit. These growers, however, were completely subject to the will and whim of the Company. Its word was final. To illustrate, whenever the market for bananas declined, the Company would simply cut back on its purchases from the independent growers, while keeping its own production in high gear [Kepner, Jr., and Soothill, 1935:71-76].

While the Costa Rican government could have intervened on behalf of the native producers, there was one very important reason why it did not. A conflict with the "Frutera" meant a confrontation with the economic, political, and ultimately the military power of the United States—a confrontation which Costa Rica was guaranteed to lose. It should be remembered that at this time the United States was very actively pursuing its Big Stick policy in the Caribbean, and Costa Rica had received more than one taste of it. In 1917, for example, Frederico Tinoco Granados overthrew the duly elected president Alfredo González Flores. The United States, favoring González, refused to recognize Tinoco. In 1919 Tinoco was forced to resign. On August 12 of that year, Juan Bautista Quirós was named by the Congress as his successor, but on September 1 he was visited by the United States consul in Costa Rica, a Mr. Chase, and given twenty-four hours to leave the presidency and have himself replaced by one of González' men [Monge Alfaro, 1966:277]. Chase carried with him a telegram from Secretary of State Lansing, which stated in part, ". . . the government of the United States under no circumstances can consider Mr. J. B. Quirós authorized in any manner to act as President of Costa Rica" [Monge Alfaro, 1966:277]. Quirós left office the next day. With such experiences fresh in their minds, Costa Ricans were not wont to oppose the Company.

The Company operated without restraint in its treatment of the local planters. It is reported that it sold its stems for an average price of 3.60 dollars during the period 1899-1927, while it was paying an average of fifty cents[2] per stem ("count bunch" of nine hands in length) to the local growers [Zúñiga Huete, 1928:80]. All production costs had to be deducted from these fifty cents. A further abuse of the local planters was the differential rates charged by the Northern. In the Soto-Keith contract of 1884 (articles 16 and 17) it was stipulated that tariffs for rail transport would be paid by users in Costa Rican currency. But in 1886 this was modified by executive decree, so that only gold (not *either* gold *or* silver) would be accepted as payment. This decree was illegal, since the contract of 1884 was a law, and laws cannot be modified by executive decree. The modification was nevertheless accepted. Since there was a scarcity of gold pesos in Costa Rica, tariffs were paid in dollars and pounds sterling, and converted by the Company into gold at a rate considerably lower than the official one, thereby placing a surcharge on the user.

Conflicts between the Company and local planters were not uncommon, since the former did everything in its power to minimize its losses. Whenever ships heading for the port of Limón were unable to dock be-

---

[2]Growers with contracts were paid sixty cents per stem, whereas those without contracts were paid only thirty cents [Kepner, Jr., and Soothill, 1935:71].

cause of bad weather, for instance, fruit which had been cut on Company orders would rot at the railheads, and the Company refused to be responsible for the losses. In order to eliminate this practice, the 1930 law provided for formal contracts between buyer and seller and created an arbitration board to resolve conflicts [Salas Marrero and Barahona Israel, 1973:562-63]. There is no record of the board's ever having been utilized, probably because of the fear on the part of the planters that the Company would take retribution for such appeals. A recent prize-winning novel [Gutiérrez, 1973] depicts the ways in which the Company inexorably moved against planters who fell out of favor.

Reluctant to come to the aid of their countrymen, the coffee oligarchy let the Company work its will unopposed and undertaxed. Their policy turned out to be a double-edged sword, however, for the Company was the one alternative to increasing taxes on the coffee industry, an alternative which the coffee oligarchy did not want to pursue. A previous section has outlined the history of the taxation of the coffee industry. It will be illuminating, in the present discussion on the comparison of the coffee and banana industries, to examine the history of taxation in the banana industry.

Until 1910 bananas were exported with no tax whatsoever. This was guaranteed by the "Contract-Law" ("Contrato-Ley") Pacheco-Scott, which exempted the Company from the payment of export taxes until 1910 [Salas Marrero and Barahona Israel, 1973:561]. As a consequence, millions of dollars of bananas were exported, but not a single cent of tax was paid to the Costa Rican government. During this period, therefore, with the exception of the source of employment which the Company provided, banana cultivation had little impact on Costa Rican economic development. Even the wages paid to the workers did not enter the economy, because most of this money went back to the Frutera through its company stores, whose stock was imported duty-free. During the years that the tax exemption was in force, there raged a national debate over the issue. Diputado Ricardo Jiménez Oreamuno (a direct descendant of Juan Vázquez de Coronado [Stone, 1971b:5]) and representative of the coffee oligarchy, broke with the coffee barons and forged a continuing battle to tax the Company. In 1907, when the discussion was under way concerning the type of tax to be imposed on the Company when the exemption ran out, Jiménez sought a tax of two cents per stem, limited to a ten-year period [Woodbridge, 1961:212]. Yet when the Echandi-Hitchcock law of 1909 was signed, it provided for only a one-penny tax and exempted the Company from all other taxes for a period of twenty years. Jiménez lost his battle. The only real concession made by the Company was that it agreed to pay the tax retroactively for the years

1908 and 1909. Many of the diputados argued that if the government imposed too high a tax, the Company would abandon its operations or at the very least would stop expanding its plantations [Salas Marrero and Barahona Israel, 1973:562].

In 1925, following an aborted attempt in 1916, an income tax was levied in Costa Rica. It was argued by some that the Railroad was obliged to pay this tax since, under the Soto-Keith contract of 1884 (article 23a), it was exempt only from import duty. Yet the Northern refused to pay the new tax [Zúñiga Huete, 1928:87].

In 1929 a new contract was passed into law, providing for a sliding tax scale, the purpose of which was to stimulate production by reducing the tax rate as exports increased. This contract, however, never went into effect. As early as 1927 it was reported that the Company was openly bribing diputados to secure their support for a favorable contract (one bribe was reported to be as high as 5,000 colones [Diario de Costa Rica, January 22, 1927; La Tribuna, January 23, 1927]). As a response, a group called La Sociedad Económica de Amigos del País was formed to pressure the Congress into providing a contract more favorable to the local growers and to the nation as a whole. It pointed out that the past contracts had been entirely discriminatory, since they exempted the Company from taxes which the local growers, as Costa Rican citizens, had to pay [Guerrero et al., 1927]. The Company won this struggle, and the 1929 law was revoked and replaced in 1930 by a law which increased the tax to only two cents per bunch and did away with sliding scales. Furthermore, this contract exempted the Company from all other taxes, including income tax, for a period of twenty more years [Grupo de Productores, 1929; Kepner, Jr., and Soothill, 1935:78-80; Salas Marrero and Barahona Israel, 1973:563; Woodbridge, 1961:214].

A comparison of the taxes imposed on coffee with those placed on bananas is revealing. It is reported that in 1928 coffee export taxes amounted to 11.8 percent of total valuation, whereas banana taxes comprised only 1.4 percent of it. Moreover coffee tax contributions to the national economy were six times greater than those contributed by bananas [Kepner, Jr., and Soothill, 1935:213]. By 1937, coffee growers were paying an ad valorum export tax of 8 percent, all import duties on materials used in the growing of coffee and in the maintenance of the beneficios, and the income tax. The Company, on the other hand, was paying a total tax of two cents per stem and was exempted from all other taxes. Since prices fluctuated, it is not possible to provide an exact figure on the percent of the selling price that this tax represented; since the average value of exports reported in the 1930s was about 2 million dollars and the average number of stems exported was about 4 million dollars, however, the Company was being taxed at approximately 4 percent of the *export* value. This figure is misleading, however, since the export value of the product is only a small fraction of its wholesale selling price. If we take the 3.60 dollars average price per bunch given earlier, we see that the two-cent tax per bunch comes out to a tax of only a fraction of 1 percent. Furthermore, all of these calculations are based on the assumption that the export data are accurate. In fact, since the Company (not the government) had the exclusive right to tally all exports, underreporting was apparently very common.[3] Coffee, on the other hand, was exported under the eye of government-paid administrators.

Since the Company was exempt from import duties, its savings on this tax far exceeded what it paid in export taxes. The original law did not contemplate providing import tax exemptions for operations other than the construction of the railroad, but little by little the Company was able to expand the narrow exemption to cover the costs of its banana operation. In 1917, for example, diesel locomotives were substituted for the coal and wood-burning types. The Company began importing the fuel without paying taxes on it, despite protests from the Ministry of Finance. Once imported without duty, the fuel could be used for banana operations [Zúñiga Huete, 1928:86]. Furthermore, there were persistent rumors that a lot of what the Company imported duty-free was later sold on the black market; in this way the Company was provided with another source of revenue, and the state's income was further reduced. The Company still continues to avoid taxes by stretching the interpretation of its contracts. Thus, during the period 1967-70 the Company purchased without sales tax 285,000 colones of liquor, arguing that the item was not a luxury (and therefore not taxable) but a necessity for the improvement of labor relations [*La Nación*, August 17, 1973:61].

The Company demonstrated an uncanny ability to avoid the spirit and often the letter of the laws which governed its relationship with Costa Rica. In 1933 a Costa Rican congressional committee issued a report [Comisión Especial, 1933] regarding the ways in which the Company violated the 1930 contract. The committee charged that the Company was avoiding taxes because it would not permit state inspectors to count the number of stems actually exported; the government had to take the Company's figures as final. Furthermore, the committee found that the Company refused to renew numerous purchase contracts with domestic growers, refused to give information to the investigative committee, and was not increasing plantings as stipulated in the 1930 contract. In addi-

---

[3] It is perhaps worthwhile to point out that underreporting of banana exports is probably still common, according to recent reports of a similar practice in Guatemala [*Latin American Economic Report* 6 (no. 11: March 17, 1978), 83].

tion, promised mobile dispensaries had never gone into use and a promised hospital in Siquirres turned out, on inspection, to be nothing more than a shack with a few odd medicines and no doctor in attendance. The Company's reply to the committee, made during the investigation [United Fruit Company, 1932], was that it was indeed fulfilling the provisions of the contract. With regard to the hospital in Siquirres, for example, the Company stated that the hospital was operating "with the necessary efficiency," avoiding mention of the nature of the equipment and personnel. The Company also reported that it had signed contracts with a number of local growers, thereby fulfilling the provisions to that effect in the 1930 contract. The congressional committee contacted these growers directly and found that the Company had signed contracts only with those individuals who it was sure would not plant more bananas (since the demand for bananas had dropped on account of the Depression). In one instance, the Company had signed a contract with a party for the planting of 200 hectares, but the growers were told by the Company that the land would be sublet to others who would do the growing. The subleasee never appeared. In another instance the Company signed a contract for 221 hectares of bananas, but the local planters testified to the committee that of their 221 hectares, only 100 were suitable for planting, and that 50 of those were already planted in coffee, so that they had planted only 22 hectares. Out of a total of 3,000 hectares which the Company was obliged to bring into production through local growers, the committee found that only 238.5 had actually been planted [Comisión Especial, 1933].

The example mentioned above is only one case out of many that could be cited in support of the contention that the Company avoided fulfilling its contractual obligations. Other examples will be presented below in regard to labor contracts. The transfer of the Costa Rica Railway to the Northern Railway and unfair pricing on the Railway have already been discussed. The central reason that the Company was able to get away with these violations was the special, almost extralegal nature of the contracts signed between United Fruit and the Costa Rican government. These contracts, called Contract Laws (Contrato-Leyes), were drawn up by the executive branch of government and submitted to the Congress for ratification, *not for approval*. The courts held that since it was not the Congress that drew up the laws, they were not laws but contracts and, as such, could not be modified without the joint consent of both parties. Such an interpretation placed these contracts in a special legal position and gave them the character of unmodifiable constitutional principles [Woodbridge, 1961:266]. By ratifying such Contrato-Leyes, the Congress forfeited its own right and responsibility to reexamine the laws at a later date and to change them whenever necessary. The Company, of course, was well aware of this fact, and has consistently taken advantage of it.

The latest round of contract making coincided with the period subsequent to the Revolution of 1948. Although the revolution was essentially bourgeois and anticommunist in nature, there were elements of nationalism within it. Perhaps for this reason the Company, fearing the imposition of more radical measures, agreed in 1949 to pay a number of minor taxes (for example, a tax on foreign consuls), a land tax, and, most important, a 15 percent income tax on net profits. This was raised to 30 percent during the term of José Figueres Ferrer in 1954, with the understanding that the state would take over the schools, hospitals, and airports which had been under the private control of the Company.

This comparison of the coffee and banana industries in Costa Rica demonstrates that while coffee exercised a major impact on the economy of the country both in terms of savings and government revenue, the banana industry had a minimal impact on it. Furthermore, the monopolistic practices of United Fruit interfered with the development of a strong sector of local producers who, in turn, might have made a substantial contribution to the national economy.[4] Finally, Costa Rica's experience with United Fruit helped established a pattern of dependency and helplessness with respect to foreign business operations. In self-defense, the Company argues [Garrido Guerrero, 1968:8-12, 41-7] that it has made a major contribution to the economy by opening up to cultivation areas that had been unfarmed by Costa Ricans. Furthermore, it points to its heavy investment in infrastructure (railroads, roads, ports, docks, schools, hospitals) as evidence of its contribution. These investments, however, have been ephemeral and have tended to disappear as the Company abandons spent, disease-infested lands for newer terrain. The history of the blossoming and rapid withering of the banana plantations on the Atlantic coastal plain in Costa Rica was, as Salazar Navarrete [1973] has pointed out, akin to the development and subsequent abandonment of Macondo by the fruit company in Gabriel García Márquez' epic novel *One Hundred Years of Solitude*. When the Company departed, it took everything that was worth removing. All it left behind was scrap and gaping holes in the ground where installations had once stood.

The debate as to the value of United Fruit for Costa Rica overlooks an essential point, one which is a major theme of this book: the banana

---

[4]It was not until the late 1950s, long after United Fruit had abandoned its operations along the Atlantic coast and had moved to the Pacific area, that a fairly large sector of independent growers developed them. See below for details.

industry served incidentally as an escape valve for peasants who had been driven from their land by the advance of coffee. Precisely at the time when coffee production was having its most devastating effect on smallholders in the meseta region, new opportunities for work opened in the banana plantations of the Atlantic. Had these opportunities not developed it is unlikely that peasant pressure could have been contained. As we shall see in the following sections, however, work in the banana fields was not a pacifying experience for the peasantry who moved there. It served as the basis for the first organized movements of rural labor, and eventually the banana areas became the sites of major incidents of rural unrest.

Rural Labor Organizes

The construction of railroads and the cultivation of bananas require a large labor force. The small groups of blacks who had once lived in the Atlantic lowlands disappeared with the cessation of cacao cultivation during colonial times. In this section it is shown how the labor force which constructed the railroad and manned the banana plantations was established. It was this group of workers which was to be Costa Rica's first large group of rural proletarians. The banana plantations served as both an escape valve for landless peasants and a nucleus for peasant organization.

The Migration of Jamaicans

As railroad construction got underway in the early 1870s, a shortage of labor developed immediately. In the first years of construction the Atlantic lowlands became infamous for their hostile climate, marauding Indians, and disease-ridden jungle, all of which deterred many Costa Ricans from venturing into the region. The labor shortage had, however, been anticipated, and the railroad contracts included a clause which specifically stated that Keith had the right to import laborers for the construction job. Fortunately for him, there existed in Jamaica a ready pool of workers who were suffering a severe economic crisis as a result of the exhaustion of the island's sugar plantations. By the early 1860s almost no work existed for the ex-slaves who had been freed in 1833. In 1865 bloody riots broke out, but were suppressed by the government in a massacre in which several hundred people lost their lives [Hall, 1959:242-88]. Some Jamaicans in search of work migrated to Panama, where they helped de Lesseps build the canal; others went to Costa Rica, where they worked for Keith and his railroad. As early as 1872, one year

Bananas and the Rise of the Rural Proletarian 65

after the approval of the 1871 contract, there are records of shiploads of Jamaicans arriving in Costa Rica. By 1874 some 1,000 Jamaican Negroes are reported among the railroad work force of 2,500. Between 1881 and 1891, 43,000 Jamaicans out-migrated, nearly 10,000 arriving in Costa Rica [Meléndez, 1972:55-85; Olien, 1967:5-11; Olien, 1968]. By 1927, the census of that year reports 19,136 Jamaican Negroes (4.1 percent of the population), 94.1 percent of whom resided in the Province of Limón [Meléndez, 1972:73-74].

Contrary to popular myth, Costa Rica did not react well to the new settlers. Costa Ricans were very proud of their white European ancestry, and often compared themselves favorably to their darker-skinned neighbors in Central America. Despite an obvious mixture of Indian blood in the majority of the population, most Costa Ricans thought of themselves as white. The first action taken against minority groups of nonwhite background was aimed, interestingly enough, not at blacks but at Chinese. Keith had managed to import coolies, but they did not take well to the work and most of them returned home. The Costa Ricans reacted so negatively to oriental labor that in 1897 a law was passed prohibiting the immigration of Chinese [Beeche, 1935:477].

Since blacks were a major source of labor on the newly constructed railroad and on the banana plantations which grew up around it, it was impossible to prohibit their entry. Keith most certainly would have protested any such restrictions. Yet Costa Ricans took steps to prevent blacks from migrating to other parts of the country. An aging document found in the National Archives illustrates the measures. The government had built a sugar refinery near Nicoya, Guanacaste province, in order to establish an agricultural colony, but the project failed and the refinery was left unused. To remedy this situation, the government signed a lease on April 14, 1899, with an Italian, one Eugenio Morice (about whose descendants I shall have more to say in chapter 5) and a Spaniard, Manuel Velázquez. These men agreed to reconstruct, repair, and put into operation the refinery (located in "Colonia Cuba") in return for the lease and a grant of five hundred hectares of land. The most revealing part of the document appears in clause III, paragraph g. It gives the contractors the right, "to introduce into the country immigrants dedicated to the work on the farm . . . with the precise condition that said immigrants cannot be of the black race nor of the yellow race . . ." [Archivo Nacional, Sección Histórica-Congreso, no. 2507]. A further restriction on immigration was imposed by a law approved in 1904 which prohibited the entry of Arabs, Turks, Armenians, Syrians, and Gypsies [Beeche, 1935:477], a rather odd collection of nationalities, indicating that the country was trying to protect itself against various ethnic and racial groups which it considered undesirable.

It has long been asserted that in the first quarter of the twentieth century there existed a law prohibiting the migration of blacks to the meseta central. Numerous researchers have sought in vain for a copy of such a law. If one ever existed, it has apparently been lost. Nevertheless, it is quite clear that such a law operated *de facto*, if not *de jure*. The control of the movement of blacks was quite easy, since the railroad was the only route to and from the banana zone. When the trains pulled into the town of Turrialba, the last outpost of the banana zone, white train crews substituted for black ones and the train then proceeded to San José [Meléndez, 1972:76-7].

With steady employment available for them in the banana zone, there was no real motivation for blacks to leave for the meseta. In Limón they were able to retain their language and cultural patterns, transplanting a part of Jamaica to Costa Rica [Bryce-Laporte, 1974]. When, as a result of factors discussed below, the plantations began closing, things changed rather quickly. In order to prevent a massive out-migration, the government passed a law prohibiting the movement of blacks to the new banana zones. How that law came into existence can be understood by an investigation of the circumstances surrounding it, namely the development of the labor union movement in Costa Rica.

The Genesis of the Labor Union Movement

The first union-like organizations were formed in 1854. They consisted of craft workers, and were called Sociedades de Socorro. These were followed in 1886 by the Sociedad Mutualista de Artesanos de Panadería, and in 1905 by the Federación de Artesanos, Panaderos, Construccionistas y Carpinteros. Added to these groups were the Sociedad Mutualista de Tipógrafos in 1908 and la Sociedad de Artesanos of Puntarenas in 1916 [Dammers, 1965:7]. Little is known about the activities of these organizations, but there are no recorded instances of strikes until 1921, when under the influence of Spanish anarchists, the bakers won a 35 to 40 percent wage increase and an eight-hour work day.

The first major strike did not hit Costa Rica until the Great Depression. In 1930, after their work week had been cut to three days and their salary reduced, four hundred shoemakers went on strike. Some 98 percent of all shoemakers in San José walked out, and a bitter five-week struggle ensued that was eventually won by the workers. Out of this strike came the formation of the Sindicato Nacional de Calzado [Cerdas Cruz, 1972:65]. In 1933, in the depths of the Depression, a minimum wage law of one colon per day was passed, and a regulatory commission was established, largely as a result of the efforts of Jorge Volio and his Partido Reformista [Volio, 1972:277-84; Backer, 1974:14].

The above-mentioned unions were strictly urban in nature, but their organization provided the leadership for the labor struggles which were later to take place in the rural zones. Labor disputes, although frequent, with one exception never amounted to full-fledged strikes until 1934. That exception occurred in 1888, during the construction of the railroad. A group of Italians had been brought in to supplement the labor force already there. They were appalled by the living conditions, and when Keith failed to pay them a month's wages, they went on strike. They came to Cartago in bands of several hundred, demanding better food, better treatment, and back wages. In the end, when when their demands went unmet, most of them returned to Italy [Stewart, 1964:69-80].

The strike of the Italians was only the tip of the iceberg of labor discontent in the region. Disputes between Keith and the workers were common, but the blacks were unorganized and therefore did not have the power to oppose his will. This lack of organization was to change gradually with the introduction of larger and larger numbers of Costa Ricans who were moving to the zone to take up work on the banana plantations.

It will be recalled that throughout the nineteenth century peasants were being displaced from their small farms by the larger growers. As the expansion of coffee production slowed in the latter part of the century and the need for labor began to diminish on the coffee haciendas (except, of course, during harvest time), greater pressure was put on the peasant population. Many were attracted by the high salaries being offered in the banana zone, and planned to spend no more than a year or two there to save enough money to start a small farm in the highlands. As Carlos Luis Fallas has shown in his novel *Gentes y gentecillas* [1947], this plan was rarely fulfilled, since workers squandered their salary on liquor and prostitutes. The census of 1892 reveals that fully 70 percent of the population of Limón province were male and only 5 percent of the population were married. In comparison, 25 to 30 percent of the population of the meseta were married. The imbalance of the sexes was a major factor increasing tensions in the banana-growing region [Costa Rica, 1893]. Conditions in the zone were truly subhuman, "un horrible infierno" [Fallas, 1970:193], and as a result, interpersonal relations were brutal. Machete fights broke out daily, and policemen were nowhere to be found [Mejía M., 1973].

The Great Depression exacerbated the deplorable conditions of the banana zone. Bananas, during such rocky financial times, were a luxury. Consequently the market began to dry up in the United States and Europe. At the same time, the Company began to lose its battle against the stubborn banana maladies, Sigatoka and the Panama Disease, beginning about 1925. By that year the diseases were so virulent that a plantation would last for only two to three years before production would cease. As a consequence of the Depression and the diseases, exports fell sharply (see figure 6). By 1933 the Company had only 870 of its 274,000 hectares under cultivation, compared to the 20,000 it had cultivated in 1913. In 1933 production was the lowest it had been since 1902; it dropped even lower in 1934. As a result of this drop in production, huge numbers of laborers lost their jobs. Many did not have enough money to return to the meseta, where, in any event, the job market was no better. Most blacks, of course, were unable to finance the expensive trip back to Jamaica; in any case there really was not much purpose in doing that either, since economic conditions on the island were very bad as well. So in Limón, as in many other areas of the world blighted by the Depression, labor discontent reached new heights.

Other factors were to add fuel to this fire. At an early date the Company foresaw the complete infestation of the Atlantic lowland areas and began to cast an eye toward the Pacific lowlands. It realized that until the diseases were conquered in the laboratory, the only method of field control was the abondonment of infested plantations and the establishment of new ones some distance away. This practice of course, was reprehensible from an ecological point of view, but that was of no concern to the Company, or for that matter, to the Costa Rican government. The acquisition of land on the virgin Pacific coast became a number one priority of the Company. Using the Ley de Gracias of 1907, which gave municipal governments the right to sell their uncultivated land at ten colones per hectare, the Company acquired some 70,000 acres of land in this region [Kepner, Jr., 1936:79]. Under the 1930 Contrato-Ley, the government agreed to permit the Company to begin cultivation on the Pacific coast, and even insisted that it plant some 3,000 hectares in that area. This action would have been encouraging to the unemployed workers in the Limón area, but a clause in the 1930 contract specified that the Company was to give employment preference to those of Costa Rican nationality when workers with similar aptitude and capability applied for the same job [Salas Marrero and Barahona Israel, 1973: 562]. The immigrant Jamaican blacks were in deep trouble; they could not return to Jamaica, and their prospects of getting employment with the Company were reduced. The preexisting racial tensions in the zone rose to new heights with the approval of the contract in September 1930.

Fears about the Company's pulling out of the Atlantic zone and leaving the black workers with no employment possibilities were exacerbated further in 1934 when details were revealed of a new contract law between the Company and the government. One clause of that contract provided that "the proportion of Costa Ricans who should work for the banana industry be determined, *and colored people be prohibited from being employed in the Pacific zone*" (emphasis added) [Beeche, 1935:512]. Some claim that Company officials insisted on the inclusion of this clause because they feared that the blacks were becoming too highly organized, and that therefore it would be best to start out with "fresh" (that is, unorganized) workers on the new Pacific plantations. Evidence for this argument, however, is quite weak. Apparently, the Company had better relations with blacks than it did with whites. Since the former were aliens in Costa Rica and had few legal rights, they tended to be more submissive to the demands placed on them by the Company. The whites, in contrast, felt very much a part of Costa Rican society and believed that they were protected by its legal institutions. For them, losing their jobs meant a trip back to the meseta, where family and friends awaited them. For the blacks, Jamaica was a long, expensive trip away. Furthermore, blacks had one big edge on the whites: being Jamaican, they could speak English to the American foremen. For this reason, blacks were often given better positions on the work crews, and not infrequently a black would be put in charge of a white crew. The most prestigious and high-paying jobs, those with the railroad, were predominantly in the hands of blacks.

Clear-cut evidence of the white banana workers' prejudicial attitudes toward the blacks is revealed in a little-known document stored in the National Archive. The document is a Petition to Congress signed by 543 whites of Limón in July of 1933 [Archivo National, sección legislativa], and states the following:

> We want to refer especially to the problem of the negro—which is of transcendental importance, because he constitutes in the Province of Limon a situation of privilege for this race and of manifest inferiority for the white race to which we belong. It is not possible to live with them, because their bad customs don't permit it: for them the family doesn't exist, nor the honor of women, and because of that they live in promiscuity which endangers our homes, founded in accordance with religious precepts and good Costa Rican customs. . . . A law definitely ought to be passed which prohibits the entry of negroes into the country and prohibits their naturalization because they are of a race inferior to ours.

The above quotation demonstrates that all of the standard racist stereotypes were virulent in Limón at this time and that, for the Costa Rican, the solution was to stop further immigration and to prevent the naturalization of this "inferior race." Moreover, as was mentioned earlier, although no copy of a law prohibiting black migration to the meseta has ever been produced, the signers of this petition clearly felt that one existed:

When the railroad to the Atlantic was constructed, contractors were permitted to bring negro workers on the condition that they could not settle farther west than the city of Turrialba. That restriction has not been fulfilled and the negros already invade the cities of the meseta—in truth, these cities are congested with negros [Archivo Nacional—sección legislativa]

Thus, the whites in Limón were telling the Congress that the blacks were invading the meseta and that something had to be done about it.

By 1934 the banana zone was a seething cauldron. Outside factors were to make the pot boil over. It cannot be said with certainty whether a strike would have occurred without the organization of the newly founded Communist Party of Costa Rica. However, it is unlikely that the strike would have been so widespread, would have lasted so long, or would have achieved what it did if it had not been for the support of the Party. On June 16, 1931, the Partido Comunista de Costa Rica was founded by a small group of intellectuals in preparation for the 1932 special municipal elections of San José. The Congress, however, ruled that the Party was illegal; thus in order to be allowed to participate in the campaign, it changed its name, calling itself the Bloque de Obreros y Campesinos (Bloc of Workers and Peasants), and managed to win two seats on the municipal council. In 1933, May Day was celebrated for the first time in Costa Rica, and tensions generated that day eventually produced bloody street riots on May 23 of that year. Then in 1934, the Party had a major success when it managed to have two congressional deputies and eight municipal councilmen elected from among its ranks [Herrera García et al., 1971:10-17]. The connection between growing communist strength and unrest in the banana zone might never have been made if not for an individual by the name of Carlos Luis Fallas.

Fallas, born in the city of Alajuela in 1909, was of peasant extraction. Despite his poor background he managed to finish two years of school past the primary grades, but was then forced to go out and work. At the age of sixteen he went to the banana zone and worked on the docks as a stevedore, and later took on various and sundry jobs on the plantations. At the age of twenty-two, he returned to Alajuela on the occasion of his mother's death. There he learned the profession of shoemaking and soon became involved in labor struggles. As a result of his activities he was tossed into jail on many occasions. In 1933 he made an inflammatory speech to the May Day gathering in San José for which he was sentenced to one year of exile to (of all places) Limón. It was like throwing Brer Rabbit into the briar patch. For the judges, Limón was the Siberia of Costa Rica; for Fallas, it was the Nirvana of union organizers [Fallas, 1970:11-12; Arroyo, 1973:39-50].

Having been exiled to the banana plantations, Fallas immediately set out to organize the workers. His major problem was the severe split between blacks and whites. He felt, however, that the discontent generated by the struggle between the races could be channeled and directed against the Company, since there lay the enemy common to all the workers. Fallas was successful in his efforts and managed to persuade the workers to petition the Company for a six-hour work day, a salary increase to six colones a day, payment in cash instead of in scrip, the provision of work tools by the Company, better housing, dispensaries, and recognition of the union (the Congreso de Trabajadores del Atlántico). This petition, which was sent to the president of the Company and to the president of Costa Rica, Ricardo Jiménez, came on the heels of a much more limited proposal that had been made directly by the Communist Party deputies in the Congress. The first proposal—which demanded only that the Company make available to the workers quinine (for malaria treatment) and snake bite serum, and that it pay them in cash rather than scrip—was rejected by the Congress at the insistence of the Company.

After the rejection of the first proposal, Fallas presented his more extensive petition, backed by a threat to strike. The proposal of the workers was ignored by both the Company and the president of Costa Rica. On August 6, a copy of the demands was again sent to the president of the Company; this time, by way of reply, the three workers who delivered the petition were arrested. On August 9 the strike was declared. Fallas' genius at organization was demonstrated by the fact that within a few days nearly all the workers, numbering some ten thousand and spread over a vast area, had walked off the job. The Company had managed to break strikes in other countries in the past, and was determined that this was to be no exception. But United Fruit had not counted on Fallas' ability to maintain the spirit of the workers despite hardships, arrests, provocation by the police, physical violence, and racial tension. Fallas organized a mail system, food committees, shock brigades (for defense), and several strike committees. The strikers held on, learning to survive on turtle eggs, fish, and bananas [Fallas, 1934:3; Fallas, 1970:193-206; *El Trabajo*, August 12, August 19, 1934].

In the second week of the strike the Company tried to exploit the tension between blacks and whites by using the English/Spanish newspaper *La Voz del Atlántico,* which was apparently subsidized by the Company. On August 18 an article appeared entitled "Coloured Labourers Warned." The article was written by "The Sojourner's Committee," and said, in part:

> The Government of Costa Rica is a capitalist government, and this capitalist government is and has been administered by white

men of the highest social and intellectual standing, some from the most noble of the Spanish caste inhabiting Costa Rica during the colonial age, yet none of these men constituting the governing class of the country has ever shown any aggressive tendency toward the negro population.

Nevertheless, since 1925, repeated petitions have been made to the legislative and executive branches of Governmeht requesting the removal of negroes from such employment as clerks, salesmen, foreman and other skilled occupations. And who have been the agitators of such discriminations against us on account of our colour? THE VERY GROUP THAT ARE NOW DIRECTING COMMUNISM IN COSTA RICA, the greater majority of whom are propertyless foreigners from adjoining Spanish-American countries; then how could we expect that the same treatment that is being accorded us by the noble statesmen of Costa Rica would ever be accorded to the coloured workman if that group of anti-negroes for some reason come into power?

A number of rather obvious distortions appear in this quotation. In particular, the omission of the several anti-black pieces of legislation passed by the "noble caste" of white men and the attempt to pin the blame for the anti-black petitions on the Communists stand out as gross misrepresentations of the facts. Another misrepresentation was blaming the strike on "propertyless foreigners from adjoining Spanish-American countries," that is, pointing the finger at Nicaraguans. While it is true that there were some Nicaraguans in the banana zone, there is no evidence that they participated in the leadership of the strike. The article concludes by stating that "passivity and lawfulness" have always protected the blacks against persecutions and that, therefore, participation in the strike would be dangerous. In all probability, this article was inserted at the behest of the Company in order to split black and white, although no direct evidence of this is available.

When the strike was in its third week, the government interceded. The union leaders came to San José and signed an agreement on August 28 in which the Company agreed to increase the salary to 4.20 colones a day (20 céntimos over the old wage), eliminate scrip, make available free hospitalization, improve hygiene and housing, provide some work tools, and recognize the union. The president of the United Fruit Company refused to sit in the same room with the strikers, and simply gave his word to the Minister of Labor that he agreed to the terms [*El Trabajo*, September 2, 1934]. The strikers went back to work, but immediately the word was spread that there was no contract and that Fallas had sold out for 30,000 dollars and was now on his way to the United States. Fortunately for Fallas, he had returned to the zone after signing the agreement in San José, and thus was able to disprove the rumor about the payoff [Fallas, 1970:206].

The fact that the Company had no intention of living up to the agreement soon became abundantly clear, and a new strike was called. This time, the organization and discipline characteristic of the first strike were absent, as the workers, feeling cheated, resorted to violence. The police were called in and a serious confrontation resulted in which the strikers were eventually subdued [Fallas, 1970:206-7; *El Trabajo*, September 9, 1934].

The Rural Proletarian Labor Unions Mature

Although the strike of 1934 failed to fully achieve its goals, it initiated a long series of strikes, some of which were ultimately quite successful. The first strike demonstrated the power of organization and the pressure that the workers could bring to bear against the Company and the government. At the same time it demonstrated the Company's capacity for deceit, a lesson which had to be learned if future negotiations were to prove successful. In any event, the days of the Frutera on the Atlantic side were numbered. In 1938 the Cortés-Chittendon contract was signed which provided for the cultivation of a minimum of 4,000 hectares and the construction of ports and railroads along the Pacific coast. By that time the Company already owned 118,000 hectares in this region. In exchange for the contract, the government was given a one-million-dollar loan from the Company [Salas Marrero and Barahona Israel, 1973:563]. The blacks, prohibited from moving to the new area by the 1934 contract, were left behind to fend for themselves. They took up cacao cultivation, which many of them continue today, on lands leased to them by the Company. The departure of the Company from the Atlantic side destroyed the economy of the province of Limon [Meléndez and Duncan, 1972:94-5].

The Company's move to the Pacific did not free it of labor problems, however. One year after the signing of the 1938 contract, the first strike was called. It took place in the Parrita area and was led by Danilo Jimenez Veiga (who served as Minister of Labor in 1971, when the banana unions managed to win their first collective bargaining contract from the Company) [Jiménez Veiga, 1971:6-9]. Another strike was called in 1943 and resulted in a salary increase. Then came the Civil War of 1948, a consequence of which was the dissolution of the Communist Party [Bell, 1971:158]. Without the support of the Party the strength of the banana unions faltered. Thus, although some 12,000 workers participated in a new strike in 1949 in the Quepos and Golfito areas, the effort was a failure, owing to a lack of union organization.

To replace the Communist-led unions, the government sponsored new ones. In the Pacific banana zone a new union, called the Unión de Trabajadores de Golfito (UTG), was formed in 1950, along with the Federación de Trabajadores Bananeros Anexos (FETRABA). The latter was a parent organization into which the regional banana unions were organized. Shortly thereafter, however, the Communists managed to regroup their forces, although their party remained outlawed. They formed the Federación de Obreros Bananeros (FOBA), which is affiliated with the Communist-led national organization, the Confederación General de Trabajadores Costarricenses (CGTC), formed in 1952. By the early 1970s the CGTC had thirty-three unions and 5,989 members affiliated with it [Backer, 1974:18]. In 1953 a strike in the Golfito Division involved close to 10,000 workers. The basis for the strike was the dismissal of some 100 workers for their participation in that year's May Day parade. The strike lasted eleven days, leaders were arrested and one was killed, but in the end the victory was the strikers', since they won free hospitalization for the lower-paid workers, occupational hazard insurance, and an increase in salary.

In 1954 FOBA and FETRABA unified for the first time, and waged a strike with the participation of some 1,500 workers, but the unity did not last and the strike was broken. The following year, a strike broke out in Puerto González Víquez. Although the plantations in this area were located on the Costa Rican side of the border, they were administered by the Chiriquí Land Company, the Panamanian division of the United Fruit Company. Since the Panamanian workers had been putting considerably less pressure on the Company than their Costa Rican counterparts, the wages and working conditions offered by the Chiriquí Land Company were not as good as those provided by the Costa Rican division of the Company. Thus, Costa Rican workers employed by Chiriquí did not do as well as employees of the Costa Rican division. After a strike of several weeks, the workers were partially successful in having their demands met [Fallas, 1970:210-14; González Muñóz, 1966:8-22; Cerdas Cruz, 1972:79-81].

Other minor work stoppages and strikes occurred in 1955 and 1958. Then in 1959 the *aguinaldo* (the Christmas bonus which is the equivalent of a month's salary) was made mandatory for all large business firms; when the Company refused to pay it, the workers went out on strike again. Both FOBA and FETRABA participated in this strike, unifying forces in a drive against the Company which, despite this pressure, remained resolute. In order to avoid a major strike and serious violence, the government decided that it would pay the aguinaldo, thereby using state tax money to cover the payment that the Company should have made [Cerdas Cruz, 1972:80-81]. With the strike only a partial success (since it did not get the Company to pay the aguinaldo), the unions sought remedy through the courts. The Company argued that its 1949 contract did not oblige it to conform to any law that did not apply to the *majority* of farmers. Since only five farmers in the country (clearly not a majority) filed income tax returns showing an income of greater than 300,000 colones, the Company did not have to pay the aguinaldo, because that law applied only to farmers with yearly gross incomes greater than 300,000 colones [Woodbridge, 1961:228-29]. The courts accepted the Company's argument and ruled against the workers. Here, again, it can be seen that the Contract Law offered the Company protection beyond that which was available to any other producer in the country; the intent of the Congress in passing the aguinaldo law of 1959 was that it apply to all large businesses, but the Company was able to circumvent the regulation.

Another major strike in the banana zone occurred in 1971 and resulted in a major victory for the union. Led by the UTG (which was originally anticommunist in nature but by the early 1970s was Communist controlled), the strike lasted twelve days and resulted in ninety arrests and several incidents of tear-gassing. The Company agreed to sign a collective bargaining contract with the UTG and the Sindicato de Trabajadores Bananeros Unidos Independientes (SITRABUNI), a union promoted by the Company [Convención Colectiva de Trabajo, 1971]. The contract covered salaries, vacations, aguinaldo, housing, and health, but left many large loopholes through which the Company could escape. In several places in the contract it was left up to the Company to carry out a particular clause or to determine the circumstances of special situations without the participation of the unions. For example, the Company (and not the unions) was responsible for punishing administrators and foremen who were guilty of taking reprisals against union leaders (clause 5). In another part of the contract, it was left to the Company to decide which situations were so urgent that workers should be forced to work on holidays (clause 7). Another section of the contract (clause 10) read that the Company would make a number of improvements in housing "in the least possible time," yet did not set limits on that time. Nevertheless, the contract was considered a major victory for the unions, and with the achievement of this victory, the UTG was greatly strengthened. From 1962 to 1970 it had an average of 35 members, but in 1973 it counted among its ranks 3,000 of the 6,000 workers in the Golfito Division [Union Leaders, 1973].

Before closing this discussion of the banana unions in the Pacific region, it is important to clarify, if only briefly, the role that the

Communist Party plays in their functioning. There is no doubt, as has been shown by the preceding discussion of the history of the labor union movement in Costa Rica, that the unions have received their major impulse from the Communist Party and its organizers. Just as Fallas, the leader of the first strike, was a Communist, so too are the leaders of the UTG. However, few workers of the United Fruit Company are Communists, and most of them flatly reject Communist ideology. These attitudes were manifested by the great majority of the banana workers (nearly 100) whom I interviewed in 1973. They recognize, however, that their strongest allies are the Communists and that it has been through Communist leadership that they have won the wage increases and fringe benefits that have been wrested from the Company [Union leaders, 1973]. At the same time, the union leaders are quite aware of the fact that most members do not "buy" the Communist line. This awareness is vividly demonstrated by a large poster which hangs in at least one union hall in the banana zone, proclaiming: "Sindicalismo no es Comunismo" ("Unionism is not Communism").

One final point regarding the banana unions needs to be made. In 1956, after two decades of abandonment, plantings were begun again on the Atlantic side. This time, however, the United Fruit played no role. Rather, the plantings were made by the Standard Fruit Company, part of the Castle and Cook conglomerate (known to the consumer as Dole.) The discovery of a new variety called Giant Cavendish or Valery, a variety resistant to the Panama Disease, led to the reinitiation of banana cultivation on the Atlantic coast. The experiment was successful, and exports were begun in 1959. Within a few years the population of the zone went from 18,000 to 31,000. As many as fifty Costa Rican companies have farms in the area, as have several foreign corporations such as the Del Monte Corporation, Afrecanische & Laeisz, BANDECO, and COBAL [Equipo Técnico Interinstitucional, 1970; Salas Marrero and Barahona Israel, 1973:556-57]. By 1972, production in the Atlantic zone far exceeded that of the United Fruit Company (the latter produced some 18,000,000 boxes on 9,800 cultivated hectares, while the former produced 31,000,000 boxes on 18,242 hectares [*La Nación*, October 20, 1972:50; Salas Marrero and Barahona Israel, 1973:557]).

Thus, the Unión de Trabajadores Agrícolas de Limón, along with a new union, Trabajadores Agrícolas de Heredia, became actively engaged in disputes with the companies. Strikes were common [*La Nación*, October 18, 1972:29; September 11, 1973:6], but from all appearances, the relation between worker and producer was not as tense as it had been with the United Fruit Company and its workers. Perhaps the experiences of the Company served as a reminder to the producers, but it is more likely that the government's support of many of the union demands was a major factor in improving the worker/producer relationship. In any event, by the mid 1970s, the unions in the Atlantic zone had become a powerful force.

Plate 1: Typical Costa Rican oxcart used for hauling coffee

Plate 2: Female *peones sueltos* (day laborers) working on a sugar harvest

Peasants of Costa Rica 79

Plate 3: A coffee *recibidor* (receiving station) in the central valley

Plate 4: Harvesting coffee

Plate 5: Preparing for the daily weigh-in after the day's coffee harvest is complete

Plate 6: A cluster of migrant worker shacks on a coffee hacienda

Plate 7: Freshly cut banana stems being transported to the packing plant on overhead cables. Plastic bags are used to protect the crop while it is developing

Plate 8: Two-family homes provided by the United Fruit Company for its workers. Note electric lines and television antennas

Plate 9: A squatter settlement carved out of the jungle. Note log bridge in lower right side of picture

Plate 10: Squatter's shack surrounded by young coffee and plantain plantings

Plate 11: A squatter

Plate 12: A rural mass being conducted by a Franciscan priest in a remote village. Rural school house is in background

Plate 13: A rural military outpost

Plate 14: A coffee farmer and his family

Part II
The Peasant in the Modern World:
The Impact of Agrarian Capitalism

The preceding chapters have presented a diachronic analysis of Costa Rican development. Without a doubt, the most influential force in the shaping of that development has been agrarian capitalism, since it has provided the elite with economic sustenance, laid the foundations for a nascent middle class, and totally transformed the social order in the countryside. It is appropriate at this point to move to a synchronic analysis, and focus attention on the contemporary countryside.

Part II of the book is divided into four chapters. Chapter 4 explores the impact that agrarian capitalism has had on the yeoman. Capitalist agriculture has resulted in the progressive downward mobility of that group. The once-proud class of yeoman farmers has been so decimated that in contemporary rural Costa Rica only a minority of the peasants are landholders. The progressive loss of land which peasants have undergone as a result of the onslaught of agrarian capitalism has made them acutely aware of their growing economic insecurity. An empirical examination of the social hierarchy which peasants use to distinguish among the various types (or classes) of rural folk reveals that the primary basis for the hierarchy is the degree of economic security each type of peasant possesses.

The implications of the security basis of social stratification are explored in the next two chapters. In chapter 5 it is shown that one way in which peasants attempt to overcome the problem of economic insecurity is to join peasant leagues whose goal it is to assist the peasants in land invasions. Peasants who embark upon land invasions are shown to be ones who have lost faith in their government's ability to assist them. It is projected that as more and more peasants lose their land, squatting will become a more frequent occurrence.

Chapter 6 explores the government's reaction to the land tenure problem. The development of the agrarian reform program is discussed, and its impact on peasant attitudes is demonstrated empirically with the use of survey data. Although the program is highly successful in reorienting peasant attitudes (e.g., increasing trust in government), the scope of the program is far too limited to have a significant impact on the overall problem of landlessness.

The final chapter views the Costa Rican case in comparative perspective. It concludes by taking a look at the future, and attempts to predict the final outcome of the long struggle which Costa Rican peasants have had with agrarian capitalism.

4 The Social Impact of Agrarian Capitalism: Stratification and Insecurity

> The fact is that peasantries nowhere form a homogeneous mass or agglomerate, but are always and everywhere typified themselves by internal differentiation along many lines.
> [Mintz, 1973:93]

The coffee boom left in its wake a large mass of landless peasants as a form of social debris. These people, having been forced off their lands by the onrush of coffee, sought shelter on the coffee plantations, where they could sell their labor. For those who were unable to find work on the plantations, and for the more independent-minded who preferred not to work there, homesteading became the chosen vocation. With the stagnation of the coffee industry and the consequent leveling off of work opportunities on the plantations, a second form of agrarian capitalism came into the picture. The banana industry served to siphon off the peasants displaced from the meseta by the coffee industry. In the present decade, however, with the world market for bananas nearly saturated, this industry, too, has lost most of its labor absorptive capacity. The closing off of the territorial frontiers has further increased the numbers of peasants who have been unable to find their niche in the economic system, and who have consequently become a floating force of day laborers, seeking out work wherever and whenever it appears. Increasing numbers of these people have, in desperation, turned to squatting.

The Costa Rican countryside no longer presents the relatively unified picture it did when the yeoman was dominant. Today he makes up only a small minority among the much larger mass of peasants. This chapter discusses the social hierarchy which was created by agrarian capitalism and which continues to exist in contemporary rural Costa Rica. First the various types of peasants are described. Then data from an attitude survey is analyzed in order to determine the underlying basis of the hierarchy.

Types of Peasants in Costa Rica

Two basic hypotheses underlay the research conducted on peasant types in contemporary Costa Rica. First, it was hypothesized that the vast changes which have gone on since colonial days, when nearly all residents were smallholders, must have produced a rather complex social stratification. Hence, just as sociologists have devised a rather complex portrait of social classes and occupational categories in urban areas, it was expected that considerable complexity would be found in rural Costa Rica. It was also recognized that because all peasants by definition (see appendix 1 for the definition of peasants used here) are rural cultivators, and therefore basically have the same occupation (farming), the complexity of social stratification among peasants would not approach that found in urban areas.

The second hypothesis was that social strata among peasants would vary as the peasant's relationship to the land varied. In particular, it was assumed that the means of production would be fundamental in the determination of stratification.

Of the two hypotheses which were used in exploring social stratification among peasants in Costa Rica, only the first was fully supported. As will be shown below, considerable diversity of peasant types does exist. However, the peasant's relationship to the land, it was found, was only a superficial manifestation of a deeper basis for social stratification, namely degree of security.

Fieldwork was accomplished by first conducting an extensive series of informal interviews with peasants in various parts of the country. All were asked to describe to the author the types of peasants found in the area in which they lived. These interviews slowly produced a picture of nine separate and clearly identifiable peasant types: three landed, two tenant, and four landless. The approximate English translations[1] of these

---

[1] The Spanish version of these nine types, in the same order, is: *dueño de finca con escritura; dueño de finca sin escritura; precarista o parásito; agricultor que paga alquiler de*

Stratification and Insecurity 89

types are, of the landed: landowner with title, landowner without title, and squatter; of the tenant: renter and sharecropper; and of the landless: steady nonplantation (hacienda) laborer, steady plantation laborer, day laborer, and migrant laborer.

Peasants in the landed category comprise perhaps the most diverse and difficult to define group. In this category fall the landowners with title, the landowners without title, and the squatters. The basic lines of stratification for this group, however, follow those for the other categories: each lower type in the list has progressively less control over land than does the one above it.

The titled landowner represents the elite among peasants, at least insofar as his control over the means of production and his security of tenure are concerned. Peasants in this category may make all decisions with reference to planting, harvesting, marketing, etc. It is critical to note, however, that not all landed peasants are necessarily the economic elite in the hierarchy. For many reasons, most important among which are the amount of land owned, the quality of the land, and the type of crops planted, the titled landowners vary considerably in their income. Within the sample of peasants interviewed for this research, the mean area of the land owned was 17.5 hectares. However, this figure is a greatly distorted representation of the size of landholdings among the titled owners, because it is inflated by the presence of a very few respondents who own unusually large tracts of land. Closer inspection of the data reveals that 53 percent of the titled owners hold less than four hectares of land, and 81 percent hold less than ten hectares. Hence the great majority of the titled owners are truly smallholders, with plots just large enough to sustain a family. In nearly one third of the cases (32.7

---

tierra con efectivo; agricultor que trabaja a medias o a tercios; peón fijo de un solo patrón (de hacienda); peon fijo por las compañías bananeras; peón suelto u ocasional; peón ambulante que anda atrás de las cosechas.

It should be noted that in some cases a descriptive phrase was used rather than, or in addition to, the standard Spanish term, and in other cases two terms were used. The reason for this is that in talking with peasants from different regions of the country it was found that in some cases more than one term was used to define the same type. Hence, in some regions of Costa Rica the term *peón suelto* was more frequently heard than the term *peón ocasional*. Although both terms were readily identified in all regions, it was felt that by providing the greatest number of cues to the respondent as to the type of peasant being referred to, confusion would be reduced to a minimum.

It should also be noted that these nine types correspond closely to categories proposed by numerous other researchers who have focused on Latin America [Ford, 1955; Wolf, 1955; Barraclough and Flores, 1965; Schulman, 1966; Smith, 1970] including ones suggested by those who have focused exclusively on Costa Rica [Norris, 1952; Castillo, 1954; Goldkind, 1961].

percent) the holdings were no larger than one hectare. Peasants with holdings as small as this almost certainly supplement their income with wage labor, or have children who provide supplemental income (see plate 14).

Although compared to most urban Costa Ricans the landed peasants are quite poor, among the peasantry they represent an economic elite. At the time of the survey their average weekly income came to the equivalent of about forty-five dollars, nearly twice the mean for all peasants interviewed and substantially higher than any other group (see table 4). It is perhaps easiest to understand the elite position of the landed peasants when it is realized that their income is nearly five times the legal minimum wage paid to agricultural workers.

Table 4. Characteristics of Land Tenure Types

Tenure Type	Mean Weekly Income in Dollars	Mean Years of Education Completed
Landed		
Landowner with title	45	2.9
Landowner without title	23	3.1
Squatter	18	2.7
Tenant		
Renter	13	1.8
Sharecropper	21	3.3
Landless		
Steady nonplantation laborer	11	2.4
Steady plantation laborer	33	3.3
Day laborer	9	2.8
Migrant	9	1.7
Grand Mean	25	2.9

Source: Seligson, 1974: 248-67. The total sample N consisted of 531 peasants. Data on all but ten respondents is reflected in this table. The remaining ten were unclassifiable because in addition to working in agriculture, they also worked at non-peasant jobs (waiter in a restaurant, for example).

The economically superior position of the titled landowners over other peasants, however, is not paralleled by a superiority of educational attainment. As is shown in table 4, the titled owners average slightly fewer years of education than do the untitled owners, sharecroppers, and banana workers, although they clearly do stand out above the lowest ranks (e.g., migrant laborers).

Of all the peasant types, the landowner without title is the most difficult to differentiate from the other landed types. This group shades off

Stratification and Insecurity

at the two extremes: on the upper end, it merges with the titled owners; and at the lower end it merges with the squatters. In conducting the field work, at least four separate subtypes of landowner were found without title, distinguished from each other by varying degrees of control over land. The least secure of these peasants had no documents at all to prove ownership of their property. They had perhaps once squatted on land, and, as a result of the laws regarding squatter's rights discussed in chapter 2, obtained some claim to ownership. Somewhat more secure were owners who had a private bill of sale (*carta venta privada*) showing from whom the land was purchased and the date of the transaction. Rarely do these private bills contain accurate references to the location or size of the farm. Moreover, since no legal note is taken of the transaction, close inspection often reveals that such documents are forged.

Nevertheless, in the sample interviewed, private bills of sale were the most frequently possessed proof of ownership among the untitled owners. The popularity of this form of proof undoubtedly stems from the costs and difficulties involved in obtaining more formal proof, such as the notarized bill of sale or the official survey plot. The notarized bill (*carta venta protocolizada*) requires that both buyer and seller present themselves to a notary for verification of the signatures of the two parties. A transaction such as this involves some cost (notary fees, travel, etc.), but serves to enhance the value of the property by helping to assure prospective purchasers that the owner will be unable to make a claim on the land once he has sold it. Hence the security of ownership is markedly increased with the notarized document. Only with an authorized survey plot (*plano catastrado*), however, can a buyer be assured that the notarized bill of sale really refers to the particular property under consideration. Such a plot must be drawn up by a certified topographic engineer (a member of the Colegio de Ingenieros) and approved by the national office of land titling (Catastro Nacional).

Such survey plots are very expensive to have drawn up, since they require the services of an engineer as well as a lawyer (a lawyer is required to process the document through the land-titling office). The document is very important, however; it is a requirement for the granting of official title. Nevertheless, even with an official plot the owner does not automatically obtain title, because several other steps are required for full legal title, as was described in chapter 2.

It is roughly estimated that one-fourth of all farms in Costa Rica are untitled [Agency for International Development, 1970: VI, 4 n.6]. In regions off the meseta central, areas now farmed by those who were displaced by agrarian capitalist coffee cultivation, the barriers to titling have traditionally been so great that most of the land has gone untitled. In a study conducted in 1970 [Saenz and Knight, 1971], it was found that 91 percent of the land in the most remote areas studied was untitled.

The legal position of the untitled owners is somewhat confused, since until legal title is obtained, they have no way of proving their right to a given plot. While absence of title has not prevented peasants from buying and selling land, it has made it nearly impossible for them to get bank credit, so long as the land remains untitled. The banks do not advance any money at all, even on a short-term basis, for improvements on untitled farms. The National Production Council (Consejo Nacional de Producción), which grants credit to peasants, also requires proof of title for loans.

At the bottom of the hierarchy of landed peasants are the squatters (see plates 9, 10, and 11). They are the poorest and least well educated of all the landed types (see table 4). The mean size of squatter farms in the sample interviewed was 7.6 hectares, but 54 percent owned one hectare or less. It is more appropriate to contrast squatters with day laborers and migrant workers than with landed types, since it is from these landless peasant groups that the squatters emanate. The squatters earn an average of twice what these landless peasants earn, and therefore probably have made a wise decision to risk the squatting venture. The previous statement is qualified because I have no data on those squatters who have failed (who were evicted from the property they took). Further details on squatters are presented in chapter 5. According to the 1973 agricultural census, squatter lands constitute 2.4 percent of the total number of parcels and .9 percent of the total land area [Dirección General de Estadística y Censos, 1974a].

Sharecropping usually appears in one of two forms. One form, called *esquilmo*, is found mostly in the Pacific coast province of Guanacaste. Under this system, the owner grants to the peasant (who is frequently a relative or employee), the right to work a piece of land for one year. No rent is charged, but the land must be cleared and planted in pasture before it is returned to the owner [Clark, 1971:94]. The *aparcería* system, commonly called *a medias* (halves), requires that the sharecropper return approximately one-half of the crop to the owner as payment for the usufructuary rights.[2]

---

[2]Two other minor forms of land tenure are found in Costa Rica but have not been specifically listed here. One of these is the "free use" system, called *gratuito*. This form is generally found among family members and on large plantations, and entails the granting of a small plot by the owner to a worker, as a perquisite. In 1973, 2.3 percent of the farms and .2 percent of the farmland area were used under this system. The other form is the *colono* system [Norris, 1952], a perquisite granted to steady nonplantation laborers, by which the plantation owner permits the peasant to plant permanent crops on a small piece of hacienda property, and to reap most of the profit from the harvest. Under the gratuito

Stratification and Insecurity

The landless peasants have been divided into four categories: two steady types, and two floating types. It has been necessary to distinguish between the steady plantation workers (banana workers) and the steady hacienda workers (coffee workers), because of the very different nature of these two systems of employment.[3] To begin with, the plantation workers are more highly paid than the hacienda workers. By law, the minimum wage on coffee haciendas in 1973 was 12.9 colones daily, whereas the minimum wage on banana plantations at that time was 28 colones, 54 percent higher. As shown in table 4, the plantation laborers earned an average of 33 dollars a week, or three times that earned by the nonplantation laborers. The extra wages frequently earned in overtime (at time-and-a-half and double-time rates) on the banana farms help to explain the three-fold increase in earnings when official wage rates for banana workers are only double the nonplantation rates. A second major difference between the two systems is that on banana plantations a large number of the workers are unionized, as was shown in chapter 3, whereas few coffee hacienda workers are. Third, banana workers are provided better housing, better recreational facilities, and more accessible medical treatment than are the large majority of coffee hacienda workers.

The survey data collected for this research clearly reveal the differences between the two groups. Virtually all (99 percent) of the banana workers interviewed lived in houses with cement floors, whereas only 25 percent of the houses of hacienda workers had cement floors. Similarly, 87 percent of the banana workers had electric or gas stoves for cooking, and 56 percent had indoor plumbing, whereas only 7 percent of the nonplantation workers had gas or electric stoves (the others cooked with fire wood), and only 13 percent had indoor plumbing (see plates 7 and 8). The improved working conditions on banana plantations are, however, of

---

system, in contrast, permanent crops are normally prohibited. The colono form of usufruct is very rare; in 1963 it amounted to .2 percent of the farms and .1 percent of the farmland area. The 1973 census does not even report on this form of tenancy. Both of these forms exist to ensure a reliable supply of labor on the plantation or homestead. In this way the owner can guarantee himself a steady source of labor when he needs it (at harvest and planting time), while not being forced to pay for the worker's services during the other times of the year. The few respondents in the sample who held land in either of these two ways were classified as either steady nonplantation laborers or sharecroppers, depending on the number of weeks a year they spent working on the plots they had been loaned.

[3] For the purposes of this discussion the non-banana plantation workers will all be referred to as coffee plantation workers. There are, of course, other kinds of plantations in Costa Rica (e.g., sugar), but the coffee workers are by far the most numerous, and are the focus of this study.

relatively recent origin. As was shown in chapter 3, when the United Fruit Company operated in the Limón area, conditions were truly subhuman. Over the years, however, the Company has come to recognize that its goals are better realized by satisfying at least a modicum of the demands made by the unions, since by not doing so it will be faced with financially ruinous strikes.[4]

The primary reason that the United Fruit Company has been able to provide considerably better working conditions than have coffee haciendas is the substantially greater margin of profit earned by the banana industry. The low rate of domestic taxation on the banana industry and the oligopolistic world price structure established by the major banana companies help provide the greater profits earned in bananas. Peasants are very well aware of this difference between the two operations. For this reason, the banana worker knows that his strikes ultimately have the potential of succeeding, for if the Company yields, all it has to do is increase banana prices in order to recover what it is losing in the salary increase. The coffee worker is equally aware that his patrón has no such power over the market, and therefore would have to take the loss out of his own (small) pocket; thus, the coffee workers realize that their chances of waging a successful strike are minimal.

The last two categories of landless peasants are composed of those workers who are unable to find steady work on any one farm and are, therefore, forced into a ceaseless search for work opportunities. In some areas of the country, day work of this sort is available in sufficient quantity and with sufficient regularity that a substantial permanent population of workers can be supported. These day laborers, called *peones sueltos* or *ocasionales* in Costa Rica and *afuerinos* in some other

[4]Stone [1969:197-201] argues that in the past there was a close interdependence between peón and patrón on coffee haciendas, since the former needed the latter for his salary, and the latter depended on the former for labor. Out of this relationship grew a strong mutual respect, Stone argues, in which there were very clearly defined rights and privileges. This would appear to contrast sharply with the totally impersonal relationship prevailing on banana plantations, where the patrón is an almost mythical, money-hungry gringo who is never seen by the workers. The picture which Stone paints is far too idyllic. With respect to the question of interpersonal relationships between patrón and peón, coffee workers are not treated too differently from banana workers. Stone admits that today the peón-patrón relationship on coffee haciendas is becoming more and more impersonal, but then goes on to say that "in the view of the Ministry of Labor, the laborer has as many rights as the owner. . . . The Ministry maintains the large plantations under its constant vigilence" [1969:200]. In reality, any examination of cases brought before the Ministry of Labor will demonstrate that for the laborer, winning is the exception to the rule. Moreover, the Ministry of Labor's "constant vigilance" over the large plantations is more theoretical than actual, especially in the areas off the meseta, where work inspectors are rarely seen outside of the banana zones.

Latin American countries, tend to live in rented houses or in their parents' home, while they work in neighboring haciendas (see plate 2). In areas where work is too scarce to support this type of existence, day laborers are forced to leave their villages and pursue the harvests around the country, thereby becoming migrant workers.

The day laborers and migrants had the lowest income of all the peasant types studied, and the migrants had the lowest educational levels. These two groups were less likely to have gas or electric stoves than any other peasant types, only 5 percent of the day laborers and none of the migrant laborers having this luxury. Similarly, only 11 percent of the day laborers, and none of the migrants, lived in dwellings with indoor plumbing. Fully one-fourth of the migrants had no sanitary facitities, not even a latrine (see plates 5 and 6).

Social Stratification Among Peasants

Methodology

Careful consideration was necessary in the formulation of a research methodology designed to elicit the peasants' image of rural social stratification.[5] First of all, since the concept of status is likely to be either unknown or poorly understood by the majority of peasants, it is not possible to simply ask peasants to rank the nine types described in the previous section in terms of that concept.[6] A further complication with the word *status* is that its translation into Spanish is rendered as either *estado legal* or *posición relativa*, neither of which conveys very accurately the idea we have in mind for the term. Another alternative is *prestigio* [Haller, Holsinger, and Ulhoa Saraiva, 1972], but this option entails a two-fold problem. First, its meaning in Spanish tends to connote "good standing" and thus it is questionable if the notion of *low* prestige would be meaningful at all to the respondent. Furthermore,

---

[5] I would like to thank Paul Allen Beck for suggesting that the respondents verify the a priori rankings.

[6] Other studies have asked peasants to provide an ordering of urban as well as rural occupations [Haller, Holsinger, and Ulhoa Saraiva, 1972], but I have chosen to limit my investigation to the rural types alone. This was done for two reasons. First, the peasants' knowledge of the status hierarchy in urban areas is likely to be extremely limited, and therefore the questions posed to them about status in urban areas are not likely to be very salient. Consequently, one would expect to obtain extremely "noisy" data from such an investigation. Second, my interest in terms of the historical background presented in the previous chapters is social stratification in the countryside, rather than in the entire society. The latter would obviously have required field work in both urban and rural areas.

prestigio is a term rarely used among Costa Rican peasants, and its meaning is probably not well grasped. Eventually it was decided that no single term taken from our urban, educated vocabulary would be fully translatable into peasant speech. Instead, it was decided that an operational equivalent of the word *status* would be constructed. After much thought it was decided that the best operational equivalent would be the following interrogative: "If you could choose, which of the following occupations would you choose to be? What would you rather be?" ("Si Ud. pudiera escoger, cuál de las siguientes ocupaciones escogería? Qué le gustaría ser más?").[7]

Pretests in the field demonstrated that this phraseology was readily understood by peasants. The only difficulty with it is that it is possible for the respondent to add a qualifier to the question by going through something akin to the following mental process: "I would rather be a landowner, but that is beyond my wildest dreams, so instead I will choose the renter, which is not beyond the realm of possibility for me." There is no way of determining precisely how many peasants made this mental addition to the question, but conversations with many respondents after the interviews were completed indicated that this was a rare occurrence.[8]

How well were the peasants able to handle the task of ranking the nine peasant types? In particular, were the categories salient for the respondents, and were they able to discriminate among the categories in the rank order procedure?

For the most part, the respondents were able to identify all of the nine peasant types presented to them, and had little trouble choosing one type over another. This fact is demonstrated by the very low nonresponse rate. In all, only 1 percent of these questions were left unanswered by the respondents.

Findings

The rank orderings provided by each respondent were used to compute the mean scores of all respondents for each category of peasants.[9] Before

---

[7] I would like to thank Charles Cannel of the University of Michigan for suggesting this approach.

[8] A discussion of alternative rank order procedures is found in appendix 2.

[9] The rank orderings for each of the respondents were computed by examining each pair of peasant types and scoring a given type "+1" each time it was chosen over the one with which it was paired. The "losing" type within each pair was scored "0." If the respondent did not indicate a preference between the two elements of a pair of types, that pair was scored a zero and thus nothing was added to the summing procedure. Only one percent of all pairs were given a score of zero. This procedure provides a theoretically maximum

the ranks were computed, however, it was decided to eliminate from the sample all those respondents who presented highly inconsistent responses to the questions, since the reliability of their answers was open to doubt. The procedure for eliminating these respondents is explained in appendix 3. Removing them (26 out of the sample of 531, or 4.9 percent of the sample) considerably reduces the "noise" in the data.

In table 5 the rank orders are presented for the entire sample (with the "noisy" interviews removed). An examination of the far right column of the table reveals a surprising finding: the banana workers rank just below the owners with and without title, and above the squatters, renters, and sharecroppers. This finding is of critical importance, and raises a question as to why the plantation workers rank so highly, a question that can be answered in light of the historical material presented in the preceding chapters.

Table 5. Ranks of Peasant Types

Type	Mean	S.D.	Rank
Landowner with title	1.26	0.96	1
Landowner without title	3.89	2.50	2
Steady plantation laborer	4.48	1.93	3
Renter	4.74	1.63	4
Steady nonplantation laborer	4.76	1.60	5
Sharecropper	5.14	1.66	6
Day laborer	6.65	1.47	7
Squatter	7.16	2.13	8
Migrant laborer	7.28	1.49	9

Note: N = 505. See appendix 3 for the explanation of why 26 out of the sample of 531 cases were dropped.

The story of the Costa Rican peasantry has been one of a social group moving from landed to landless status. In the poverty-stricken colonial society, the right to work a piece of land and to reap its harvest was tantamount to the right to survival. During this period, therefore, land served as the basic assurance of survival for the peasantry. With the introduction of agrarian capitalism, a new alternative appeared: earning a

---

mean score of 8 and a minimum of 0. In order to make the rankings easier to interpret, +1 was added to all means, so that the final order would range from 1 to 9, thereby paralleling the nine peasant types. Then these means were converted into rank orders, the highest mean being scored a rank of 1 (first-ranked), and the lowest mean having a rank of 9 (last-ranked).

wage through the sale of one's physical labor. Because of high wages and the pressure of the large coffee growers to force the peasant off his plot, this alternative became an attractive one. Thus, sometime in the middle of the last century, wage laboring became an acceptable (even attractive) surrogate for the security of landownership. The data in table 5 reveal, therefore, that today there are two alternative routes to security: one is land, and the other is a steady, well-paid job. More specifically, the peasants are stating that if land cannot be owned (with or without title), then it is best to seek security in the banana zone, for example, rather than to attempt to obtain usufructuary rights over land through renting and sharecropping. The latter two situations are quite risky, because the possibility always exists that the landowner can raise the rent or the crop can fail. If either of these should occur, disaster would strike the family of the renter or sharecropper, whereas the steady plantation laborer is guaranteed (up to a certain point) that his wage will be paid to him every Saturday. Even more risky is the situation of the squatter, who can lose his land at any moment. It is not surprising, therefore, that squatters are ranked very low (rank 8).

Further evidence of the importance of security is provided by the rank orders given to the other peasant types (see table 5). Day laborers and migrant workers are ranked below renters and sharecroppers. That is to say, when faced with a choice of unsteady work or a usufructory situation, the peasant finds that the former is less secure than the latter, and therefore, despite the risks involved in renting and sharecropping, this type of work is preferable to the absolute insecurity of unsteady day work.

Precisely these findings were obtained by Allen W. Johnson [1971:149] in his study of sharecroppers in Brazil. He notes the following:

> Peasants at the margin of subsistence can never forget that they have no possessions or wealth to cushion them from a stroke of bad luck. Even without some calamity such as bad weather or disease, they watch helplessly as they and their children lose weight each year before the new harvest begins. The uncertainty of the weather, the chronic shortages of cash and food, and an insecure relation to the land are matters over which the poor [the landless] peasant has no direct control. He has no reasonable alternative but to respond by emphasizing his own security.

Another indication of the importance of security is the fact that the migrant worker was the category most frequently placed in last position. By definition, the migrant worker is an insecure type, his subsistence depending upon his ability to hustle up a new job as each crop is harvested. Many migrant workers stated in the course of the interviews that the wages were higher than in steady work, since owing to labor shortages during periods of peak demand, wages for harvest work are always substantially above the year-round wages. Most of the migrant workers went on to say, however, that if offered a steady job they would take it at once, since the constant travelling was very hard on their families and prevented them from sending their children to school. Moreover, after the harvest season they earned no income at all.

Further insight into social stratification in the countryside is revealed by the surprisingly high ranking that plantation workers were given. It will be recalled that in the early days of banana cultivation, conditions on those plantations were subhuman, but that over the years the situation has improved markedly. In the course of the interviews it was found that few plantations provided their workers with as comfortable housing as did the United Fruit Company; in fact, most coffee plantation housing, especially in the more remote areas, was deplorable.[10] Salaries have always been substantially higher in the banana zone, thereby making work there even more attractive. During the course of the interviews several banana workers voluntarily offered the opinion that the United Fruit Company is the best patrón in Costa Rica. They ranked their line of work as third, coming behind landed with title and landed without title, and ranked the non-banana fixed worker fifth, coming after renters. An even more positive appraisal of banana workers was given by the non-banana steady workers and migrants, who ranked banana workers second, placing only landed owners with title above this category.

The conclusion to be drawn from this examination of the rank orders is that status in the countryside is not determined by land tenure considerations alone, but by other factors as well. Quite clearly, the most important of these factors is security. From a broader perspective, one could argue that land tenure itself is actually a surrogate for a more important underlying dimension of security, in that those who own land tend to be more secure than those who do not. From this perspective, one could hypothesize that the landedness dimension itself has little contemporary meaning and that it is subsumed under the dimension of security.

---

[10] On the United Fruit plantations there are three types of dwelling units: individual, double, and barracks. The individual units are the newest, and according to Company officials, the only type now being constructed (see plate 8). They are primarily reserved for families, whereas the multiple units are more frequently used by single men. The rooms in these multiple units, and particularly those in the barracks, are quite small, stark, and uncomfortable, but always have cement floors. Even these barracks, however, are superior to the veritable shacks found on the more poorly capitalized coffee plantations located in areas off the meseta (see plate 6).

It is possible to probe the data presented in table 5 for further underlying dimensions. To do this it is necessary to resort to the use of a rather complex statistical program called MDPREF. An explanation of the manner in which this program converts rank-order data into a graphical representation of the dimensionality of the data would take us too far afield in this book. Moreover, the technique is explained in some detail elsewhere [Seligson, 1977b:38-44]. Rather than repeating that explanation here, only the findings of the analysis are presented.

The MDPREF analysis of the data yields two clearly interpretable dimensions. Figure 7 portrays these dimensions with the axes labeled. Individual preferences are indicated with representative vectors (drawn with arrow heads denoting their end points).[11] The solution yielded a very good fit to the data; the first dimension explained 56 percent of the variance in the rank orders. The second dimension explained an additional 16 percent of the variance for a total of 72 percent. The relatively small proportion of unexplained variance not only reveals that the solution makes a good fit with the input data, but also testifies to the need for a two-dimensional rather than a unidimensional interpretation of the stratification hierarchy. Interpreting the data in a unidimensional way would result in discarding a significant amount of the variance for which MDPREF is capable of accounting.

It is quite clear that the horizontal dimension of figure 7 cannot be interpreted as a landed/landless one. This is so because there are certain anomalies in the location of types which make the landed/landless interpretation specious. Most important, the squatter, a landed type, is located on the left-hand side of the continuum, right in the center of the landless types and far removed from the two landed types. A second reason for the inappropriateness of the landed/landless label is the location of the two steady worker types on what would be the landed side of the continuum, mixed in quite closely with two landed types.

An examination of the horizontal axis reveals that the peasant types are actually arrayed along a continuum from more to less secure. The horizontal dimension groups the types in such a way as to clarify the rank orders presented in table 5. It is seen that the titled landowner is placed at the extreme right-hand end of the continuum as the most preferred type. This type is followed by the landowner without title. Next, located near the center of the plot, comes a tightly knit cluster composed of the two tenant types and the two steady worker types. Finally, at the extreme left-hand side are the three types least preferred: day laborer,

[11] Only representative vectors could be drawn in, because of the impossibility of including all 505 vectors on the plot. In many cases more than one subject provided an identical or near-identical rank order.

Stratification and Insecurity

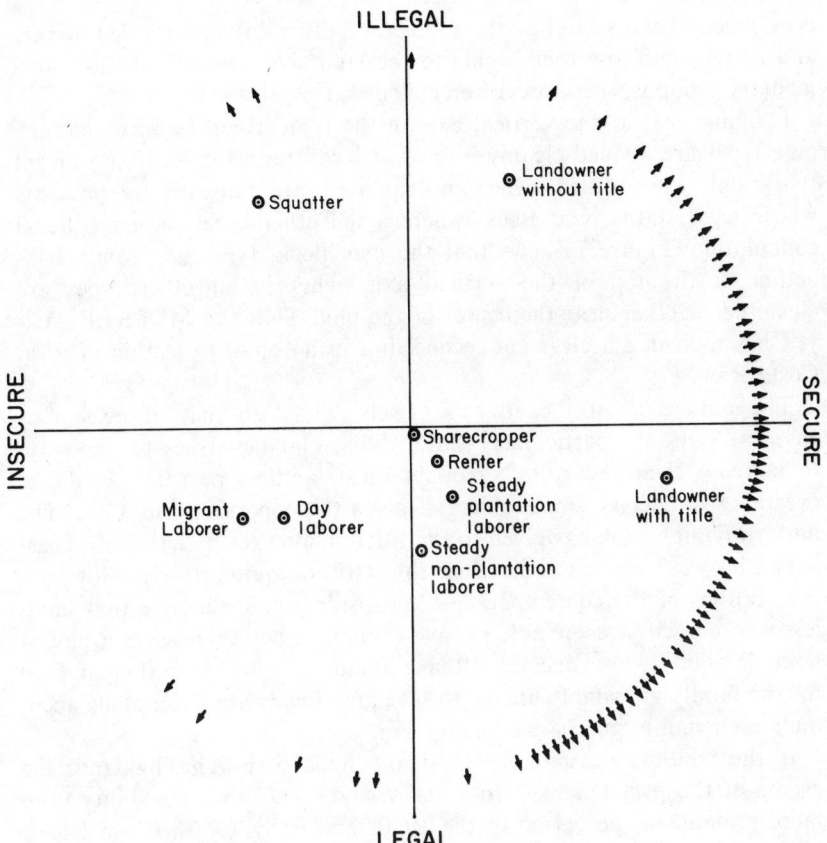

Figure 7. Two-dimensional plot of preferences and subjects

squatter, and migrant laborer. Thus, as one moves from right to left on the horizontal dimension, the types become progressively less secure. Titled owners are the most secure type, while at the other extreme, unsteady workers, migrant laborers, and squatters are the most insecure. Unsteady workers and migrant workers can never be sure of their next day's work, while squatters live in fear of losing their land. The types of peasants in the center of the plot have an intermediate level of security which is derived from different sources. The untitled owner is aware that he could lose his land in a legal dispute. Thus, although he has the security of owning a piece of land, that security is limited by his lack of title. The two steady worker types are secure in that they have a permanent job, while the tenant types obtain their security from the land they till. These five types, however, are not nearly as secure as the landowner type, since workers can lose their jobs (and often do) and untitled owners and tenants can lose their rights to the land. The security of this intermediary group is, therefore, often ephemeral.

Looking next at the vertical axis in the plot, it can be seen that the nine types are divided cleanly into what I will term the legal and illegal types: only the untitled owner and squatters are categories of peasants whose legal status is at issue, whereas the other types have no illegal connotation. Figure 7 shows that the two illegal types are grouped together at the top of the vertical axis, whereas all other types are clustered together near the center of the plot. Thus the MDPREF analysis has indicated a clear-cut second dimension of stratification in rural Costa Rica.

The dimension of illegality is closely linked to that of insecurity. Insecure peasants, particularly those who are landless, seek to find ways to increase their security. No doubt most landless peasants would be overjoyed to become smallholders, if given the opportunity to do so. The uniformly high rankings given to the titled landowner by nearly all peasants who were interviewed reflect this attitude quite clearly. However, the realities of the contemporary countryside give little hope that landless workers will ever be able to save enough to buy themselves a plot of land. Peasants whose income often is unable to provide sufficient food for the family are simply unable to save any money at all, let alone accumulate enough to purchase a small farm.

If the landless peasant ever had any hope of purchasing land, the events of the past ten to twenty years have made that possibility even more remote. In the period of the 1950s and early 1960s, Costa Rica's birth rate was among the highest in the world. Although in recent years the urban birth rate has dropped significantly, the accumulated population increase, along with high birth rates in rural areas, has placed enormous population pressure on the land (Seligson, forthcoming-b; Sandner, 1962; Saenz P., 1969:75). No longer are there vast tracts of unsettled land on which the enterprising peasant can settle. The Costa Rican frontier is virtually closed to further settlement. As a result of population pressure and land scarcity, land prices have risen steadily in the past decade. Added pressure is put on the land by the expansion of large cattle plantations, many of which are owned by multinational corporations. Costa Rica has developed a strong cattle industry in recent years, but unfortunately, it is an industry which is highly capital and land intensive, but labor extensive. As a result, land values continue to rise, but employment opportunities stagnate. Finally, the automation of many tasks which had previously been labor intensive (spraying of fungicides, for instance) has diminished the need for labor on coffee haciendas and banana plantations.

There are but two principal alternatives left for the peasant: either he can react to his insecurity by invading land, or the government can give him land through a land reform program. Both of these alternatives are explored in the two succeeding chapters.

5 The Peasant's Response to Insecurity: Organization and Land Invasion

Three Types of Peasant Organizations

No sector of the Costa Rican peasantry other than banana workers is well organized. Some limited success at organizing other landless peasants, however, has occurred. Nevertheless, almost without exception the purposes of the organization are extremely narrow, being exclusively directed toward the goal of obtaining land. There is no indication that peasant organizations are hoping to achieve a major transformation in the political system, nor for that matter is there much serious discussion of a transformation of the agrarian sector. This chapter outlines the major types of such organizations.

Peasant organizations in Costa Rica may be distinguished by the nature of their leadership, either Communist Party, government agency, or peasants themselves. The difficulty in dividing organizations into three separate types is that in most cases, once the movement is well under way, everybody wants to get into the act, and so the three types often blend into one. The reason for this is the desire of Communists and government agencies alike to get involved in peasant conflicts in order to enhance their public image, increase their legitimacy with peasant groups, and build their constituencies. Thus, one highly placed government bureaucrat told me that his agency was pressing for the organization of peasant leagues so that when it petitioned the legislature for a larger budget, it could call on the organized peasants to march on Congress in support of the petition, much in the way that the Bolivian MNR party called on armed peasants and miners to support its program [Malloy, 1970a].

Peasant Leagues Fomented by the Communists

The first type of organization is the Communist-supported "comité campesino" or peasant league.[1] In 1973 there were seventy-eight of these committees scattered throughout the countryside, with a total of some five thousand dues-paying members. The dues amount to a nominal sum (less than twenty cents a month), of which 20 percent is paid to the parent organization, FUNTAC, the Federación Unitaria Nacional de los Trabajadores Agrícolas y de Campesinos (The National United Federation of Agricultural Workers and Peasants). Each committee has an organizational secretary, a finance secretary, and a secretary for recording the minutes.

In recent years FUNTAC has been trying to change the structure of these committees by establishing within each one a "Consejo Agrario" (Agricultural Council) whose purpose it is to plan in detail the way in which the committee is going to accomplish agrarian reform. As the leader of FUNTAC [Sierra Cantillo, 1973] stated, "It is not from the top down, but just the opposite, from the bottom up that one makes an agrarian reform." That is to say, the agrarian reform called for by FUNTAC is not going to be made by the official government agencies, but by the peasants themselves. For such reform to be successful, the leaders believe careful planning is needed in order to avoid disorderly squatting, which ends up creating conflicts among the peasants themselves. Quite clearly, such planning is necessary, because in the majority of cases where squatting has taken place in recent years, severe conflicts have broken out among the squatters. As one Johnny-come-lately squatter told me, "The most serious problem here is not with the police, it is with the squatters themselves. Some grab more land than they are entitled to and others have nothing" [Squatters, 1972].

It would be misleading to overemphasize the strength of the Comité Campesino: these are not labor unions which periodically seek to negoti-

[1] Much of the information related to the internal structure of this mode of organization was given to me by Gonzalo Sierra Cantillo, Secretary General of the Federación Unitaria de Trabajadores Agrícolas y de Campesinos (FUNTAC) [see Comisión Nacional Campesina, 1965:19-20].

ate new contracts, but organizations established for the sole purpose of obtaining land for landless peasants. Apparently, the only time these committees become active is right before a land seizure. If the seizure is successful, the committee quickly disappears, since its function has been fulfilled. Once its goal has been attained and each peasant has his plot, the committee has little else to do.

FUNTAC, in its new organizational scheme, is trying to broaden the concerns and prolong the life of the committees by having them deal with the interpeasant conflicts which develop after the initial seizure. If FUNTAC is successful in expanding the role of the committees, it will have taken an important step toward the establishment of a rural power base outside of the banana zones, its traditional areas of strength. In some cases the peasant leagues have succeeded in establishing permanent organizations, and have even become officially recognized unions. In recent years the following peasant unions have been formed: Unión de Pequeños Productores Agrícolas de Pérez Zeledón, Unión de Pequeños Productores Agrícolas de Villa Neilly, Unión de Pequeños Productores Agrícolas de Guanacaste, and Sindicato de Pequeños Productores Agrícolas de Limón. Throughout the middle 1970s, however, few peasants identified with a larger peasant movement. Their actions were directed toward the resolution of their own insecurity problem, and once this problem was solved, "revolutionary" fervor was extinguished.

The ephemeral nature of the Comité Campesino has been altered in instances where the original land seizure failed. Paradoxical as it may seem, peasant movements in Costa Rica which initially fail become the most fertile territory for long-lived peasant leagues. This is because an unsuccessful movement means that the peasants are left confronting the dual problems of unemployment and land scarcity. Thus it is only a matter of time before new attempts are made, each new frustrated effort leading to greater resolve on the part of the peasants to succeed.[2]

[2] In other countries of Latin America such movements are often smashed brutally in the early stages, so that future attempts at land seizures by the group are rendered impossible. In Costa Rica, however, official force of this nature is rarely used, and peasants do not expect that it will be. In the early 1970s, however, as land seizures became more common, the government began to show a firmer hand. In November, 1973, a violent conflict broke out in the southern Pacific region of Costa Rica between a group of some four hundred to five hundred squatters on the one hand and a consortium of Cuban-Americans on the other. After one Cuban's hand was cut off in a fight and a rural policeman was killed [*La Nación*, November 16, 1973:10A], President Figueres declared a state of emergency and sent down a large contingent of heavily armed troops [*La Nación*, November 16, 1973:1,6,30]. A bloody conflict was avoided when the squatters, outnumbered and outgunned, agreed to abandon the land they had taken. In 1975, however, under the revitalized land reform program of the Oduber regime, the government purchased 18,678 hectares from the United Fruit Company and turned it over to these peasants. The troops, however, remain stationed in the zone.

Protracted conflicts only serve to temper the metal of the participants, mold the leadership of the group, and forge the basis for a permanent league. In most cases, however, this line of development is stunted by the introduction of outside organizers from government agencies. Once the peasant group has made repeated attempts at land seizure, it attracts sufficient national attention for government agencies to intervene, and thereby usurp the influence of the existing leadership. It is out of such repeated, frustrated attempts to obtain land that the second form of peasant organization develops, that which is led by government agencies.

Peasant Leagues Led by Government Agencies

Two autonomous institutions of the Costa Rican government have been directly involved with peasant movements. The first is the Instituto de Tierras y Colonización (ITCO), discussed at length in the next chapter. The second is a new agency formed during the last administration of José Figueres. Called the Instituto Mixto de Ayuda Social (IMAS) it is an omnibus antipoverty organization [Leiva Rojas, n.d.]. One division of IMAS is devoted to peasant problems and is specifically charged with the responsibility of training peasants. Although the IMAS program was originally conceived of as vocational training, elements within the organization believed that such training would be better left to already established organizations, such as the Instituto Nacional de Aprendizaje (The National Job Training Institute). Thus, in its place, IMAS officials sought to introduce leadership training—more correctly, "consciousness raising"—along the lines developed by Ivan Illich [1971] and Paulo Freire [1971]. Whenever a case of squatting has been sufficiently serious to warrant national attention, ITCO and IMAS have intervened, often clashing with each other over issues of jurisdiction. Both institutions attempt to impose their own solutions. Unfortunately, it is not at all unusual for the peasants' interests to be ignored in the midst of such interinstitutional conflicts.

Perhaps the best illustration of how a peasant movement can become coopted by such institutions is the now famous case of "El Jobo." Sometime in the last century, the Morice family began accumulating vast amounts of land in the area around La Cruz in the peninsula of Guanacaste. In 1947, using the Ley de Poseedores en Precario of 1942, Luis Morice exchanged 5,000 hectares of his hacienda, which he alleged had been squatted on, for new lands. When the government engineers came out to survey the squatted on land, Morice offered them free food, drink, and lodging. In addition, he was such a congenial host that he traveled with them wherever they went, pointing out to them exactly what was his, what was squatted on, and what the names of the squatters were.

Morice's plan was to have the squatted on land titled to fictitious persons, so that when the squatters received their titles, they would be worthless. When the titles were given out some years later, Morice challenged the squatters on the rights to the land, and when the judge saw that the titles were not in the names of the squatters, he awarded the land to Morice, since the latter held a prior claim to it. As a result, Morice managed to retain the land that he had allegedly offered in exchange for the new land, while keeping the new lands as a gift from the government [Fallas, 1960:2-10].

The peasants, many of whom had worked those plots for over twenty years, were infuriated by this turn of events. Their protests, however, only managed to get them arrested, since Morice appeared to have considerable influence over the local judicial system and police force. Thus, in 1960, eight peasants were arrested in La Cruz, accused of taking down one of Morice's fences. Actually, what they were doing was removing a fence which Morice had put up on land that belonged to them. Nevertheless, the peasants are reported to have been tortured by the police until they provided full "confessions" [*La República*, May 20, 1960:1,4; May 21, 1960:3; May 24, 1960:1,9]. The crisis heightened in the late 1960s. Up until that time Morice had held a lease on the land adjoining the beach on the peninsula called El Jobo. According to Costa Rican law, coastal land can never be privately owned, but can only be rented from the state for limited periods of time. For this reason, Morice was unable to own this coastal land, which was important to him in the care of his cattle, for which he needed access to the salt deposits on the beach. When ITCO was created in 1961, it became the agency to grant such leases. At first ITCO renewed his lease, but when the lease came up for a second renewal some years later, it was denied on the grounds that Morice was a *latifundista*. This occurred in 1970. The land-hungry peasants of the area had been under the impression that Morice owned the Jobo peninsula, and when they got wind of the fact that ITCO had denied him the lease, a small group of them decided to invade the land. Morice went after the squatters with bulldozers and destroyed their shacks, but the peasants held on, moving to the area adjacent to the beach. On November 10, 1970, ten peasants were arrested on grounds of "preventive detention." By this time, the struggle was beginning to make waves, and ITCO sent a team to investigate [*La Nación*, July 25, 1971:32-33; Bonilla Genaro Duarte, 1973:197-98; Instituto de Tierras y Colonización, 1973:4-5].

On November 18, 1970, ITCO called a meeting in a place called La Coyotera. To attend the meeting, the squatters had to cross a narrow stretch of beach on which Morice had set up a roadblock in an effort to prevent them from passing. When Gil Tablada Corea, a saddle maker from La Cruz who sympathized with the squatters, refused to heed Morice's warning, he was fatally shot in the face by Morice after a brief struggle. In an effort to cover up the murder, Morice placed a pistol in the victim's left hand to make it look like a suicide. What Morice did not realize was that Tablada was right-handed. Furthermore, the pistol had no magazine [*La Libertad*, November 28, 1970:9; January 9, 1971:9]. After the murder, the peasants recognized that the rules of the game had been changed and that it was now a do-or-die issue. Not only was Morice not initially brought to trial, but the squatters, within hours after the murder, were put under arrest and sent off to jail in Liberia, the capital of Guanacaste province, where they remained for twenty-eight days until bail was arranged with the help of ITCO and IMAS.

ITCO then began an extensive study of the area and discovered that Morice had only 613 hectares legally titled, whereas he had fenced in an area of 5,797 hectares. Counting the rest of the farms to which he claimed ownership, Morice claimed a total of 9,400 hectares. Under the ITCO law, any farm that is uncultivated and larger than 1,000 hectares may have its untitled portions expropriated. Since Morice had only 613 of the 5,797 hectares titled, ITCO began expropriation proceedings, with the plan of turning part of this land over to the squatters. To subvert this plan, Morice transferred part of his land to a Nicaraguan relative of his, and had it titled in her name in order to reduce his total holdings. He then brought in cattle, in order to begin working the land that had been abandoned for years. As a result of this maneuver, Morice succeeded in establishing his right to work part of the Jobo peninsula, and temporary rights were given to the squatters to work another part. Unfortunately for the squatters, in order for motor vehicles to gain entrance to their part of the peninsula, it was necessary to use a road which crossed Morice's section. In December of 1972, a "goodwill caravan" prepared by IMAS and consisting of clothes, medicines, doctors, and dentists, to aid the ailing squatters, attempted to reach the squatters' part of the peninsula, using Morice's access road. In order to stop them, Morice tore up the road with bulldozers and diverted a stream so that it would cut across the roadbed, thus making entrance impossible [ITCO, 1973:4-6; IMAS, 1973:4-6; *Diario de Costa Rica*, December 27, 1972; *La Nación*, July 21, 1971:28-29; *La Nación*, July 25, 1971:32-33; *La República*, May 10, 1971:10; *La Libertad*, November 4, 1972:5].

As of this writing, the struggle in El Jobo remains unresolved. The courts have not decided what to do with regard to the land. Morice, however, ultimately was tried in abstentia and convicted of the murder of Tablada, but continues to live in freedom as a fugitive from justice.

Allegedly he is in Nicaragua, evading the eight-year prison term which faces him in Costa Rica. In late 1976 a movement toward extraditing him was was begun [*Pueblo*, June 21, 1976:3].

This case illustrates the fact that once government agencies become involved in a case of squatting, the nature of the conflict changes drastically. The landowner feels more seriously threatened, and the peasants feel that they have more support. As a result, violent conflict is much more likely to be the outcome. Moreover, the peasants often have little better chance of winning the case with government support than they do without it, because the agrarian reform law contains loopholes; a shrewd lawyer can often win a case against ITCO. Furthermore, the judges, as representatives of the propertied classes, have rarely ruled in ITCO's favor in court cases.

One typical example of an unjust court ruling is brought out by James Rowles [1973] in his analysis of the Miravalles case. In this case, ITCO expropriated a huge farm measuring nearly thirteen thousand hectares that had been squatted on in 1954-57 by some five hundred families during a massive invasion. The expropriation clauses of the ITCO law state that the payment of expropriated land shall not exceed the value declared by the owners for tax purposes. The value of the farm listed in the tax office was 438,000 colones, and this is what ITCO offered the owners. They refused to accept this sum and claimed that ITCO had to pay them the actual worth of the farm, some 4,000,000 colones. The case dragged on for a number of years, passing from one court to another. Eventually, in 1969, the court of appeals, using bizarre reasoning, ruled in favor of the owners. The courts reasoned that the value listed in the tax office was not the value *declared* by the owners, and therefore had no bearing on the value of the farm. The judges failed to ask, however, what value the owners had actually declared for tax purposes, since they were required to make such a declaration under the law in force at the time. One can assume that the value they declared could not have been higher than the assessment made by the tax office, since all property owners in Costa Rica typically understate the value of their land so as to avoid paying more taxes. Furthermore, since the owners did not object to the assessed value listed in the tax office, it should have been assumed that they accepted that value. Finally, if the assessment was in fact too low, the owners were defrauding the tax office. But the judges failed to consider any of these points (and a number of others), and forced ITCO to pay the full value of the property in cash, refusing to let it pay in bonds unless the bonds were valued at their market value rather than at their maturity value. This payment nearly bankrupted ITCO.

The long-run consequences of government interference in peasant organizations seem to be negative ones, because on the one hand the movement loses its leadership in exchange for the coopting forces of the government agencies, and on the other hand such intervention does not improve the peasants' chances of success in their struggle for land.

Spontaneous Peasant Leagues

In marked contrast to these coopted peasant movements are the movements that are led totally by peasants themselves, without interference from either the Communist Party or government agencies. This type of movement has been characterized as "pre-political" [Hobsbawm, 1959:2], and operates with indigenous (peasant) leadership alone.

When peasant motives become intermingled with larger political goals, the movements take on a different character. Such intermingling may be seen, for example, when peasants are encouraged by outsiders to invade land that is either near some populated center, or owned by some government official or influential foreigner. Such invasions are designed to be political statements, since they are sure to be detected, and confrontations almost always develop. In contrast, invasions which are carried out in remote areas on land that is known to be state land, or whose owner either has not appeared in several years or has little political influence, have a good chance of going undetected and have a high probability of success. If such movements are successful, they are rarely reported in the press, and for that reason little is known about them. Since I was able to interview several peasants who had participated in one such movement, including one of its leaders, it is worthwhile to describe briefly how it operated.

Los Pinos, the fictitious name I will use for the farm where this squatting movement occurred, was once owned by a multinational foreign consortium. Original plans of the owners had included the development of a highly profitable agricultural operation, but because of mismanagement, a lack of capital, and waning interest on the part of the owners, the project never got off the ground. A small part of the farm was planted and was being worked by a contingent of peones, but the major operation consisted of small-scale lumbering. Since Los Pinos is located in a remote area, rarely, if ever, did government inspectors from the Ministry of Labor make an inspection of conditions on the farm. As a consequence, the legal minimum wage was never paid, and housing facilities were far below standard.

As the years passed, conditions on the farm began to deteriorate. The most serious problem for the workers developed when the foreman stopped paying them on a regular basis. A few weeks would pass and partial payment would be made. Then a few more weeks without pay, and another payment. Since this occurred during the nonharvest time of year, the workers could not find work elsewhere and had to accept the situation.

Finally an entire month passed without pay. A group of four workers decided that they had no choice but to head up into the mountains, the uncultivated part of the farm, and plant some corn and beans in order to prevent starvation. They did not do this openly but continued to work on Los Pinos, living off the unsteady wages paid there and in the afternoons and weekends, with the help of family labor, working the land they squatted on. When the first crops came in, other workers who had originally resisted the idea of squatting came to realize that it was the only solution to their plight.

At this point, Benito, a peasant who had been involved in squatting incidents before, was sought out for advice. He told them that the only way to succeed was to operate in groups of ten to twenty and to mark off their plots in a contiguous area so as to avoid isolation. They followed his advice, but by now the number of squatters had risen to close to fifty and it was no longer possible for them to work undetected; the foreman soon discovered their plots. He immediately called in the police, who went to the squatters and told them that they had better stop work or their crops would be set afire and they would be arrested. The squatters, frightened by the threats, again sought the advice of Benito. He suggested that instead of abandoning their plots, they raise the stakes of the conflict by moving their families onto the plots and constructing small shacks for them to live in. This tactic was designed to make it more difficult for the police to move in on the squatters, for now there would be women and children involved.

When the police returned, with the intention of burning the crops, they found that right in the middle of the cultivated fields stood small wooden shacks. A fire, of course, would have trapped the squatters in their homes, burning them alive. Unable to proceed with the burning operation, the police went to the shacks and demanded that the squatters get out. Anticipating that this was what was going to happen, all the members of the group agreed that they would respond, "When you get out all of the rest, I will go with pleasure." Thus, the police were placed in the position of having to arrest everyone at the same time, a task for which they did not have the manpower (by this time there were some one hundred families living in the area). The police responded to the squatters by saying, "These lands are owned by don Fulano and you have to get off." The squatters responded with, "They can't belong to him because he doesn't live here; we've never seen him and he doesn't work these lands, but we do."

The constant threats of the police deeply upset the squatters and induced them to think of further ways of frustrating them. They decided to write a petition to the president of the country, telling him to order the guards away so that they could dedicate all their time to farming. When Benito heard this, he objected. He realized that such a course of action would attract national publicity to the case, forcing the government to take action on it. That would have meant the intervention of ITCO and the national guard and probably the ultimate defeat of the squatters. He proposed a different solution. He said, "Let's build a school right at the entrance of the squatted lands, and put up a big sign saying, 'School Zone—Respect!' " There was no teacher, of course, but in Costa Rica the Ministry of Education readily responds to petitions for new schools, even in remote areas, so long as the minimum number of children are available in the area. Since the squatters now had their families with them, there were more than enough children to start a small school. One Saturday the squatters gathered at the entrance of their land and put up a small, very rustic shack, placing in front of it the sign, "School Zone—Respect!" On Monday morning the foreman approached the building and asked the nearby squatters, "Who built this?" Their response was, "The People." When he pressed them, insisting on knowing who the leader was, they simply replied, "Everyone." The foreman turned away in a fury of frustration, saying that he would be back the next day with the police, to burn down the school.

The police did return the next day, and approached the school. The implied threat of the squatters was all too evident to everyone; if the police burned down the school, they would be destroying public property and would consequently become involved in a serious conflict with the Ministry of Education. Not knowing how to cope with such a situation, the police left, recognizing that they had been beaten. After this, they refused to return to the area, fearing repercussions from San José. The foreman now had no one to defend his position. The squatters had won.

When I asked Benito what had moved him to lead this group, he answered in the following way. He had come to that zone as a young man, looking for work. At first he had had no trouble getting any, but after a few years, when the task of clearing the mountains had ended, work became scarcer. He had thought to himself, "What happens when there is no more work, what will I do then?" He concluded that "if a person wants to work and doesn't have a place to work, he must look for a place to work." Thus, he decided that the large landholders who had been given huge tracts of land in the area and would not be able to work more than a fraction of them in their lifetimes had no right to the unworked land. As a result of that reasoning, he began to encourage his fellow landless peasants to take the land they needed. There is no doubt in my mind that Benito was not trained in Cuba or Russia and that he had no links with the Communist Party of Costa Rica. He is a genuine example of a leader of an indigenous peasant movement that was totally successful. In all likelihood there are many more examples of such movements, but few are ever recorded.

Peasant Activism: An Explanation

Linking Attitudes and Behavior

Costa Rican peasants have not been passive in their reaction to the spread of agrarian capitalism. As has been shown, many peasants migrated to new areas of the country rather than be forced into peonage. In the present century, however, the acquisition of new lands has disappeared as an alternative. Peasants are increasingly turning to squatting in order to obtain land—but not all peasants do so. Why do some peasants become involved in land invasions, while others do not?

For many years it has been acknowledged that discontent alone does not make an activist. Many are unhappy with their lot, feel that they have been exploited in their work, or are resentful of government policies, but few take action. William A. Gamson [1968] has suggested that a certain combination of attitudes is required to move a person to political action. In particular, he has hypothesized that the combination of a high sense of efficacy and a low degree of political trust "is the optimum combination for mobilization" [Gamson, 1968:48].[3]

Clarke [1973:537], going beyond Gamson, has presented a more elaborate model of the relationship between attitudes and protest behavior. A modified version of a figure presented by Clarke is shown in figure 8. On the right side of the figure are those who trust government and who will be either "allegiant activists" or "allegiant apathetics," depending on

[3]Research in the United States has supported Gamson's hypothesis. Student activism during the Vietnam War protest days has been shown to be a product of a combination of high efficacy and low trust [Block, Haan, and Smith, 1973]. Protest approval by a cross-section of the United States electorate has also been predicted by this combination of attitudes [Balch and Kellstedt, 1975]. Perhaps the most extensive support for the Gamson hypothesis comes from the evidence available on black participation in the urban riots of the 1960s. In an extensive review of the literature on this subject, James W. Clarke [1973] concludes that structural variables such an unemployment, low education, poor housing, etc., do not explain why some blacks participated in the riots and others did not, since in the ghetto environment, these factors are more nearly constants than variables. Clarke finds that feelings of personal efficacy and lack of trust in government are the most important predictors; only those blacks who are *both* efficacious and distrustful of government are likely to riot [Paige, 1971].

Organization and Land Invasion

whether they feel efficacious or powerless. These individuals are not prone to protest participation. On the left side of the figure are those with low trust, often referred to as "cynics" [Aberbach, 1969:86-90; Miller, 1974:952]. The low-trust (cynical), low-efficacy (powerless) individuals feel that their protest is unlikely to be effective. They are called the "alienated apathetics." The low-trust/high-efficacy individuals, on the other hand, believe that their actions will be noticed, and are more likely to become involved in riots. They are termed the "alienated activists." Seen in this light, the riot is the black ghetto dweller's rational means of attempting to have his demands satisfied; it is an effective, if costly, way of making the white community take notice of the ghetto's problems. Gamson [1977:139] aptly puts it this way: "Rebellion, in this view, is simply politics by other means. It is not some kind of irrational expression."

We can use the Clarke framework to help explain land invasions in Costa Rica. Such invasions must be considered a radical act in the Costa Rican context, because they challenge the dominant political power

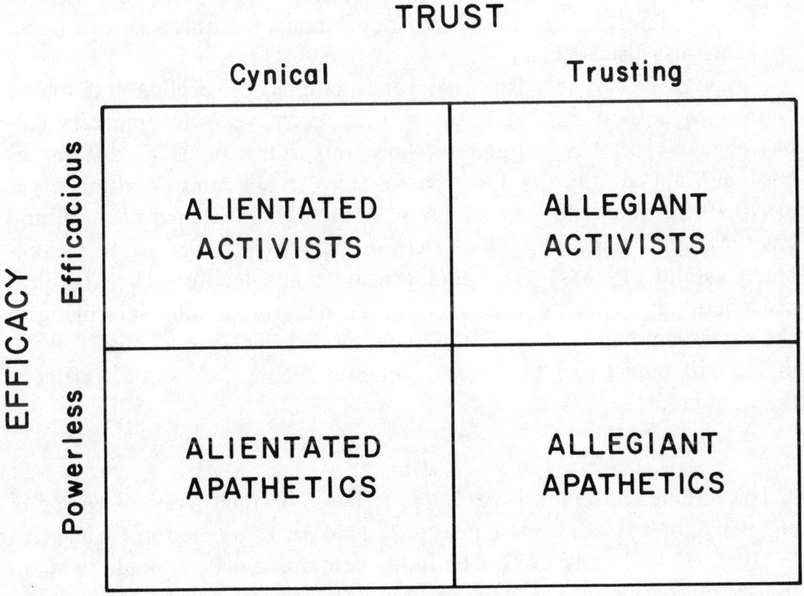

	TRUST	
EFFICACY	Cynical	Trusting
Efficacious	ALIENTATED ACTIVISTS	ALLEGIANT ACTIVISTS
Powerless	ALIENTATED APATHETICS	ALLEGIANT APATHETICS

Figure 8. Hypothesized relation between trust and efficacy

structure and provoke the threat of severe sanctions for the invaders. While some 78 percent of rural families in Costa Rica are landless, only on occasion do peasants resort to squatting to improve their situation. What is it about those landless peasants who turn to squatting which makes them distinct from others who, in similar circumstances, do not? The theoretical framework proposed above would suggest that peasants who have a higher sense of efficacy and a stronger distrust of government than the average landless peasant are more likely to have demonstrated political activism through land invasions, that is, squatting.

What of the landed sector of the peasantry? The peasants in this group are better off than their landless counterparts (see chapter 4), and perhaps more important, have long-term economic security which the landless do not. In addition, landed peasants have a stake in their community far beyond that of landless laborers, who may be frequently forced to change jobs and move to other communities owing to a scarcity of work. Thus it is reasonable to hypothesize that landed peasants are significantly more trusting and feel more efficacious than landless, nonsquatting peasants. In this section these hypotheses will be tested by comparing levels of trust and efficacy among the three categories of peasants just discussed.[4]

Although researchers have not yet attempted an explicit test of the Gamson hypothesis in Latin America, in recent years fragmentary empirical evidence has begun to show important political differences between landed and landless peasants. Van Es and Whittenberger (1970:19-22) found that Brazilian wage laborers participate less in, and have less knowledge of, politics than do peasant proprietors. In Colombia, Cartano (1968:84-85) found peasant wage laborers (i.e., landless peasants) significantly more anomic than peasant smallholders living in the same community. Mathiason and Powell (1972) found that Colombian smallholders had significantly greater feelings of political efficacy than did landless peasants.

Data

The findings to be presented here are based on the survey, discussed in chapter 4, of 531 adult male peasants, a survey conducted in Costa Rica in late 1972 and early 1973. The fundamental distinctions made in chapter 4 between landed and landless peasants are retained here. However,

---

[4]An analysis of attitudes among Costa Rican peasants which explores different types of political participation (conventional and unconventional) as well as different measures of efficacy is contained in Seligson, 1979b.

in order to simplify the analysis, the small group of tenant farmers (renters and sharecroppers) are grouped together with the landless peasants.[5] Furthermore, since the attention in this chapter is on the distinctiveness of the squatters, these peasants are treated as a separate group. Hence the analysis performed is based on three groups: landed peasants, landless peasants, and squatters. Of the 531 respondents, a total of 521 were categorized unambiguously into one of these three types: 203 smallholders (titled and untitled owners), 263 landless peasants, and 55 squatters.

The basic set of questions used to measure political trust are a slightly modified version of the University of Michigan's Survey Research Center "trust in government" scale. The efficacy questions are drawn from the "problem-solving efficacy scale" developed by Seligson [1979b; 1979c; forthcoming-a], based on the work of Mathiason in Venezuela [1972]. Details concerning the items and the distribution of responses is contained in Seligson [1979c], and the text of the questions is contained in chapter 6, tables 7 and 8, of the present work. (See appendix 4 for scale construction techniques.)

Results

The results of the data analysis are presented in two parts. First, the analysis of the trust and efficacy attitudes is presented. Second, the joint effect of these attitudes is discussed in relation to the three types of peasants (smallholders, landless laborers, and squatters), who are categorized into their appropriate position in figure 8.

Figure 9 presents the results of the analysis of the trust scale. Those peasants whose mean trust score is above zero (the mean for a Z-scored variable) are placed in the "trusting" category, and those with a score below zero are placed in the "cynical" category. The relative position of the mean values of each peasant type is illustrated by the position of the points on the line. Figure 9 shows that trust is highest among the smallholders, drops among the landless laborers, and is lowest among the squatters.[6]

---

[5] When the analysis is performed with the tenants removed from the sample, the results remain substantively the same.

[6] The differences among the means of the three groups are statistically significant (F ratio probability $<.001$) when a one-way analysis of variance test is applied to the data. A Duncan post hoc test (sig. = .05) reveals the three groups' means are significantly different from each other.

The analysis of the efficacy scale is conducted in the same fashion that has been used to examine trust. Figure 10 displays the mean efficacy score of the three peasant types. The smallholders and the squatters are both highly efficacious in contrast to the landless laborers.[7]

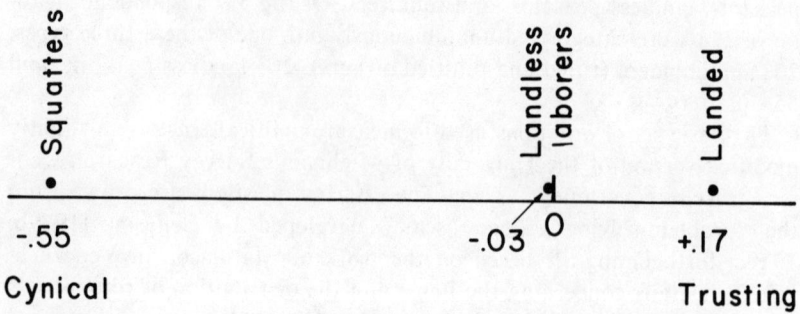

Figure 9. Trust among types of Costa Rican peasants

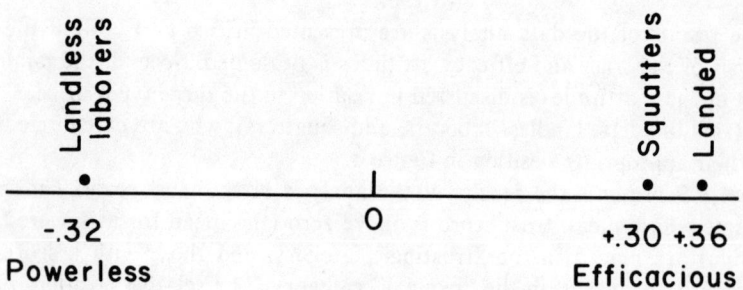

Figure 10. Efficacy among types of Costa Rican peasants

Now that each land tenure type has been discussed with regard to its score on the trust and efficacy dimensions, it is appropriate to turn to an examination of the relationship between these two dimensions, in order

---

[7] A one way analysis of variance on the efficacy indicator reveals a significant difference (F <.001). The Duncan post hoc test (sig. =.05), however, reveals that the difference between the squatter and smallholder levels of efficacy is not significant. Rather, only the difference between the landless laborers on the one hand and the squatters and smallholders on the other is significant.

Organization and Land Invasion

to see where each group of peasants falls on the theoretical framework.[8] Figure 11 displays the three types of peasants as located within the trust-efficacy framework.

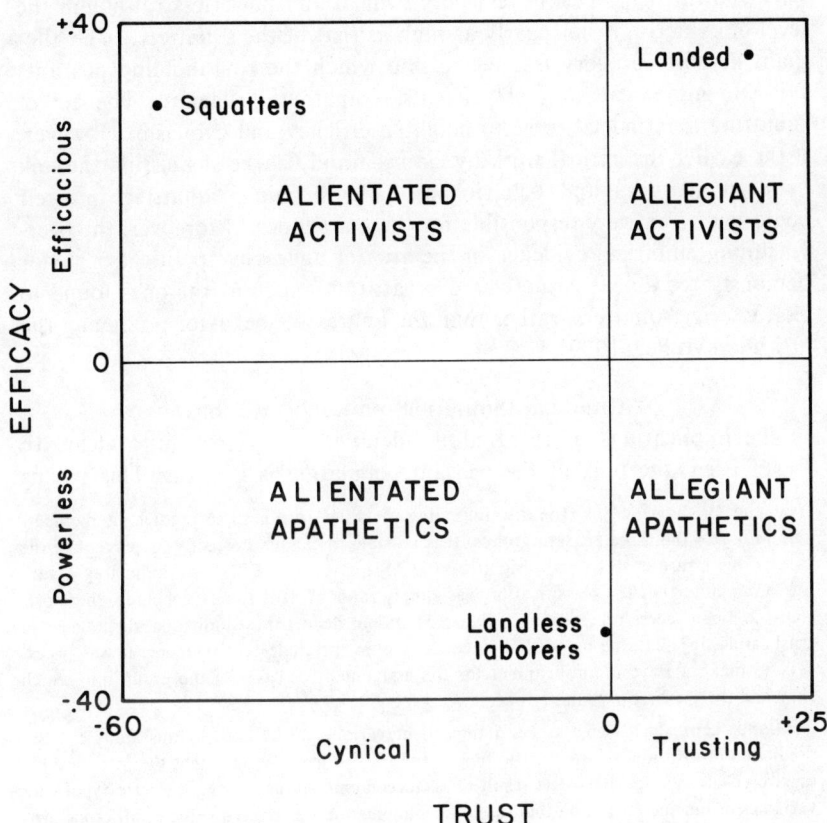

Figure 11. Trust and efficacy among types of Costa Rican peasants

[8]The mean scores of each peasant type on the trust dimension appear to confirm the theory. These mean scores, however, may be deceiving, for while the mean of each type may indeed fall in the predicted order, (e.g., landed, landless, squatter) the trust scores of *individual* peasants may be different from those predicted. In fact, it would be unreasonable to expect all smallholders to be more trusting than all laborers, and similarly, all squatters would not be expected to be more cynical than all of the other peasants. What needs to be determined is whether a statistically significant number of the smallholders are more trusting than the landless peasants and the squatters, and if a significant portion of the squatters are more cynical than the landed and landless peasants.

In order to make this determination, discriminant analysis was employed [Cooley and Lohnes, 1971]. Discriminant analysis is a classification technique which identifies the probable group membership of each respondent based on the information contained in the discriminating variable or variables. In this case, the scores each peasant obtained on the

Looking first at the category of alienated activists, it can be seen that only the squatters are both highly cynical and highly efficacious. The alienated apathetic category is populated by the landless laborers, who have shown themselves to feel both cynical and powerless (although the level of cynicism is not nearly as high as that of the squatters.) The allegiant activist category is the one into which the smallholding peasants fall. No major category of peasants is apathetic allegiant. The act of squatting may indeed serve to heighten efficacy and cynicism. However, if the earlier theoretical work by Gamson and Clarke suggesting the link between attitudes and behavior has any meaning, squatting in itself could not be entirely responsible for these attitudes.[9] Moreover, the overwhelming empirical evidence in the area of aggressive political behavior demonstrates that it is motivated by attitudes such as the ones found to characterize squatters, rather than the aggressive behavior producing the attitude [Muller, 1979].

Attitudinal Limitations on Land Invasions

The implications of the findings detailed above are quite clear. In Costa Rica, the bulk of the peasant population is landless. This means

---

trust and efficacy indexes (the discriminating variables) are used to predict his membership in one of the three peasant groups. It is possible to classify correctly 59 percent of the cases. This figure is statistically significant (Chi-square) at <.001 level, indicating a very low probability that the classification was simply random. It is fair to conclude, therefore, that the mean scores represented in figure 11 do not distort most individual differences in trust levels. It should be noted that since the groups differed greatly in size, it was necessary to make a Bayesian adjustment for the assignment of cases to the group into which they had the greatest probability of falling.

[9]Land tenure has been the sole independent variable to be used in this study for the prediction of attitudes of trust and efficacy. In order to make certain that the relationships uncovered are not spurious (the result of socioeconomic status, not land tenure type), the variables of income (based on total cash income plus total estimated value of all crops produced) and education have been examined. Examination of the data reveals no significant difference with regard to the education variable. There are significant (F ratio <.001) differences between the income levels of the three types, however. The squatters comprise the poorest group, with an average weekly income of 70 colones (less than 10 dollars). The landless laborers earn an average of 142 colones, double that of the squatters. The landed peasants earn an average of 365 colones weekly—more than twice the salary of the landless peasants. (Such a high figure for the landed peasants is somewhat of a distortion, since there were a few landed peasants who had a very high income which inflated the mean. The 215 median figure for these peasants, however, is still relatively high.)

Since these differences are significant, it is necessary to control for income in the examination of the relationship between peasant type and the attitudinal variables. This has been done by dividing the sample into two groups, those with incomes above it and those with incomes below it, and then rerunning the analysis. The findings are quite clear: the same relationship between peasant type and the trust and efficacy variables which appeared earlier is evident within each income group.

that the countryside is dominated by individuals who feel politically cynical and politically powerless when compared to the landed peasants. While such a situation is not a particularly desirable one from many points of view, it is not one which presents a serious threat to national stability; only a tiny minority of peasants are *both* cynical and efficacious. Only this minority is likely to embark upon land invasions.

Many factors can intervene to change this situation. Perhaps the most important of these would be the impact of the organization discussed earlier in this chapter. Landless peasants who feel politically powerless on an individual basis may become involved in strikes and other forms of protest behavior upon being organized into peasant leagues. Masses of cynical peasants, effectively organized into such leagues, have at times been successful in their efforts to obtain land (as they were in the northeast of Brazil in the early 1960s, and in Chile in the early 1970s). Landless peasants in Costa Rica may well alter their present political passivity if organized into peasant leagues. Whether such a development would ultimately reward the peasant with a plot of land is an open question, however. In Brazil the military takeover of 1964 brutally crushed the peasant leagues, and in Chile the coup of 1973 resulted in the immediate return of land that had been seized in land invasions. In Costa Rica the government has attempted to avoid such clashes by satisfying peasant demands for land through an agrarian reform program; the successes, failures, and limitations of that program are discussed in the next chapter.

6 Government Response to Agrarian Capitalism: Land Reform

The introduction of coffee cultivation in Costa Rica has brought about the steady downward social mobility of the peasant. The once proud yeoman who constituted the social backbone of the nation has slowly slipped into a position of insignificance alongside the powerful coffee giants and banana magnates. The bulk of the peasantry is landless, and those who have land own very little.

It has been shown in chapter 4 that one major result of the deterioration of the peasant's relative economic position and the diversification of peasant social structure has been the development of an intense concern with security. Peasants faced with an intolerably insecure economic situation have been forced to invade land as the only course of action left to them. Squatting, however, does not solve the peasants' problem. Many land invasions are unsuccessful, and the peasants are thrown from their newly acquired land into prison cells. Invasions which do succeed rarely provide a tranquil existence for the squatter, since he suffers continual threats of eviction from angered landlords and unceasing pressure from other squatters who attempt to snatch away his new land. The squatter has no security.

Where are the landless, unemployed peasant masses to turn? The paucity of jobs in the city makes urban migration a viable alternative for only a very few peasants. Peasants are increasingly turning to the government for a solution. This chapter discusses the development of agrarian reform in Costa Rica: the government's response to the problems created by agrarian capitalism. It outlines the history of agrarian reform and demonstrates that up until the early 1970s the effort was only a token one. Recent efforts to expand the reform program are then discussed. The impact of reform on peasant attitudes, based on data gathered in two opinion surveys, are then presented. The data demonstrate that peasants who have received land under the reform program develop attitudes which reflect more trust in government, more positive orientation toward the future, and higher feelings of political efficacy than do those who have not been beneficiaries of land reform. Land reform is seen as an imperative for the future stability of the Costa Rican countryside. Finally, the impact of reform on land distribution is analyzed, using data from 1963 to 1973.

First Efforts to Help the Peasant: The CNP

The first contemporary effort to provide relief to the peasant was not directed to the landless sector at all, but to the subsistence smallholder. The government hoped to help stabilize the price of basic grains. It did so by creating, in 1949, the Consejo Nacional de Producción (the National Production Council). In most years the price of grain would drop as the harvest began to come in. Since most farmers had no storage facilities, they were forced to sell the grain at low prices. Later in the year prices would climb, but then the small farmer would have no grain to sell. The CNP was to regulate prices by purchasing corn, beans, and other basic grains directly from the producer and at fair prices. The Consejo, by constructing storage facilities, was able to buy the grain at a reasonable price and then sell it later in the year when prices rose.

The CNP assisted small farmers in three other ways. First, it made credit available to those who were unable to get it through the national banking system. Agricultural bank credit has traditionally been largely directed toward coffee-, banana-, and cattle-raising. Subsistence farmers generally have been unable to obtain the small bank loans required to expand farm production [May, 1952:61-62; Banco Central, 1960:29; U.S. Department of Agriculture, 1970:28]. In recent years, only about 3 to 4 percent of agricultural bank credit has gone to the subsistence farmer [Ministerio de Agricultura, 1973:34-39; González-Vega, 1973:23-29]. A major factor in the limitation of credit to small farmers was that banks generally do not make loans to farmers who can not offer titled land as collateral [Salas Marrero and Barahona Israel, 1973:498]. Since most small farmers living off the meseta did not have title, they were excluded from receiving credit.[1] The CNP, however, was not as restricted in its collateral policies in the way the banks were. In the early 1970s the CNP was granting two thousand loans a year at an average of a little less than 250 dollars each. This meant that only approximately 6 percent of all of the smallholders (defined as holdings of less than five hectares) received CNP credit. Added to the 3 percent of the smallholders who received bank credit (assuming no overlap), less than one-tenth of the smallholders received agricultural credit. A 1969 survey of more than four hundred small farmers revealed a substantial excessive demand for agricultural credit [Vogel and González-Vega, 1969], and there are signs of an increasing imbalance of supply and demand in the mid 1970s [Vogel, 1978:10]. Despite the rapid growth of the rural population, there were fewer rural credit loans in the early 1970s than in the early 1950s [González-Vega, 1973:50].

The next way in which the CNP assisted the small farmer was through the establishment of general stores (*expendios*) with fixed prices on basic consumer items. These stores guaranteed the peasant that he could buy food at prices which were not subject to the whim of the local *pulperos* (the general store owners), who were notorious for overcharging their customers, especially in remote regions where competition was limited or nonexistent.

The final method which the CNP employed to assist the farmer was the provision of high quality seed. One of the most difficult agricultural problems in Costa Rica is fungus disease, caused by the unusually high rainfall, which affects crops in most areas of the country. (Some regions have an average of fifteen feet of rain a year.) As a result, seeds gathered from the harvest are often diseased and result in low yields in subsequent crops. The CNP supplied specially grown healthy seeds at a low cost and thereby helped insure farmers a higher yield. In addition, new fungus-resistant seed varieties were developed by the Instituto Interamericano de Ciencias Agrícolas (IICA), located in Turrialba, Costa Rica, and introduced by the CNP for use by the peasants.

The CNP, helpful though it has been to a limited sector of small farmers, has been of virtually no benefit to the landless peasant.[2] The smallholder, while by no means well off, did have the economic security

---

[1]Since 1914 the Banco Nacional has operated Rural Credit Boards (originally called Cajas Rurales de Crédito but later called Juntas Rurales de Crédito). These Juntas are active, giving about 28,000 loans a year at an average of about 800 dollars each. Other commercial banks make a total of fewer than 8,000 loans a year to small farmers [Brown, 1973:19].

[2]The general stores could be used by all, landed and landless alike, and therefore were of some benefit to the latter group as well.

of his land; the landless peasant was in a more difficult position. Unfortunately, no governmental aid was forthcoming for the landless peasants until the 1960s, and even then, it came in such small doses that its impact was, until just recently, negligible.

Land Reform Gets Underway

When the first effort at reform appeared in the 1940s, it came through the back door. The Costa Rican state, as a result of the serious economic dislocations produced by World War II, began to take steps to modernize its structure. In 1942 the Ministerio de Agricultura y Ganaderia (Ministry of Agriculture and Livestock) was organized, and within it the Oficina de Colonización y de Distribución de Tierras del Estado (Office of Colonization and Distribution of State Lands) was created. This office was established, not to effect agrarian reform, but to administer state forest reserves. Since sections of these reserve lands were being occupied illegally by private individuals (both large landholders and peasants alike), the Office was inexorably drawn into the business of settling land disputes. The Office of Colonization was not equipped to handle the problem which it found itself confronting. It was staffed primarily by agronomists and agricultural technicians whose expertise did not include handling land disputes. As a consequence, very little was accomplished.

By 1949 it had become clear that a more effective bureaucratic structure had to be created to cope with the land problem. As a result, a legislative committee was formed with representatives from the Ministries of Agriculture, Finance, Justice, and Labor, as well as representatives from the private sector. Unfortunately the reform effort was stillborn, and no legislative action was taken. Perhaps the task was too complex, too revolutionary for Costa Rica to confront on its own. What model was it to use? The models provided by the Mexican and Bolivian Revolutions provided little guidance, since Costa Rica had not undergone an agrarian revolution as had those two countries.[3]

The Cuban Revolution and its subsequent radical agrarian reform did much to create a responsive atmosphere for the passage of reform legislation in Costa Rica. In fact, there is some evidence that the United States foreign mission was attempting to encourage the passage of some

[3]The so-called Revolution of 1948 in Costa Rica should in no way be misconstrued as an agrarian revolution. The peasants who did get drawn into the conflict did so as a result of party loyalties, their stand (pro or con) on communism (a major issue in the "revolution"), and their opposition to electoral fraud. The Revolution is more appropriately termed a civil war [Aguilar, 1969:192-94; Bell, 1971:41-61,106-30; Acuña, 1974:33-141].

sort of reform law [Riismandel, 1972:203-222]. The United States' position on the need for reform was made known in August, 1961, at the Conference of Punta del Este, which laid the foundations for the Alliance for Progress. A major concern of the Alliance was the promulgation of agrarian reforms in the participating states. Perhaps as a consequence of the Cuban experience, internal pressure for reform began to grow. In 1961 the Partido Agraria was formed in Costa Rica with the slogan "land for the man who tills it." As talk of agrarian reform grew, peasants were encouraged to invade land in the hope that their possession would be legalized under the anticipated law. As a consequence, landholders whose property had been invaded put pressure on the government to pass a reform law so that they could receive compensation for their loss. A few months after the Punta del Este meeting an agrarian reform law came into being, on October 14, 1961 [Hill, 1964:46-48].

There has been much debate over whether the law was a vehicle for a true agrarian reform or just a sop to domestic and foreign pressure [Flores, 1963:8-9]. Certainly the goals of the law were ambitious enough: (1) to better the socioeconomic conditions of peasants; (2) to conserve natural resources; (3) to promote an increase in the productivity of the land; (4) to prevent the concentration of land in the hands of those who would use it for speculative purposes; (5) to support the development of small- and medium-sized farms; (6) to avoid the creation of *minifundios*; and (7) to promote cooperatives. Critics argued, however, that these goals would never be met and that the peasantry would not find relief.

The key grounds for criticizing the law lie in the issue of compensation for expropriation. The law places heavy emphasis on "respect for private property." It does so for two reasons. First, the legislators wanted to do all they could to prevent peasants from interpreting the new law as an open ticket for further land invasions. It was felt that unless the law contained a strong statement supporting private property, mass squatting would result. In fact, despite the legislators' efforts, incidents of squatting did increase after the law went into effect. The second reason for the emphasis on respect for private property is much more important, and lies at the heart of the controversy over the law. The law provides for *prior* full compensation for expropriated land, based on the value of the property as declared by the owner for tax purposes. Hence, the extent of the expropriations (and consequently the scope of the entire agrarian reform) became directly and inexorably tied to the financial ability of the state. This was so because for every latifundio that was expropriated, funds had to be found to pay the owner in full for his property, or bonds had to be issued for payment. Either way, each expropriation had a direct impact on national indebtedness. In a country like Costa Rica, which relies on the export of agricultural commodities for the greatest share of its income, the state's capacity to absorb debts is quite limited. Hence the scope of the reform program, despite the best intentions of those whose job it was to implement it, was severely restricted. The evidence to support this statement can be found in the records of the Instituto de Tierras y Colonización (The Lands and Colonization Institute), which was established in November 1962 as the bureaucratic apparatus for the execution of the law.

Phase 1: The Colonization Program, 1962-66

ITCO went through several stages in its evolution, each with its own characteristics. The first of these phases placed an emphasis on colonization schemes. At first blush the colonization idea seemed like a good one. It promised to resolve the land hunger of many peasants at the lowest possible cost to the government. The limited financial resources of the Institute conflicted with its desire to benefit the largest possible number of peasants. As a way out of this conflict, inexpensive lands in remote areas were acquired by ITCO to be set up as colonies. Even following this course of action, after five years of effort only 1,272 peasant families were settled on 11 colonies, covering a total of 35,412 hectares (see table 6).

Table 6. ITCO's Colonization Program

Year	Number of Projects	Area in Hectares	Number of Settlers
1962	0	0	0
1963	2	4,371	247
1964	5	23,073	685
1965	2	2,129	124
1966	2	5,839	166
1967 to present	0	0	0
Totals	11	35,412	1,222

Source: Instituto de Tierras y Colonización, 1974.

Extraordinarily high hidden costs in the colonization scheme limited its success. In 1962 the Institute did not fully appreciate the fact that for a peasant to make a go of things he had to have more than a plot of land and his two hands. Roads, more than anything else, were essential; roads make it possible to obtain seed, fertilizer, and tools for the production of crops, and also provide access to markets once the crop has been harvested. Roads also permit the sick to be transported to hospitals, and make it possible for agricultural agents (*extensionistas*) to visit the farms and provide technical advice. Upon their establishment, most of the ITCO colonies had neither external roads linking them to the outside world nor internal roads linking one farmer to his neighbor. The regions chosen for the colonies were often so remote that all-weather roads connecting them to the outside world were too costly to construct. It is not surprising that 32 percent of the colonists who were interviewed responded that roads were the most pressing problem they had.[4]

It is not that ITCO did not want to provide roads in these areas; it is simply that it did not have the resources with which to do so. Road construction in Costa Rica is an extraordinarily expensive affair, because of the uneven nature of the terrain and the extremely high rainfall. Problems of drainage and landslides are insurmountable without a large investment in machinery and materials. It is no accident that the last completed section of the Inter-American Highway linking the United States with the Panama Canal was in Costa Rica. And even in this case, despite thirty years of construction efforts, large foreign loans, and the most up-to-date machinery and engineering advice, sections of the road wash out almost every rainy season. ITCO had none of the resources of the Inter-American highway builders, but nevertheless it was confronted with the construction of road networks to eleven remote colonies scattered over different regions of the country.

Roads, however, were not the only unforeseen problem in the colonization scheme. Other kinds of infrastructure projects were needed as well. Houses had to be erected for the colonists, water systems had to be installed. ITCO argued that other government agencies responsible for such specific needs as housing and potable water (the Instituto Nacional de Vivienda y Urbanismo, or INVU, and the Servicio Nacional de Acueductos y Alcantarías, or SNAA, respectively) should take over these projects. These agencies in most cases replied, however, that the colonies were ITCO projects and that they were, therefore, ITCO's responsibility. The same reply was often heard from the Ministry of Public Works (Ministerio de Obras Públicas) when it came to the establishing of roads linking the colonies to the nearest town. As a result, ITCO, the agrarian reform agency, was saddled with the responsibility of being a road builder, house builder, water system builder, etc. In the 1976 survey

---

[4]These data come from a study conducted in April-June 1976 by the author and Elena A. Wachong, with the assistance of ITCO and the Ford and Rockefeller Foundations' Joint Population and Development Policy Research Program. Further results of the study are presented later on in this chapter. Total sample: N=753, of whom 303 were colonists.

referred to above, in which 32 percent of the colonists responded that bad roads were their major problem, 16 percent of the remaining respondents said that the absence of a water system was their central problem, and another 12 percent named the absence of bridges. Roads, bridges, and water systems accounted, therefore, for 60 percent of the colonists' major problems.

Some important lessons were learned from the colonization program. The first of these had to do with location. It became abundantly clear that future reform should take place in at least partially developed regions. The few colonies located in such regions had fared relatively well. ITCO data show, for example, that Colonia La Trinidad, located in a well-developed area, achieved production levels of 44,535 colones ($5,178) per capita in 1974, while remote La Esperanza produced only 4,815 colones ($560) per capita in the same year [ITCO, 1975].

A second lesson ITCO learned had to do with the selection of the colonists themselves. It is not entirely clear how the colonists were selected; ITCO did establish procedures which required some sort of background check on the individual, but apparently political considerations were often important. Hence, it has been alleged that in some cases landowners with political connections were able to obtain parcels of an ITCO colony. They in turn would rent them out to some friend or relative, or would simply sell the property for profit even though the sale of property was strictly forbidden by ITCO rules. In other cases, it has been alleged, the colonization program was used as a way of exiling disruptive members of a community: individuals who were drunks, vagabonds, or political dissenters are said to have been sent off to these remote regions to be gotten rid of. Another problem with selection involved finding highly motivated peasants willing to endure the sacrifices of colonization. Interviews with 303 members of six colonies revealed that many complained about being forced to leave their old home towns and having to move to remote areas. As they saw it, the colonies should have been established nearer their families and friends so that they would not have felt so isolated. The poor roads made visits back home costly, difficult, and time-consuming. In many cases family members were cut off from each other for years. Not only did the colonists feel isolated, they also felt betrayed by ITCO. It appears that in an effort to sell the idea of the colonies to peasants, ITCO often promised more than it could deliver. Peasants report that they were promised houses but were given only a few pieces of corrugated tin roofing. Others state that they were promised farms and given inaccessible, uncleared jungle. Some say that they were promised technical help and in many cases given none. It is difficult to say if those promises were official ITCO policy or whether they were unauthorized remarks made by ITCO staffers in order to encourage reluctant prospective colonists to settle in remote locations. Official policy or not, colonists believed that they had been deceived.

All in all, the colonization program was not particularly successful. In 1966 the final two colonies were established, and after that no new colonies were created. The eleven extant colonies went through some very rocky times, and in some cases large numbers of colonists abandoned their farms. By the 1970s, however, as national development proceeded, many of these remote areas were finally linked to the national highway system, and other pressing infrastructure projects were completed. A number of the colonies began to increase their productivity, and some have become relatively successful operations. Many colonists, however, retain bitter memories of the early days of the program. Moreover, it was generally agreed that the costs of the colonization program were too great to make it a practical alternative.

Phase 2: Settling Squatter Conflicts, 1966-70

By late 1966 serious reexamination of ITCO's programs was underway. It was clear by this time that the limited resources of the Institute made further colonization impossible. Officials within the Institute began searching for a new role more compatible with its desperate economic situation. By default, perhaps, the settlement of squatter conflicts became the only activity which the Institute was able to pursue.

From the first days of its establishment, ITCO began receiving requests from peasants and large landlords alike to intervene in and resolve squatter conflicts. The 1961 law emphasized this aspect of the program, since squatting conflicts were a source of considerable tension in the countryside. The squatters steadfastly refused to be evicted, while the landowners demanded eviction or compensation. In addition, the government found itself in conflict with peasants who squatted on public domain land. There were also some cases of squatting on Indian reservations (*reservas indígenas*). In the years 1966 to 1969, ITCO dedicated itself to the resolution of these conflicts. In cases where peasants could prove their legitimate right to the land they were granted legal title. In other cases, where the landlord had the law on his side, the peasant was offered a small plot on one of the colonies in exchange for his agreement to abandon the squatted on land. The cost to the Institute was minimal, since all that was required was the utilization of the legal and administrative staff that ITCO already had on its payroll. Capital expenditures were largely unnecessary.

The program met with some success. In 1966, the year the project began, only 79 titles were granted. In 1967 the number rose to 303, and in 1968 to 705. In that year an additional 217 titles were given to individuals in the colonization program. In 1969, the last year of this phase, 747 titles were granted to squatters plus an additional 42 titles for the colonists. The entire four-year period saw the granting of 2,093 titles, compared to only 224 titles in the previous four years.

Despite successes in the titling program, its small size limited its effectiveness. Moreover, the program sought to deal with the consequence of inequality in land distribution rather than its cause. That is to say, rather than attempting to restructure land distribution in Costa Rica in order to avoid squatting conflicts, the program attempted to resolve the conflicts that had already occurred. It became evident that such a program was not acceptable to either the peasant or the political elites. The peasants wanted land and preferred to get it legally. They preferred to avoid the risks involved in squatting if at all possible. Political elites, in turn, sought to avoid rural unrest, and tranquility could only be accomplished by providing land to peasants before serious conflicts erupted and squatting occurred. ITCO recognized that some new efforts had to be made that would not only resolve existing conflicts but avoid new ones whenever possible. This recognition brought about the next phase in the development of the Institute, the one adhered to in the 1970s.

Phase 3: The Formation of Agricultural Enterprises, 1970-78

By the end of the 1960s, ITCO had accumulated enough experience from its past efforts to embark upon a program which promised greater success. ITCO had learned from the colonization programs that the total cost of setting up colonies in undeveloped regions was far too high and that, while the initial costs of purchasing land in more developed regions were higher than acquiring land in undeveloped areas, the total cost of the project promised to be far lower. ITCO had also learned that potential recipients of land had to be self-motivated and fully aware of the realities of the project at hand, rather than be misled by pie in the sky promises which could not be fulfilled. Finally, ITCO had become convinced that time was growing short and that a major effort to satisfy peasant land hunger had to be made.

With accumulated experience under their belts, ITCO planners began searching for a new model of reform. In 1969, on the flood plains of Guanacaste province, the opportunity arose and ITCO acted. The upshot was the establishment of an entirely new style of agrarian reform in Costa Rica, which came to be known as the Río Cañas Model.

The Río Cañas Model. The story of the peasants of Río Cañas takes us back to 1959 and to a village called Río Caña Vieja.[5] In that year, as

[5]The information in this section comes from personal interviews with peasants, Peace Corps volunteers, and from Instituto Mixto de Ayuda Social [1973:n.p.].

a result of unusually heavy rains in the area, the two rivers which border the town overflowed their banks and swept away all of the houses, cattle, and crops. The peasants of the village were left destitute. Costa Rican disaster relief agencies quickly stepped in and transported the homeless to the city of Santa Cruz, Guanacaste.

Once in Santa Cruz, the peasants formed an emergency committee, and with the help of INVU (the housing agency), forty-nine houses were built on high ground near the site of the old village of Río Caña Vieja. With the housing problem solved, the most pressing concern became that of finding work. In Guanacaste, more than in any other region in Costa Rica, day work was scarce and low paid. Rarely were there sufficient *jornales* to satisfy the demand for them, and frequently the minimum wage laws were ignored.[6] After years of frustration, the Río Cañas peasant emergency committee decided to rent a parcel of land from a large landholder in the area so that its members could cultivate basic grains.

For two years the peasants worked the nearly four hundred hectares of rented land, turning an unused farm into productive fields. Then tragedy struck once again, but this time it was not nature which was playing tricks on the peasants: it was the landowner. When the peasants asked for a renewal of the rental contract for a third year, the landlord refused. The peasants were desperate; they had invested two years of sweat in clearing the land, and now that the crops were beginning to come in, the landlord refused to let them continue their work. The committee then sent a delegaton to San José to talk to ITCO officials about the problem. ITCO sympathized with their plight and promised action, but none was immediately forthcoming. ITCO was faced with its chronic shortage of capital and could not, without outside help, assist the Río Cañas peasants. The peasants then presented their case to the national legislature, arguing that years had passed since they had lost their homes in the 1959 flood and still there was no relief. When the story was picked up by the news media, the national conscience was touched and action was taken. ITCO was given the go ahead to purchase the land. When the owner refused the price offered, ITCO used its legal powers and ordered expropriation (with full compensation).

On March 12, 1969, the cooperative of Río Cañas was organized with forty-four members. The peasants decided to work in common the bulk of the 309 hectares of land that they had acquired, rather than divide the land into small plots. It is difficult to ascertain why they did not

---

[6]Because of the bleak employment situation in Guanacaste and the high concentration of land in large cattle farms, this province has experienced the largest out-migration of any of the seven provinces of the country since the 1950s [Fernández, Schmidt, and Basauri, 1976: 91-103].

make the division into individual plots, but it is likely that their years of working together on the emergency committee had helped weld the group into a functioning interdependent unit. Working the land in common would help them to maximize the resources at their disposal. With the assistance of some Peace Corps volunteers they began growing and selling watermelons, and with the assistance of agricultural agents they planted rice. They were given credit to buy three tractors, a harvester, electric saws, and an assortment of other farm equipment. They also began using improved seed provided by the CNP. By 1975 the cooperative was producing 1.4 million colones annually, or an average of 32,442 colones per capita ($3,770). Of course the lion's share of this money went to repay the outstanding debts, but nevertheless, the results impressed observers.

The Río Cañas model has served as a stimulus to both ITCO and peasants alike. The former finally had a success to which it could point with pride, and the latter saw that with enough initiative they could get ITCO's help. As a result, the Río Cañas model inspired an upsurge of reform activity in Costa Rica which has been characteristic of the present phase of ITCO's life.

ITCO's New Program. In the 1970s, four basic principles have guided ITCO's rapidly expanding efforts at agrarian reform. The first is that settlements should be located in developed regions. This is not to imply that all projects will be located on the meseta central, but rather, that they must be accessible to some major marketing center. As a result, although many of the new projects are located off the meseta, they are virtually always within a short distance of some regional town which in turn is connected by all-weather roads to San José.

The second guiding principle is that, whenever possible, new projects should be formed on established farms rather than on virgin territory. In many cases such farms have been abandoned by their previous owners before ITCO takes them over; nevertheless, internal roads, wells, storage sheds, and flood control systems are usually in place, and require little additional investment to put them in working order. ITCO is particularly attracted to projects which already have installations for cash crops. For example, in some cases the farms have had installations for a small dairy, and in other cases they have had a *trapiche*.[7] In one case an entire banana packing plant with surrounding banana fields was included within the settlement grounds. ITCO has recognized that these infrastructure items raise the acquisition price but are far cheaper than if they had to be added later.

[7] These are small sugar mills which produce an unrefined brown sugar sold in cylindrical cakes called *tapa dulce*. The trapiche should not be confused with the much more elaborate *ingenio*, or sugar refinery, which produces refined, white sugar.

According to the third principle, ITCO projects are required to demonstrate potential economic viability. Each new project is carefully studied by a team of agronomists and economists in order to determine the likelihood of economic success. Crop yields are estimated, and market prices are calculated. If it appears that the project will not be a success, the plan is either modified or rejected altogether.

The final principle guides the selection of beneficiaries of the projects, namely, that peasants should select themselves for the projects. ITCO has become actively involved in the organization of groups of peasants who are seeking land. In the past, ITCO shied away from such groups, fearing that by assisting them it would possibly end up stimulating land invasions. Today, ITCO prefers to have contact with the groups, so that it can give them guidance and at the same time have some feel for their mettle. ITCO does not make it easy for such groups to get land, for to do so would only invite disaster for those not willing to put up with the hardships of initiating a settlement. Moreover, the struggle for land helps build camaraderie, as happened in the Río Cañas case discussed above. The likelihood of cooperation among members once the project becomes established is increased considerably.

Two types of projects have been developed under the new guidelines. The first type is the individual parcel program, similar to the the colonization program in its land tenure pattern (i.e., individual ownership), but different from it in that the settlements are formed following as closely as possible the four guiding principles now used by ITCO in its planning. The second program follows the Río Cañas model and is called the "self-run communal enterprise" (*empresas comunitarias de autogestión*).

Both types of reform programs have been experimented with in recent years, and ITCO is now attempting to determine which is more effective. The communal enterprise model is based upon ITCO's own experience with the Río Cañas cooperative and its familiarity with similar programs in other Latin American countries such as Colombia, Honduras, and Panama [Araujo, 1975; PROCCARA, 1975]. The essential difference between the individual parcel and the communal enterprise programs is that within the former, the farms are individual possessions, whereas under the latter, the land is both owned and worked in common. Communal ownership is considered of critical importance to the program's potential for success. Under the colony and individual plot program each peasant works on his own plot and has only his own resources upon which to draw. Consequently, individual plots are capital and labor starved, making it very difficult for a farm to become an economic success. The communal enterprise, in contrast, operates all land in common, and therefore has the potential of becoming an efficient operation through the pooling of capital investment, labor, and technological know-how. In addition, the communal arrangement permits diversification of the farm's production, thereby taking full advantage of the topography and irrigation found in various sections of the farm. For example, coffee can be planted on hilly parts of the terrain, while vegetables can be grown on the flatter lands.

One important feature of the communal enterprise which should be emphasized is that all members receive identical wages regardless of the function they serve in the organization. Thus, whereas in a typical cooperative the manager (*gerente*) normally receives an hourly wage considerably higher than that of the other members, such discrepancies in wages are not permitted on a communal enterprise. The maintenance of all salaries at the same level is intended as a safeguard against jealousy among members.

The communal enterprises are not without their problems, however. The success of any collective operation relies on mutual trust. In communal farms which I observed, a number of members expressed discontent with other members, particularly over issues related to work; some felt that others were shirking their responsibilities or were getting the easier jobs. The managers often expressed the feeling of being overwhelmed with the responsibilities for running such a complex endeavor. Internal conflicts in some enterprises have taken such a toll on productivity that they have brought the farms to the brink of economic collapse.

An indication of the difficulties encountered by members of the communal enterprises is revealed by the data collected in the 1976 study reported above. In that study, 226 members of communal enterprises were interviewed. One question asked was "Do you think that among the people in this settlement there are more disagreements or fewer disagreements than among those people who are not members." It was found that members of communal enterprises were more likely (F test for analysis of variance significant at $<.001$) to perceive that there were more disagreements than were ITCO settlers in the parcel or colony programs. However, although there appear to be more disagreements within the communal enterprises, the data also reveal that enterprise members trust each other more than do beneficiaries of the other reform projects. The peasants were asked the following question: "Some people tend to help others, while others only watch out for themselves. Thinking about the people in this settlement, do you think that the majority help the rest or do you think that the majority only watch out for themselves?" It was found that communal members were much more likely than other beneficiaries (F test $<.001$) to believe that the majority of members help others. Apparently, in spite of the perceived greater number of disagreements encountered among the communal members, their level of interpersonal trust is higher than that of peasants who work on individual parcels or in colonies. The greater disagreement probably stems from the fact that communal ownership, work, and decision-making force peasants into much more frequent interaction than is commonly found in the settlements with individual ownership.

Another ITCO project which has been implemented under the new program is directed at untitled landholders. It will be recalled that a large number of landowning peasants in Costa Rica do not hold legal title to their property. Untitled ownership creates serious difficulties for the peasant when he attempts to obtain bank credit, and also induces feelings of insecurity. As a result, ITCO has been atempting to deal with this problem by employing modernized and highly efficient titling procedures in order to speed up the process of titling. The program was made possible largely by U.S. foreign aid loans.[8]

The Impact of Reform

It has been shown that in the 1970s ITCO has made intensive efforts to revitalize what had become a stagnant reform program. What has been its overall success to date? Two questions need to be asked. First, what impact has reform had on those peasants who have already received land? Second, how large an impact has reform made in reversing the trend in land concentration?

Impact on Beneficiaries

Impact on Income. Little research has been conducted on the impact of agrarian reform in Latin America. Most reform projects are set up with no attempt to evaluate their impact on the recipients of reform. This is unfortunate, because the absence of impact data severely hampers reform planning. At least one study, however, has analyzed the impact of reform. This research, conducted by William C. Thiesenhusen [1974] in Chile, compares 56 peasant families in 1964 and 1970 in four reform projects. Three findings stand out. First, the income per hectare increased about 10 percent per year, which is more than double the rate of increase in agricultural production for all of Chile. More significantly,

---

[8]The goal is to title some 660,000 hectares, or approximately 55 percent of the untitled farmland in Costa Rica. An estimated 27,000 peasants are to benefit from this program. Because of the vastness of the project, a number of technical difficulties were initially encountered, but the program now seems to be operating fairly smoothly [Agency for International Development, 1970:VI, 1-14].

the gross family income was about twice that which would be earned by a wage laborer earning the minimum wage. Third, reform also brought about a surprising consequence: income distribution became more unequal among the reform beneficiaries. What happened was that a substantial number of peasants showed strong upward mobility, whereas another group showed downward mobility. As Thiesenhusen [1974: 325] emphasizes, "Some analysts writing on reform assume that all beneficiaries progress more or less in equal measure. That is not true; some make considerable income progress while others stagnate."

In Costa Rica, an attempt was made to replicate Thiesenhusen's analysis. To do this, use was made of two surveys. The first of these, described in detail in chapters 4 and 5, was conducted in 1973. The 263 landless peasants among the total sample of 531 will be analyzed in this chapter. The second study, conducted in 1976, was based on a sample of 753 peasants in ITCO projects (colonies, communal enterprises, and parcelization programs).[9]

For the purposes of this analysis a before-and-after research design is used. The landless peasants from the 1973 sample represent the "before" group, while the ITCO peasants represent the "after" group. The landless peasants are viewed as representing the reform peasants before they received assistance from ITCO. Differences in income, when the proper controls are made for inflation over the three years, are assumed to be a result of the reform process.[10] The best way of doing this so as to insure maximum comparability of the two samples is to use Thiesenhusen's suggestion of comparing actual income to minimum wage figures. In this way we know quite accurately what the 1973 peasants would be earning in 1976 by simply comparing minimum wage figures.

The evidence is quite clear that the results which Thiesenhusen found in Chile are also found in Costa Rica. Reform does substantially increase income. In 1973, the minimum wage was 72 colones a week. The 1973 sample of landless peasants showed that total family income (including the earnings of the head of the family plus all income earned by other family members and given to the head of the family) averaged 96 colones, or 33.9 percent over the minimum wage figures. In the 1976 sample of reform peasants, total family income amounted to 201 colones, or 67.5 percent above the new minimum wage of 120 colones. Hence, the reform peasants were earning considerably more than their landless counterparts in both relative and absolute terms.

[9] Both surveys were directed by the author. Some details of the 1976 study are reported in footnote 4 of this chapter.

[10] Data supporting this assumption are contained in Seligson [1979a].

Inequality in income distribution also increased. Applying the Gini index of inequality (described in the next section of this chapter) to the family income data, we find that the index is 25 among the landless peasants and 34 among the reform peasants. Hence, as in the reform settlement which Thiesenhusen studied in Chile, there has been a shift in the direction of inequality. It is found that the percentage of peasants in the reform sample who earn less than the minimum wage is smaller than the percentage of landless peasants who do. Among the landless, 30.5 percent of the sample earned less than the minimum wage, whereas among the reform peasants only 18.9 percent earned less than that amount. It is at the other extreme of the distribution that we find the greater inequality. A look at the percentage of the sample earning more than double the minimum wage shows that only 15.5 percent of the landless peasants earned this much money, whereas in the reform samples 21.2 percent earned this much. Finally, when we examine the very top 1 percent of the distribution, we find that the wealthiest landless peasants earn no more than an average of 4.1 times the minimum wage, whereas the top 1 percent of the reform peasants earned 14.3 percent times the minimum.

What appears to have happened in the Costa Rican reform is that not only have the recipients as a whole benefitted to an extent from the reform, but some of them have made great strides in improving their incomes. The impact of reform is particularly noticeable among those beneficiaries of the programs who have held their land for at least four years. Those peasants have incomes which average 9 percent higher than the entire sample of beneficiaries. What appears to be happening as the years go on is that those who receive land from ITCO are able to increase the yields on their farms, and hence increase income. Probably a major factor in producing these higher yields is the impact of technical assistance and credit which are made available to the peasants.

Impact on Attitudes. In addition to economic data on the impact of reform, it is possible to examine attitudinal data in order to study the impact of the reform program on peasants. A look at shifts in social-psychological attitudes reveals what happens to peasants once they have been given land. Tables 7 to 10 compare the attitudes of the sample of 753 peasants who have received land from ITCO with those of the sample of 263 landless peasants.

The attitudinal impact of reform is striking. The data reveal that those peasants who have received land from ITCO are significantly more trusting in government, and more positively oriented toward the future and feel more politically efficacious than do landless peasants, who are more cynical, more pessimistic about the future and feel more powerless than the ITCO peasants.

The ITCO peasants' greater trust in government is revealed in table 7.[11] For each of the seven questions listed the ITCO peasants responded more frequently with a trusting response than did the more cynical landless peasants, although in two cases the results are not statistically significant. The pattern of responses for the individual questions in table 7 is highly revealing. The strongest differences of opinion between the landless peasants and the reform peasants occurs in the first four questions, in which the respondent is asked to evaluate the performance of government and government officials. It is readily comprehensible that peasants who have been given land by ITCO would feel, at least in one instance, that the government is doing a respectable job. Hence we find that more than twice as many reform peasants think that the government helps them, and conversely, more than three times as many landless peasants think the government hurts them (question 1). In similar fashion, the ITCO peasants are nearly twice as likely to trust government to do the right thing, whereas landless peasants are nearly twice as likely to believe that government almost never can be trusted to do the right thing (question 2). We also find that 25 percent more of the ITCO peasants believe that government is interested in people like themselves than do the landless peasants (question 3). While the bulk of both groups of peasants feel that public servants are prepared for their jobs, more than twice as many landless peasants feel that the public servants are unprepared (question 4).

The remaining trust-in-government questions (questions 5-7) ask the peasant to make evaluations that largely go beyond his own personal experience. It is here that the trust levels of the two groups are much more similar. Hence, when asked if governnment is interested in solving the problems of the majority of Costa Ricans or if it is interested only in the problems of some important families, the reform peasants were only slightly more willing to state that government was interested in the majority than were the landless peasants (question 5). Similarly, there is no statistically significant difference between the landless and reform peasants in their view of governmental misspending of tax money (question 6), and no statistically significant difference in their view concerning the honesty of public officials. The overall pattern of the responses to the trust questions is clear: peasants who have received land from ITCO are much more favorable in their evaluation of government performance than are landless peasants.

Researchers frequently view peasants as politically incapable [Banfield, 1958:9-10]; that is, they are considered to be unable to organ-

[11] The trust questions reported in this table and the efficacy questions reported in the next table are the ones used in chapter 5.

Table 7. Trust in Government Comparisons[a]

	Landless Peasants (N = 263)	Reform Peasants (N = 753)
1. Do you think that what government (*los gobiernos*) does helps you, hurts you, or neither helps nor hurts you?		
helps	20.2%	40.5%
neither	43.3	46.9
hurts	36.5	12.6
	$p < .001$	
	Tau c = $-.32$	
2. How often do you think that one can trust government to do the right thing? Do you think you can trust them almost always, almost never, or sometimes?		
almost always or sometimes	35.7	65.0
almost never	64.3	35.0
	$p < .001$	
	Tau b = $-.29$	
3. Some say that government isn't interested in the problems of people like you. Others say that government is interested in the problems of people like you. What do you think?		
interested	46.1	71.5
not interested	53.9	28.5
	$p < .001$	
	Tau b = $-.26$	
4. Do you think that among the public servants the majority do not have the preparation necessary for their job, or the majority do have the preparation, or there are some who do and some who do not have the preparation?		
majority prepared or some prepared	73.0	89.2
majority unprepared	27.0	10.8
	$p < .001$	
	Tau b = $-.21$	
5. Would you say that government is interested in solving the problems of the majority of Costa Ricans, or is it interested only in the problems of some important families?		
majority	36.3	45.9
important families	63.7	54.1
	$p < .01$	
	Tau b = $-.09$	
6. Would you say that government misspends a lot of the money that the people pay in taxes, a little of the money, or none of that money?		
a lot	60.2	58.4
some	17.7	28.3
little	17.7	8.4
none	4.4	4.9
	p = ns	

Table 7, *continued*

	Landless Peasants (N = 263)	Reform Peasants (N = 753)
7. Do you think that among public servants there are many who aren't honest, there are some who aren't honest, or there are a few who aren't honest?		
few or some dishonest	66.7	69.3
majority dishonest	33.3	30.7
	p = ns	

[a] Includes questions directly comparable in the two surveys. Percentages include nonmissing data only. Total N varies because of missing data.

ize their communities for effective political actions. While I have argued elsewhere that this characterization is an inaccurate one [Booth and Seligson, 1978a, 1978b; 1979; Seligson and Booth, 1979a; Seligson and Salazar X., 1979], and that peasants do have a higher sense of efficacy than is generally believed, what is of interest in the present analysis is a comparison of levels of efficacy within the peasant sector. Sharp differences appear between the landless and reform peasants, as is revealed in tables 8 and 9. In these two tables efficacy is measured in two different ways, but the conclusion is identical. Efficacy is measured in table 8 by a series of questions regarding problems and problem-solving in the peasant's village.[12] The first question in table 8 demonstrates that while over 86 percent of the ITCO peasants can name what they consider to be the most serious problem in their village, only a little over 55 percent of the landless peasants are able to do so. The responses to the remaining questions in table 8 reveal similar differences between the two samples. The ITCO peasants are much more informed about how the problem arose (question 2) and how it could be solved (question 3) and have been more actively involved in solving the problem (question 4) than have the landless peasants. It can be concluded that reform peasants have a significantly higher feeling of political efficacy than do landless peasants. Communities composed of reform peasants, therefore, are much more likely to be active in trying to solve local problems. Consequently, greater communal activism in such communities can be expected. In contrast, communities populated by landless peasants can be expected to be more frequently characterized by an attitude of "let the other guy worry about it."

[12] The questions in this table form a valid Guttman scale. For further details on this method of measuring efficacy see Seligson [1979b; 1979c; forthcoming-a].

Table 8. Political Efficacy I Comparisons[a]

	Landless Peasants (N=263)	Reform Peasants (N=753)
1. All communities have problems, that is, things which make people's lives difficult. What is the most serious problem in this village, that is, the village of (name filled in)?		
problem mentioned	55.5%	85.7%
no problem	44.5	14.3
	$p < .001$	
	Tau b = $-.33$	
2. In your opinion, how did this problem arise?		
answer	53.2	80.6
no answer	46.8	19.3
	$p < .001$	
	Tau b = $-.29$	
3. What could be done about this problem?		
answer	49.0	75.6
no answer	51.0	24.4
	$p < .001$	
	Tau b = $-.27$	
4. Have you tried to help solve the problem?		
yes, helped solve	25.5	49.4
no, not helped solve	74.5	50.1
	$p < .001$	
	Tau b = $-.25$	

[a] Includes questions directly comparable in the two surveys. Percentages include non-missing data only. Total N varies because of missing data.

The second measure of political efficacy is detailed in table 9. This measure is made up of questions which probe the respondent's sense of efficacy in relation to government institutions. The first question asks for his feelings of efficacy toward the local government (the *municipalidad*). The respondent is asked what he would do if the municipality considered passing a law which he considered unjust. Whereas the majority of both groups of peasants feel that they would do something about the law, a full 40 percent of the landless peasants say they would do nothing, whereas only a little over 17 percent of the ITCO peasants say they would react this way (question 1). Similarly, the reform peasants are much more optimistic that efforts on the part of the community to stop the law would be successful. Only 4.3 percent of the reform peasants feel that they would have a bad chance of stopping the law as compared to 24.9 percent of the landless peasants who react this way. The last question in this series asks the peasant to speculate as to the way he would be treated in a government office. Here we see that the contact of ITCO peasants with government institutions apparently has been considerably more satisfactory than that of the landless peasants. Over half of the ITCO peasants feel that they would receive a lot of attention in the government office, whereas less than one-fifth of the landless peasants feel this way. It is clear from the responses to these questions that reform peasants feel considerably more capable of having an impact on government bureaucracies than do landless peasants.

Table 9. Political Efficacy II Comparisons[a]

	Landless Peasants (N=263)	Reform Peasants (N=753)
1. Let's suppose that a municipal law is being considered which you consider unjust and harmful to your community. What do you think you could do about this?		
do something (protest, strike, etc.)	50.6%	82.6%
do nothing	49.4	17.4
	$p < .001$	
	Tau b = $-.25$	
2. If a group of neighbors made an effort to stop the law, what chance would you have to stop it? Would you have a good chance, a fair chance, or a poor chance?		
good chance	40.6	75.0
fair chance	34.5	20.7
poor chance	24.9	4.3
	$p < .001$	
	Tau c = $-.38$	
3. Let's suppose that there were a matter that you had to arrange in one of the offices of the government. If you tried to explain your problem to the people of that office, do you think they would pay you a lot of attention, a little attention, or wouldn't pay attention to you?		
lot of attention	16.5	56.5
little attention	65.5	38.0
no attention	18.0	5.5
	$p < .001$	
	Tau c = $-.43$	

[a] Includes questions directly comparable in the two surveys. Percentages include non-missing data only. Total N varies because of missing data.

The final series of questions which will be analyzed are those concerning the individual's orientation toward the future. By this is meant those attitudes which reflect the way in which a respondent reacts to the challenges of a changing world; some are optimistic and believe that they can meet those challenges because man is in control of his destiny, whereas others view the future with despair, for they believe that the future is predetermined.

Questions meant to reveal the future orientation of the two groups of peasants are contained in table 10. Once again we see clear evidence of the impact of agrarian reform. Questions 1 and 2 are phrased in a general way in order to tap underlying attitudes toward the future. The first question shows that while slightly less than half of the landless peasants believe that one makes his own destiny, over 85 percent of the reform peasants believe so. In a similar fashion, although the differences are not so great as in the prior question, nearly two-thirds of the landless peasants feel that success in life depends more on luck than on the individual, whereas only half of the reform peasants responded this way. The first two general questions serve as a basis for the more specific questions (3, 4, and 5), which posit a particular situation and ask the peasant to respond to it. The responses to the first question, a hypothetical situation regarding the value of making plans, reveal that while slightly under half of the landless peasants consider it useless to make plans, less than a fifth of the ITCO peasants feel that plans are useless. The next question in this series (question 4) demonstrates that nearly three times as many landless peasants than ITCO peasants believe that planting methods should remain unchanged. The final question (question 5) demonstrates that the landless peasants are more likely than the reform peasants to rely on religion rather than medicine in curing an illness. All of the questions in this series indicate a much more positive approach to the future among reform peasants.

Impact on Land Distribution

The above sections have demonstrated quite clearly that the peasants who have received land under ITCO's programs have improved their incomes and also have taken on a set of psychological attitudes which can be generally associated with a more positive outlook on life. While this evidence gives strong support to those who would argue for a continuation of the reform efforts, however, it says nothing about the overall impact that reform has had thus far on the distribution of land in Costa Rica. Has it been able to begin reversing the trend in land concentration that began with the introduction of agrarian capitalism in the last century, or has the trend continued despite the efforts of ITCO? This section will attempt to answer that question.

Measuring the impact of agrarian reform is facilitated by the existence of the 1963 and 1973 agricultural censuses [Dirección General de Estadística y Censos, 1966a and 1974a]. The earlier census was taken

Land Reform

Table 10. Future Orientation Comparisons[a]

	Landless Peasants (N=263)	Reform Peasants (N=753)
1. Some say that one is born with his destiny, others say that one makes his own destiny. What do you think?		
make destiny	48.6%	85.5%
born with destiny	51.4	14.5
	$p < .001$	
	Tau b = $-.39$	
2. Some say that success in life depends more on luck than on the individual. Others say, on the other hand, that success in life depends more on the individual than on luck. What does it depend upon more?		
the individual	34.5	49.8
luck	65.5	50.2
	$p < .001$	
	Tau b = $-.15$	
3. Two men are talking about the bad luck a friend of theirs had. This friend, in spite of making plans to improve his farm's production, had failed. One of the two men said, "It's better not to make plans because most of the time plans go up in smoke." But the other man was not in agreement and said, "To make plans is very important." Which of the two do you think is right?		
important to make plans	53.6	83.9
useless to make plans	46.4	16.8
	$p < .001$	
	Tau b = $-.32$	
4. Two farmers are talking about how they could work it to get a bigger coffee harvest. One farmer said, "We ought to change our way of cultivating coffee." The other responds, "I disagree. We ought to continue as before." What do you think?		
change method	70.7	89.9
continue as before	29.3	10.1
	$p < .001$	
	Tau b = $-.24$	
5. A man's wife is gravely ill. What should he do? Get the medicine first and afterwards pray to God, or should he pray to God first and afterwards get the medicine?		
medicine	40.2	61.7
pray	59.8	38.3
	$p < .001$	
	Tau b = $-.22$	

[a] Includes questions directly comparable in the two surveys. Percentages include non-missing data only. Total N varies because of missing data.

only a few months after ITCO's establishment and before the first colony was founded in 1963. The 1973 census was taken after a full decade of ITCO land reform, during which 49,195 hectares of land (1.6 percent of total farm area in 1973) were turned over to peasants [Salazar N. et al., 1977:31-37].

The data from the two censuses were analyzed to help determine the impact of this redistribution of 49,000 hectares on general land distribution in the country. It was hypothesized that, all other things remaining equal, the redistribution should have resulted in some change, albeit minor, in the national land distribution. If the process of concentration continued despite the efforts of ITCO, however, it should show up in a comparison of 1963 and 1973 data.

A number of serious problems were encountered in attempting to compare land concentration for the two census years. As a result of these problems (see note to table 11), it was determined that the published census reports would be unsuitable for the purposes of the present analysis. Consequently, copies of the machine-readable computer tapes were obtained and the appropriate conversions were carried out in order to permit comparisons of the data.[13]

The data displayed in table 11 report on land distribution for the 1963 and 1973 periods. While the two distributions are similar in many respects, three major differences are noteworthy. First, although every size category experienced an increase in the number of farms, the largest absolute increase and the second largest relative increases occurred in the smallest category of farms. While the number of farms for the entire country increased 29.2 percent, the farms in the range of 1.0 to 1.4 manzanas increased 80.1 percent. This finding indicates a clear trend toward an increase in the pattern of minifundia (farms too small to sustain a family). Second, the percentage increase in the medium-sized farms, those 3 to 50 manzanas, is relatively small (averaging 23.8, or less than the overall increase), an indication that the growth in these family-sized farms is falling behind the growth of the smallest farms. Third, the growth in the number of the farms in the largest categories is nothing short of spectacular. The number of farms in the range of 1,430 to 1,499 manzanas increased by 91.7 percent, and in the largest category, farms 3,500 manzanas and bigger increased by 8.7 percent. Since the mean farm size in the largest category dropped from 11,205.9 manzanas to 8,243.6 manzanas, it would appear that some of the largest farms have been broken up into two or more smaller holdings.

[13] I would like to thank Lic. René Sánchez Bolaños, Director of the Costa Rican census bureau, for making this data available.

Land Reform

Table 11. Land Distribution in Costa Rica, 1963 and 1973[a]

Size of Farms in Manzanas	Number of Farms		Percent Increase	Mean Size	
	1963	1973		1973	1973
1.0-1.4	2,899	5,221	80.1	1.1	1.1
1.5-2.9	5,374	6,655	23.8	2.0	2.1
3.0-3.9	2,569	3,250	26.5	3.2	3.2
4.0-5.9	4,187	5,338	27.5	4.7	4.7
6.0-6.9	1,497	1,829	22.2	6.1	6.2
7.0-9.9	3,332	4,301	29.1	8.0	8.0
10.0-14.9	4,549	5,808	27.7	11.8	11.8
15.0-19.9	2,628	3,099	17.9	16.7	16.7
20.0-29.9	4,487	5,659	26.1	23.7	24.0
30.0-49.9	5,929	6,723	13.4	37.3	37.6
50.0-69.9	3,261	4,052	24.3	56.6	57.1
70.0-99.9	2,753	3,423	24.3	80.8	81.0
100-144.9	2,168	3,031	39.8	115.7	116.8
145-174.9	639	931	45.7	156.5	157.2
175-249.9	1,032	1,374	33.1	205.0	206.2
250-284.9	268	360	34.3	262.3	263.6
285-499.9	844	1,305	54.6	364.0	362.1
500-699.9	336	506	50.6	570.8	570.6
700-999.9	205	329	60.5	815.4	810.7
1000-1429.9	156	234	50.0	1,163.7	1,150.7
1430-1499.9	12	23	91.7	1,456.3	1,457.8
1500-3499.9	159	190	19.5	2,051.0	2,160.3
3500+	51	87	70.6	11,205.9	8,243.6
Total	49,335	63,763	29.2 (mean)		

[a]The data reported here were taken from the tapes of the 1963 and 1973 agricultural census, rather than the printed census documents. Several reasons dictated this decision. First, the printed census of 1963 reports figures in manzanas (.69 hectares), while the 1973 census reports data in hectares. Second, the ranges used in the two censuses were quite different, making direct comparisons of the printed figures impossible. Third, neither census reports the upper limit as a closed interval. Fourth, the printed census figures did not clearly distinguish between land that was owned and land that was rented, sharecropped, or held in other forms of tenancy. The data reported in this table refer only to land which is owned, excluding all tenancy arrangements. It should be also noted that it is not possible to include data on the smallest farms, i.e., those less than one manzana. Although the 1973 census tape includes these small farms, the 1963 tape does not. There does exist a separate listing of the smallest farms which was published as an appendix to the 1963 census; however, it appears that these figures include non-farm property (e.g., backyards), whereas the 1973 census includes only farm land.

The findings reported above give unmistakable evidence for the conclusion that the pattern of land concentration reported on in chapter 2 of this book is still found today. Costa Rica is confronted with an increase in the number of its minifundios and an increase in the number of its latifundios. Evidently the reform program from 1963 to 1973 could not offset this strong trend towards concentration. Perhaps this conclusion can best be understood by providing a summary measure of land concentration for the two periods. One such measure frequently used is the Gini index [Alker and Russett, 1966]. The index varies between 0.0 in a situation of "perfect equality" and 100 in a situation of "perfect inequality."[14] The Gini index was calculated based on the data given in table 11. In 1963 the index was 78.9, and rose slightly to 79.6 in 1973.

It is important to determine if the land concentration reported above came about as a result of a major shift in land distribution in a few isolated areas of the country or whether the shift is a product of a more general phenomenon. If the increased concentration can be attributed to shifts in only a few areas, ITCO would be able to concentrate its resources in those areas, thereby avoiding a costly nationwide reform effort.

In order to determine the location of concentration, a Gini index was calculated for each of Costa Rica's cantones for the two time periods.[15] It was found that only 21 percent of Costa Rica's cantones saw a decrease in their land concentration over the ten-year period. In no case was the decrease greater than 19.6 points, the average decrease being only 3.9 points. On the other hand, 79 percent of the cantones underwent an increase in concentration, the average increase being 7.7 points.

[14]The Gini index is derived from calculations based on the Lorenz curve [Lorenz, 1905]. It is a measure of the area between the line of perfect equality and the Lorenz curve, multiplied by two. The line of perfect equality is that line which represents the situation in which each segment of the population (in this case farm landowners) owns a proportion of the total goods (in this case farm land) equal to its proportion of the population. It should be pointed out that the upper limit of 100 is only theoretical, since the index is to some extent dependent upon the number of points used in its calculation. When there are many points (over 20), the deviation from the theoretical upper limit becomes insignificant [Ray and Singer, 1973]. Since more than 20 points were used in the present calculations, the results are very accurate. Also note that the computer program that was used to compute the Gini index presented in this chapter includes the suggested modifications of the less-accurate Leonard program [see Whittenburg and Pemberton, 1977].

[15]The cantón is the smallest political subdivision for which there is reliable data. The smallest unit, the district, is a subdivision of a cantón. Residents and census takers alike often confuse district boundaries and therefore misclassify data. Several changes were made in cantonal boundaries between 1963 and 1973, as new cantones were created out of old ones. Fortunately, it is possible to reconstruct the data so as to eliminate the impact of these changes. Information specifying the nature of the changes is contained in Bilderback et al.[1976].

Land Reform

The widespread nature of the increase in inequality is shown best in figure 12, a map of Costa Rica on which all of the cantones are outlined.[16] The cantones which underwent a decrease in inequality are left blank. The cantones with an increase are shaded, so that the greater the increase the darker the shading. The result is quite clear: hardly any area of the country escaped increasing concentration.

While it is true that the first decade of the reform was unable to offset the trend toward increased land concentration, the pace of reform quickened considerably in the years 1974-78. During this period ITCO turned over 72,139 manzanas of land, or 58 percent of all the land it has distributed to peasants since its formation. During this same period of 1974-77, moreover, 2,818 peasant families, or 67 percent of all the families to have received land, benefited from the reforms [Salazar et al., 1977:32-42]. Table 12 summarizes the agricultural enterprise program activities, most of which took place during the 1974-77 period. In early 1978, plans were underway to develop portions of Costa Rica's largest reserves, Astua Pirie (26,400 hectares), Chambacú (140,800 hectares), and Finca Coyolar (18,000 hectares). The goal is to settle 4,500 additional families on 63,000 hectares of land by the early 1980s. The long-range plan is for settling 30,000 families on 420,000 hectares of land [*La Nación*, June 2, 1975, p. 17A].

Since no new census data will be available until 1983, it is difficult to determine whether the reforms begun in the 1974-78 period have reversed the persistent trend toward land concentration. ITCO's estimates, however, are that there has been some increase in the medium-sized farms (ten to twenty hectares) and some decrease in the largest farms [Salazar et al., 1977:38]. There are some doubts, however, whether or not the reform plans of the 1974-78 period will be carried out. Since the plans were formulated by members of the Liberación Nacional party (PLN), and since that party lost the 1978 presidential election to a coalition of parties supported in part by many large landholders, it is an open question at this writing (January 1979) whether or not any of the plans will be realized. It is worth noting, however, that the more extensive the reforms, the more painful and costly they are politically. Consequently it is quite possible that the efforts of the 1974-78 period will not be continued. It is even possible that support for the projects already functioning (for instance credit, seeds, fertilizer, technical assistance) will not be continued and will result in the failure of the projects. These thoughts are pure speculation and will have to await the outcome of policy decisions by the new administration.

[16] I would like to thank the Harvard University Center for Computer Graphics and Spatial Analysis for permitting the use of their CALFORM program, and Marion Schwarz for digitizing the map of Costa Rica.

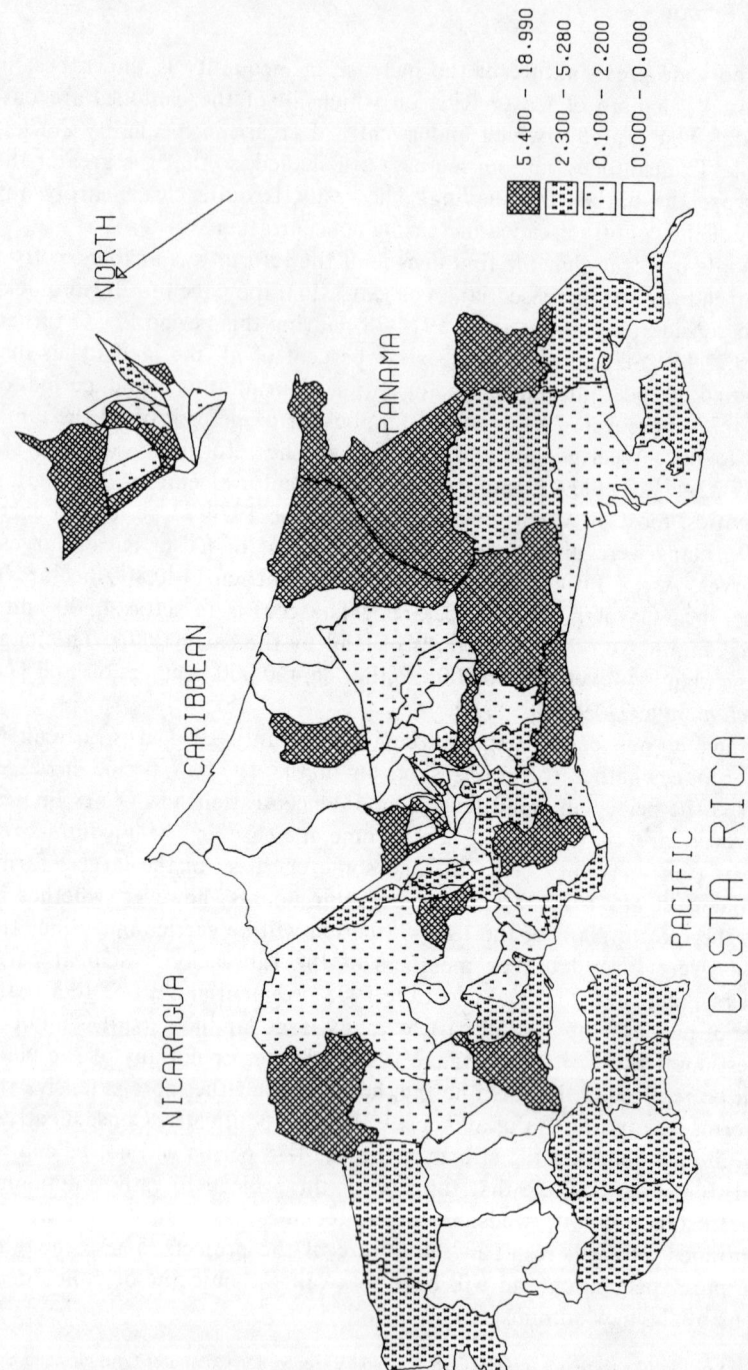

Figure 12. Change in land distribution by cantons, 1963-73

Land Reform

Table 12. The Peasant Agricultural Enterprise Program

Settlement Name	Size in Hectares	Number of Families
Communal Enterprises		
1. Coopesilencio	598	53
2. Coopecerritos	284	21
3. Coopetulga	30	14
4. Coopeutaba	43	23
5. Coopepasodanta	97	21
6. Coopezamora	325	21
7. Coopeutrapez	185	7
8. Coopegiltablada	537	25
9. Cooperíocañas	310	41
10. Coopebelén	258	36
11. Colinas	1,192	21
12. Alianza	871	59
13. Coopeisabel	317	22
14. Coopehumo	156	39
15. Coopeliberación	80	14
16. Bernabela	242	36
Subtotals	5,525	453
Individual Parcels		
1. Paso Agres*	1,608	42
2. Buenos Aires	73	27
3. Parrúas	116	38
4. El Control	517	39
5. San Luis	1,157	59
6. Thesalia*	634	75
7. Aguila	70	5
8. Las Vueltas	840	80
9. Río Frío	8,327	304#
10. Los Criques	1,111	80
11. Sonafluca	968	98
12. Coto Sur	22,270	1,500#
13. Curú	417	17
14. Las Armenias	1,708	15
15. Hnos. Jenkins	1,550	20
16. Rosemouth	370	10
17. Santa Teresita	94	14
18. Cañaza	1,083	43
19. Quebrada Azul	352	48
20. Finca Wilson	18,330	--#
21. Alcoa	3,238	--#
Subtotals	64,833	2,514
Grand Totals	70,358	2,967

Source: Salazar, et al., 1977: 36.
*No cooperative. All others have cooperatives for production and/or marketing.
#These projects are still in the process of formation.

In closing the chapter, we should note that the titling program has met with some success. ITCO estimates that 45,000 of the 81,562 farms in the country (1973 figures) are untitled. Of these untitled farms about half, some 20,000-25,000, are concentrated in eight zones: Nicoya, Santa Cruz, Cañas, Upala, Puriscal-Parrita, Providencia, Valle del General, and Coto Brus. The others are widely scattered and are not amenable to rapid titling programs, which rely on aerial photography. ITCO's goal is to title the farms in these eight zones in the shortest possible time. By 1976, 11,306 titles had been granted, covering an area of 179,893 hectares, or 14 percent of the area to be titled. The program is moving ahead quickly and should come close to meeting its set goal.

7 Conclusion: The Demise of the Peasantry

Agrarian Capitalism in Comparative Perspective

The experience of the Costa Rican peasantry with agrarian capitalism is not, of course, unique. Throughout Latin America, and for that matter in much of the rest of the Third World, coffee, tea, bananas, sugar, cacao, palm oil, rubber, cotton, and so forth are produced by peasants. It has been estimated that these agricultural goods make up three-fourths of all nonpetroleum exports from Latin America, Asia (excluding Japan), and Africa [Paige, 1975:1].

The fundamental changes that have been induced by agrarian capitalist production are generally well known. Nearly everywhere, the production of crops for the export market has resulted in the concentration of land in the hands of nonpeasant producers and the proletarianization of wide sectors of peasant populations. Beyond that, it frequently has caused the massive migration of land-seeking peasants, the destruction of cultural traditions, and the stratification of peasant society. In some countries, such as Guatemala, peasants have been able to cling to their village existence in the highlands only at the price of being forced to migrate en masse to lowland plantations for the annual harvest. Everywhere the changes have been harsh:

> In Mexico, Algeria, and Viet Nam commercialization menaced peasant access to communal land; in Mexico and Cuba it barred the peasant from claiming unclaimed public land. In Algeria and

China, it liquidated the institution of public granaries. In Algeria it ruptured the balance between pastoral and settled populations. In Mexico, Viet Nam, Algeria, and Cuba, finally, outright seizures of land by foreign colonists and enterprises drove the peasants back upon a land area no longer sufficient for their needs. [Wolf, 1969:281]

It should come as no surprise, therefore, to learn that peasants have at times reacted to these radical changes by rebelling. Not only in the countries mentioned by Wolf [1969] in his study *Peasant Wars of the Twentieth Century*(Mexico, Russia, China, Viet Nam, Algeria, and Cuba), but also in Guatemala, El Salvador, Colombia, Peru, Chile, Brazil, and elsewhere, peasants have reacted violently to the assault.

What is surprising is to find peasants who have been subjected to the onslaught of agrarian capitalism and have not rebelled. Why has the Costa Rican peasantry, in its failure to rebel, been such an exception? The preceding chapters have demonstrated, I believe, why tranquility has been the rule: in essence, it has been because of the availability of alternatives. As discussed in the introduction to this book, Scott [1976:195-206] points to factors which militate against rebellion. The present study has shown that existing alternatives served as escape valves for peasant pressure, and consequently functioned as impediments to rebellion. Thus while the growth of the coffee industry pushed many peasants off their land, these peasants found that because of a scarcity of manpower they could sell their labor for a high price to coffee plantation owners. Those who chose to reject this alternative could do so only because they had another: farming the virgin farmlands off the meseta. Finally, it has been shown that agrarian capitalism itself introduced new alternatives for the peasant: coffee cultivation was indirectly responsible for the introduction of banana cultivation and the consequent expansion of work opportunities in the lowlands.

Although all sectors of the Costa Rican peasantry have been affected by the dislocations associated with agrarian capitalism, certain sectors have been more severely affected than others. Specifically, the research presented in chapter 4 has demonstrated a rather clear-cut social stratification within the Costa Rican peasantry along the lines of security; the lower down in the security hierarchy a peasant finds himself, the more easily threatened he is by agrarian capitalism.

Landless peasants in Costa Rica, particularly those landless peasants who do not have steady jobs, are the least secure and the most likely to resist further threats to their security. Unsteady day workers (peones sueltos) and migrant workers are confronted by the fluctuating demand for labor in the planting and harvest seasons. When market conditions compel landowners to cut back production, or when machines obviate the need for manual work, the supply of jobs shrinks. Day workers and migrant workers are immediately affected by such cutbacks; the veneer of security is lost. Such peasants, therefore, are primary candidates for rebellion. Indeed, the squatting incidents reported in this book have invariably involved peasants whose job security had been lost. But as the data in chapter 5 have revealed, attitudes are also important in explaining such movements. A combination of low political trust and a strong sense of personal efficacy helps motivate squatting.

Peasants affected by agrarian capitalism set up as their first goal the reestablishment of their security. Such peasants will not become involved in broadly gauged social movements unless they are organized by outside political forces which successfully link the regaining of security to issues of larger dimensions. It was shown that peasants who had lost their land as a result of the expansion of coffee cultivation did not rebel. Rather, they took jobs on coffee plantations, moved to new lands, or became workers for the banana company. Similarly, peasant leagues formed for the purpose of organizing land invasions have the limited goal of reestablishing security. As was shown in chapter 5, peasants organize to obtain land, and once that goal is achieved their activity diminishes. For this reason, outside organizers find themselves disappointed when peasant organizations which have been successful in achieving their goals rapidly cease to function. Revolutionary elites who hope to build a power base with peasant support are not likely to be successful. As Landsberger and Hewitt [1970] have pointed out, peasant organizations are notoriously weak. The evidence from the Costa Rican case is quite clear: peasants do not rebel when alternatives, even unattractive ones, are still available. When, however, they find themselves with no options left, their actions will be single-mindedly directed toward the goal of reestablishing a modicum of their former security. When that goal is accomplished, further radical political behavior is unlikely. As Malloy [1970a] has shown, the role of the Bolivian peasant in the Revolution of 1952 was limited to regaining the land he had once owned. Once this goal was met, he showed little interest in further revolutionary activity. Indeed, to a great extent, the failure of Ché Guevara's guerrilla *foco* in Bolivia must be attributed to the success of the 1952 Revolution in meeting, at least to a small degree, the immediate needs of the peasants.

While I believe that the availability of alternatives satisfactorally explains non-rebellion in the Costa Rican case, it begs the question as to why these alternatives have existed at all. What was it that enabled the Costa Rican system to offer options to the peasant despite the fact that it was undergoing many of the same agrarian capitalist transformations that were so disruptive elsewhere? What caused Costa Rican elites to refrain from establishing repressive systems of legalized debt peonage? What can explain the absence of peasant serfdom, so common in those areas of Latin America influenced by agrarian capitalism? Why did Costa Rica resort to the importation of foreign laborers for the construction of the Atlantic railroad, when it could have pressed into service its peasantry? What explains the multitude of homestead acts of the nineteenth century which permitted peasants to colonize new lands?

One possible explanation is that the government of Costa Rica may have been more humane, more enlightened than others in Latin America, and hence refused to impose upon its peasant population the full cost of agrarian capitalism. Such an explanation, however, contradicts the facts; we know that Costa Rica attempted to take many of the same measures found elsewhere in Latin America. For example, many observers point to nineteenth-century "vagrancy laws" imposed in Guatemala, Mexico, and elsewhere in Latin America as illustrations of the tyrannical nature of the governments of those countries. These laws stipulated that peasants be required to carry cards on which landlords could record the number of days they worked each year. All were required to work a specified number of days a year (usually around 150) in order to avoid punishment for vagrancy. If it were true that Costa Rica's government was "enlightened," then such laws should not have existed in that country. However, investigation reveals that in 1883 just such a law was passed [Cardoso, 1975:26]. However, despite the existence of vagrancy laws, I can find no record of these laws ever having been enforced.

After examining the evidence from the Costa Rican case and comparing it with other cases in Latin America, I have come to the conclusion that the non-enforcement of repressive measures in Costa Rica can be best explained by the ethnic[1] homogeneity of the population. In Costa Rica the lower economic status of the peasant population is not compounded by inferior ethnic status. This is so because, in marked contrast to many Latin American nations which have undergone both agrarian capitalism and peasant rebellions (for example, Mexico, Guatemala, El Salvador, Peru), Costa Rica by the end of the colonial period had almost no Indian population. Indeed, the indigenous groups had ceased to com-

---

[1] I use the term *ethnic* rather than *racial* heterogeneity, since most (but not all) observers agree that the basis for discrimination against the Indian in Latin America is along ethnic rather than racial lines. As one student of the subject emphasizes, "concerning the Spanish American area, there is general (but not unanimous) agreement among social scientists that racial criteria of group membership are, if not entirely absent, distinctly secondary to cultural and socioeconomic criteria, and that labels such as *mestizo* or *blanco*, which at one time were racial, have become redefined in socio-cultural terms" [Van den Berghe, 1974a:4].

prise any significant portion of the population generations before Independence (see chapter 1). Consequently, Costa Rica is one of the most ethnically homogeneous countries in all of Latin America.[2]

The evidence surrounding peasant rebellions elsewhere in Latin America where there is a significant Indian population singles out the ethnic distinctiveness of peasant populations as a key factor, if not *the* key factor, in permitting elite groups to extract from them an unbearably high proportion of surplus. In essence, class and ethnicity combine for Indian groups, placing their members in a position of double jeopardy; exploitation is made all the more easy when it can be rationalized as a just punishment for "uncivilized" behavior.

In Peru, Guatemala, Mexico, and elsewhere in Latin America where there exists a significant aboriginal population, the inferior position of the Indian gave rise to a situation of internal colonialism. The ethnic basis for internal colonialism is clearly revealed by van den Berghe and Primov [1977] in their excellent study of the Cuzco region in Peru. They state:

> All evidence points to the conclusion that colonialism, whether external or internal, is in the first instance a political rather than an economic phenomenon, arising out of the conquest of one ethnic group by another. Conquest makes possible the entrenchment of the political apparatus of coercion, which in turn maintains the system of taxation, forced labor, and other forms of economic exploitation that have accompanied colonialism. One of the key elements of colonialism, besides the institutionalized inequalities in relations of power and production between groups and regions, is the *ethnic heterogeneity between the dominant and the subordinate, between exploiter and exploited.* We must, therefore, include the ethnic factor in our analysis. In the absence of ethnic diversity, one cannot meaningfully talk of internal colonialism as distinct from simple class exploitation. [van den Berghe and Primov, 1977:262, italics added]

Their distinctive language, dress, and customs make Indian peasants easy to single out as a minority group. Discrimination against Indians has made them ready targets for avaricious agrarian capitalists. When economic conditions have worsened, as a result of a drop in export prices or as a result of crop losses caused by droughts, floods, or disease, it has been easy to force the Indian to bear the cost. Moreover, because of their adherence to their traditions, Indians have often been viewed as a barrier to progress and development; therefore overworking and abusing

---

[2]Ethnic homogeneity in Costa Rica has been mentioned by many observers, and has been viewed by at least one scholar as a fundamental explanation of the viability of Costa Rica's political democracy [Busey, 1958:628-30].

them has been justified on nationalistic developmental grounds.

The Mexican case well illustrates the heavy hand of ethnic discrimination. A study of the Zapatista peasant movement has found that the conflict between peasant and landed elite

> was greatly magnified by the fact that the hacendado was generally of European or light mestizo descent, lived an urbanized, cosmopolitan style of life, and was cast in the inherently superior role of *hidalgo* (hereditary nobility). The peasant, on the other hand, was generally of Indian or mostly Indian descent, lived in the country or folk style of life, and was cast in the role of the peon, one who works with his hands. Furthermore, these racial and cultural differences were used to erect a belief and value system which defined the hacendado as inherently superior and thus tried to justify the allocation of wealth and power into his hands.
>
> The most basic difference between the peasants and the elite was racial. [White, 1969:108]

Another report [Simpson, 1952:234] has found that members of the landed aristocracy call Indians members of an "inferior race."

John Womack, Jr., considered to be Zapata's finest biographer, has demonstrated that while the peasants of Morelos who supported Zapata were no longer the tribal Indians of the pre-Columbian period, they did retain their attachment to their traditions, and their distinctive way of dress, and even preserved their Indian language to a certain extent. More important, perhaps, is the fact that the non-Indian population clearly perceived the villagers as Indian:

> In 1910 it was an old story that . . . hacienda lawyers finagled lands, timber, and water from weaker but rightful users, [and] that hacienda foremen beat and cheated field hands. *Still prevailing as the excuse was the lordly racism of viceroyal times.* For the young Joaquín García Pimentel, whose ancient and illustrious family owned the largest plantations in the state, it seemed that "the Indian . . . has many defects as a laborer, being as he is, lazy, sottish, and thieving." [Womack, Jr., 1968:41, italics added]

Once the revolution of 1910 broke out there was widespread fear of reprisals from "uncivilized" Indians:

> The scattered physical atrocities committed in Morelos loomed especially vivid and ominous: they were perpetrated close to Mexico City, and by men who wore white pajamas and sandals to work, carried machetes, and presented swarthy complexions, in this last betraying themselves unmistakably as members of an "inferior race." This was the clincher. Revolutionary executions were always distressing, but if the executioners were recognizably "white" and dressed like civilized beings in pants, boots, and shirts, their deeds remained human. That the "plebes" should execute victims was "Indian," subhuman, monstrous. [Womack, Jr., 1968:100-101]

Both supporters and opponents of Zapata perceived the Indian nature of the rebellion. One anti-Zapata general referred to the "Indians" of the revolution [Womack, Jr., 1968:140], while one sympathizer with the revolutionaries' cause said, "I will be on the side of the Indian" [Womack, Jr., 1968:150]. Even allies of Zapata despised him and his Indian followers. Writing of Huertista elements, Womack [1969:187] reports, ". . . the Zapatistas they still held in contempt, as shorter, darker-complexioned, and more countrified people, 'Indians.' "

Certainly these attitudes go far in explaining the fact that before the Revolution "half of the rural population was estimated to be bound by debt slavery" [White, 1969:119]. In Mexico, a major thrust of the policy followed by Porfirio Díaz and his científicos was to modernize agriculture by destroying the communal basis of Indian farming, and by extension, to destroy Indian culture and civilization along with it. The Díaz land reforms divested almost the entire Indian population of its land, so that "by 1910 less than one percent of the families of Mexico controlled 85 percent of the land, and 90 percent of the villages and towns on the central plateau had almost no communal land" [White, 1969:115]. The attitudes of the Mexican elites, coupled with the easily identifiable nature of the Indian groups, eased the way for the merciless exploitation of the latter by Díaz and his reformers.

The 1932 rebellion in El Salvador also reveals the importance of the role of ethnic discrimination. The introduction of coffee in El Salvador was followed by the breakup of the Indian communal lands (ejidos), and the establishment of the colono system of tenancy, in which peasants were granted usufruct rights to tiny plots in return for their labor on the hacienda. The feeling of outrage against the extreme inequities of this system eventually came to a head during the Great Depression, which devastated El Salvador's coffee-based economy. Even though all the sectors of the agricultural economy were affected by the Depression, it was the Indians who rebelled. Although census data for 1930 report that only 5.6 percent of the population of El Salvador were Indian, subsequent research has revealed that this figure derives from an excessively narrow definition of the group. Apparently, only those who spoke an Indian language were categorized as Indian in that census. More important than language is the perception of Indian ethnic identity; Anderson [1971:15] argues that "an Indian is one who thinks of himself as an Indian and is so regarded by others." Using this criterion, Anderson found that the rebellion broke out precisely in those areas where the Indian population of El Salvador was concentrated. Moreover, he emphasizes that "cultural antagonisms played a large part in the 1932 revolt" [Anderson, 1971:16], and cites others who found "definite overtones of race war" in the revolt [1971:17]. Perhaps the feeling toward the Indian is best revealed by the words of a Ladino survivor of the revolt:

> We'd like this race of the plague to be exterminated. . . . It is necessary for the government to use a strong hand. They did it right in North America, having done with them by shooting them in the first place before they could impede the progress of the nation. They killed the Indians because they will never be pacified. Here we are, treating them like part of the family, and you see the result! They have fierce instincts. [quoted by Anderson, 1971:17]

The important role of ethnicity as a factor precipitating other peasant uprisings in Latin America is equally clear. In Bolivia, for example, reports Dwight Heath [1969:178], "Many Bolivians viewed Indians as subhuman beings." It is not surprising, therefore, that a Bolivian Minister of Education, a strong supporter of Indian causes, should write:

> The Indian is a sphinx. He inhabits a hermetic world, inaccessible to the white and the mestizo. We don't understand his forms of life, nor his mental mechanism. . . . We speak of the Indian as a mass factor in the nation; in truth we are ignorant of his individual psyche and his collective drama. The Indian lives. The Indian acts and produces. The Indian does not allow himself to be understood, he doesn't desire communication. Retiring, silent, immutable, he inhabits a closed world. The Indian is an enigma. [quoted in Heath, 1969:178-79]

Malloy [1970a:190] confirms the above image, writing: "*Indio* ('Indian') was a word which conjured the image of a subhuman (uncivilized) being, locked in ignorance and bent on violent revenge."[3] The Revolution of 1952 gave the oppressed Indians

> a unique opportunity to redress old wrongs. At least so it would seem, for the first Indian uprisings in the Valley after the insurrection [of 1952] were obviously motivated as much by a desire for revenge as for land or power. . . . As the movement gained momentum, it took overtones of a racial, or at least cultural, war [Malloy, 1970:202].

The inferior position of Indians in highland Peru has much to do with the outbreak of violence there in the early 1960s [Craig, Jr., 1969]. Highland Guatemalan Indians also received incredibly bad treatment at the hands of the hacendados, a factor which motivated their political mobilizaton in the late 1940s and early 1950s [Colby and van den Berghe, 1969; Pearson, 1969].

[3] For a discussion of the use and meaning of ethnic terms in the Andean region, see van den Berghe [1974b:12-21].

These illustrations help demonstrate that under the stressful conditions brought on by agrarian capitalist production, ethnic discrimination permits dominant groups to extract unbearably high costs from peasant groups identified as Indians. Economic downturns, crop failures, national political upheavals, etc., place further strain on the peasant's tenuous existence and cut off his limited alternatives. Under such conditions, the peasant sees his security threatened with destruction and, with no alternative left, rebels. Costa Rica, in contrast, not plagued by a White/Indian dichotomy, has avoided the excesses evident elsewhere in Latin America and hence has been able to avoid peasant uprisings.

The argument here is not that Costa Ricans are immune to the attitudes prevalent elsewhere. Indeed, much of the sense of superiority which many Costa Ricans feel with respect to their Central American neighbors has racial overtones. What has prevented these attitudes from resulting in the reckless abuse of the Costa Rican peasant is the fact that on the whole it is not identified as an ethnically distinct population. As was shown in chapter 3, however, black banana workers constitute the only major peasants who are ethnically distinct and, not unexpectedly, their treatment has been significantly worse than that of other peasants. The travel restrictions placed on black workers, and the racial clashes which occurred in the banana zones during the 1934 strike revealed strong elements of racism in the Costa Rican population.

Does the absence of a sizable ethnically distinct population preclude the possibility of peasant rebellion? Obviously not. There are numerous instances of peasant rebellions in non-Indian areas of Latin America and elsewhere which are not linked to ethnic differences. Many of them, especially those in China, are related to religious groupings. Nevertheless, even without such differences in the population, peasant uprisings are still possible in situations in which the competition over scarce resources becomes so keen that large sectors of the peasant population are threatened with the loss of their security. In China, Japan, Java, and elsewhere in Asia, high population densities have long provided the conditions for peasant rebellions; competition over land and food frequently reaches epidemic proportions, resulting in a war of all against all. For example, Wolf [1969:130] reports that in China, "the introduction of commercial crops and the commercialization of land affected land prices, tenure conditions, and rent charges. Prices for land doubled and tripled in some areas, and secure tenure was replaced by short-term contracts. At the same time rents increased." The macabre picture Hinton [1966] paints of China on the eve of the Maoist revolution reveals the extent to which a situation of high population density can lead to utterly dehumanizing consequences. In the late 1940s starvation had reached such extremes that peasants were being shot on sight for eating leaves from landlords' trees and babies were being sold by desperate mothers for the equivalent of one dollar.

Similarly, Scott [1976] details the impact of economic disaster on peasants in his discussion of the "Depression Rebellions" in Southeast Asia. Closer to home, El Salvador's rapid population growth over the past eighty years has resulted in the most densely populated mainland country in the Western Hemisphere. Population growth, coupled with an extreme concentration of land in the hands of the major coffee growers, has resulted in the disappearance of alternatives for the peasants of that nation [Durham, 1977]. Peasants have reacted by resorting to rebellious activity. Hence, although the violent repression of the 1932 peasant uprising in El Salvador resulted in the extermination of many Indian communities and encouraged other Indians to conceal their "Indianness," thereby eliminating ethnically based oppression of the peasant masses, the scarcity of land is once again forcing the peasant to rebel. Instances of peasant riots and fierce government repression are reported with growing frequency. Unrest in the countryside is brutally repressed in El Salvador, however, contributing to what Huizer [1972:27-30] calls the "culture of repression."

The absence of an ethnic basis for discrimination against peasants has thus far shielded Costa Rica from peasant rebellions. It remains to be seen if population pressures like those now being felt in El Salvador will soon emerge in Costa Rica, however. If land concentraton and population growth catch the Costa Rican peasant in a two-front assault on his security, he may rebel. The final section of this book explores the possibility of such an event in the light of some data projections.

The Alternatives Disappear

In the 1960s a number of factors combined to produce what on the surface was a rather optimistic picture for the Costa Rican peasant. Industrialization in the urban sector, increasing opportunities in the agricultural sector, and land reform all promised to provide peasants with viable alternatives to rebellion.

The Central American Common Market, which Costa Rica joined in July, 1963 [Seligson, 1973:177], stimulated the expansion of industry. It was hoped that this would offer the peasant the alternative of moving to the city. This hope, however, proved unrealizable for several reasons. First, the growing mass of city dwellers quickly absorbed the available jobs, removing immigration to the cities as an alternative for their less-educated country cousins. Second, the expansion of industry which was at first rapid slowed considerably as the tiny Central American consumer market proved itself unable to absorb more products. Third, the economies of scale are such that the market is too small to support large, labor-absorptive industries such as steel mills. Fourth, industrial development in Latin America is, to use Adams' [1967] term, "secondary development"; that is, new industries tend to be highly automated (thereby requiring very little labor), in contrast to primary industrial development, which is based upon relatively primitive manufacturing techniques that require much manual labor. Finally, rivalries, political disputes, and a general lack of group feeling ("we" feeling) among Common Market members have prevented the Market from growing in recent years [Seligson, 1973:177-89]. The "Football War" between El Salvador and Honduras, in part a manifestation of the intense peasant population pressure on the land area of El Salvador, greatly reduced the chances for rapid growth of the Market. By 1978, after Costa Rica had broken diplomatic relations with Nicaragua, the market appeared doomed. For all these reasons, therefore, jobs are not readily available for Costa Rican peasants, and hence the alternative of migration to the cities is not possible for most of them. Indeed, rural to urban migration rates in Costa Rica up through the early 1970s have been much lower than elsewhere in Latin America [Fernández, et al., 1976:75-103]. However, one suspects that the low migration rates result more from the traditional availability of alternatives in the countryside than from peasant awareness of the scarcity of factory jobs. Certainly elsewhere in Latin America the scarcity of jobs has not deterred hordes of peasants from migrating to urban areas, only to end up living in slums.

Growth in the agricultural sector, for a time, showed considerable promise for Costa Rican peasants. In the decade of the 1960s, the annual growth rate of the Gross National Product generated by agriculture was an extraordinarily high 5 percent, a rate surpassed in Latin America only by Nicaragua and Panama [Oficina Internacional de Trabajo, 1972:206]. This growth resulted from the confluence of several factors. For one thing, the general easing of the Cold War meant that Costa Rica was able to open new markets for coffee among the Soviet Bloc countries. Sales to the Soviet Union alone amounted to approximately 10 percent of all coffee exports in 1968-69 [Oficina del Café, 1973a:25]. Furthermore, the economic embargo of Cuba imposed by the United States has meant a substantial expansion of Costa Rica's sugar sales to the lucrative North American market, resulting in an overall increase in sugar exports by about one-third, as compared with the pre-Castro years [Grupo de Estudio de Tenencia de la Tierra y Desarrollo Rural,

1972:10]. Third, the expanding world demand for beef and the concomitant rise in its price have permitted a marked expansion of Costa Rican beef exports: the level increased from 33 million colones in 1963 to 83 million in 1970 [Grupo de Estudio en Tenencia de la Tierra y Desarrollo, 1972:11]. Finally, the discovery of disease-resistant banana varieties has made possible the reopening of plantations on the country's Atlantic side, and the result has been a skyrocketing of exports from 171 million colones in 1963 to 597 million colones in 1970 [Grupo de Estudio en Tenencia de la Tierra y Desarrollo Rural, 1972:11].

Unfortunately, the expansion of the agricultural export sector cannot be expected to continue. All indications are that the world market for coffee, sugar, and bananas is saturated. In 1973, for example, some 36 million bags of coffee remained unsold in storehouses throughout the world [Pan-American Coffee Bureau, 1972:1]. It is true that a recent freeze in Brazil and civil strife in Africa for a time reduced world supplies and increased prices, but the long-run pattern of saturation is clear, as the sharp downturn in coffee prices in 1978 demonstrated. Whenever a freeze or a war temporarily reduces world supplies, the momentarily higher prices stimulate overplanting and consequently result in overproduction in subsequent years. And whereas beef exports show promise of continued growth, cattle ranches employ very little labor and therefore do not offer the peasant population any promise of relief.

It is projected by the International Labor Office [Oficina Internacional de Trabajo, 1972:130-31] that in the period 1970-90, the growth rate in the agricultural sector will drop to somewhere between 3 percent and 4.3 percent (falling from the 1965-70 level of 5 percent), and that overall growth will slow from the 1950-70 rate of 6.9 percent to somewhere between 4 percent and 5.2 percent. Such small drops might not seem important, but when projected a decade into the future, their serious impact on agricultural employment can easily be envisioned. It is expected that unemployment rates will rise from the 1950-63 levels of between 4.1 percent and 6.9 percent to 23 percent by 1990! Translated into more meaningful terms, there will be a deficit of some 200,000 jobs by 1985, which is to say that by that year there will be as many people without jobs in the country as there were people employed in the agricultural sector in 1963. Mexico, a country far richer in natural resources than Costa Rica, finds itself confronted with an ever worsening unemployment problem.

It is not only the international market which threatens the peasant but technology as well. Technology, which in the last century played such an important role in the expansion of coffee production, steadily reduces the need for manpower on the farms. Thus, added to the slowing of the expansion of coffee exports, which reduces the need for peasant labor, is the continued introduction of more and more labor-saving devices, such as the tractor and herbicides. Similarly, despite the growth in the production of bananas in recent years, the proportion of the agricultural labor force engaged in banana production has remained almost constant (approximately 10 percent). The mechanization of production and major advances in packing bananas have held down the demand for labor.

While the opportunities for the peasant in urban industry or in an expanded agricultural sector appear quite limited, the expansion of agrarian reform does hold out considerable promise. If the plans for future reform outlined in chapter 6 are realized, peasants will have found an alternative to rebellion. Elsewhere in Latin America, where the inferior class position of peasants is superimposed on their inferior ethnic position, land reform does not hold such promise. As van den Berghe and Primov [1977:259] point out, in Peru the massive land reform of 1968 had little impact on the Indian's life chances:

> Expropriation of the large landowners and the transformation of haciendas into cooperatives should theoretically have freed the peasants, since the alleged basis of their exploitation and subjection, namely alienation from the means of production, has been eliminated. In theory, the land now belongs collectively to those who till it. Yet, peasants remain as subordinate and dependent as ever, and attempts by the peasantry to assert their independence meet with repressive measures. Peasants remain Indians, and the rulers remain mestizos.

In Costa Rica, in contrast, peasants are *not* Indians and hence agrarian reform has a better chance of having a real impact, since peasants who receive land will not be subjected to ethnic discrimination.

There are three factors, however, which might make the observer pessimistic about the feasibility of agrarian reform as an alternative. First, it is unclear whether national financial resources will permit the expropriation of sufficient land. As pointed out in chapter 6, expropriation is legal only when full compensation is paid to the owners. Costa Rica's limited supply of capital, because of its dependent position in the international economic order, its small size, and its low level of industrialization inhibit its ability to expropriate vast amounts of land. Second, conflicts in national policy priorities and direction make it an open question as to whether there will be full support for a major land reform. The power of the large landowners in the National Assembly should not be underestimated. Beyond that, many among the new class of urban industrialists are also owners of coffee plantations; hence, they are not totally sympathetic with reform programs.[4]

---

[4] From time to time, however, large influential landowners who wish to divest themselves of unproductive rural property, or property which they no longer have the time or interest

Third, the reform process itself may serve to exacerbate the problem of rural population growth and hence add to, rather than detract from, the land scarcity problem. I have shown elsewhere [Seligson, forthcoming-b] that in Costa Rica smallholders have more children than do landless peasants. Apparently they do so in order to supply themselves with "free" family labor for farm work. Landless peasants, on the other hand, manage their family economies like those who work in an urban industrial setting; hence they attempt to hold down the number of mouths to feed, since a failure to do so means they must divide their fixed wage among a larger number of mouths. The scarcity of farm jobs makes day work for sons increasingly difficult to come by. Therefore a landless peasant sees no advantage in a large family, since jobs are not likely to be available for his children. Agrarian reform, which provides landless peasants with land, results in an increase in the desired number of children, according to a survey I conducted in 1976 among land reform beneficiaries (see chapter 3). It is estimated that if the desire for larger families among land reform beneficiaries actually results in increased family size, and if land reform affects a large sector of landless peasants, the impact on birth rates could be considerable. The resultant increase of the rural population may cancel out the beneficial impact of reform, as the wave of new children grow to adulthood and begin demanding land. Eventually there will be no land left to expropriate.

One solution to the problem of increased birth rates among land reform beneficiaries may lie in the communal enterprise model of reform described in chapter 6. It has been found [Seligson, forthcoming-b] that communal enterprise peasants of Costa Rica desire a smaller family than do individual parcel holders. Since communal peasants receive a fixed wage, as do their landless counterparts, they too have a disincentive for producing large families. However, it is unclear whether the communal enterprise program will be accepted by peasants, since most would prefer to own their own plots. In the 1976 survey, it was found that even among the 222 communal enterprise peasants interviewed, 54 percent preferred to have their own farms. Much research and experimentation needs to be done before it can be said that the communal enterprise program will offer a workable alternative to the individual parcel reform programs.

In summary, conditions in the countryside show strong indications of continued deterioration. And although the peasants know little about statisticians' projections of growth and unemployment rates, they very

---

to manage, have urged the government to expropriate their properties for agrarian reform. In this way an owner can sell the land at a fair price and know that the purchaser (the government) will pay for it. ITCO frequently has been charged with "making a land reform for the rich" when it expropriates properties of such influential individuals.

clearly see the handwriting on the wall. Increasingly, they see their villages turning into what Gerhard Sandner [1964] describes as "rural slums," where scores of families are jammed into areas in which only a few lived before. With every year, Sandner notes, there are fewer steady jobs available. Thus, while in the past sons of steady workers could count on jobs on the coffee plantations which employed their fathers, this is no longer the case. Instead, the patrón permits a family to "share" a job. Under this system an adult male in the family works for twelve weeks on the plantation and then rotates with another member of the family.[5]

The peasant sees the future and is frightened. Under the best of conditions, his economic security is limited; in the present decade, it is almost nonexistent. In the light of this fact, the dimensional analysis of peasant social status presented in chapter 4 takes on new importance in interpreting the contemporary peasant's state of mind. It has been found that the most important dimension is security: nearly all peasants prefer being smallholders above any choice on the list. Since land is normally too expensive to purchase and very risky to obtain through squatting, secure jobs such as steady banana plantation labor are ranked high. The second dimension, the legal/illegal one, can be viewed as a desperation dimension to which peasants resort when neither land nor a secure job is tenable. Under such conditions, and when irregular day-work is not obtainable, peasants will turn to squatting as a last resort. It bears repeating that an estimated 11.4 percent of all rural families are squatters. Figures such as these reveal the severity of the problem at a time when the growth of the agricultural sector has been at record heights. As this growth slows down and unemployment increases, land invasions can be expected to increase in frequency.

Squatting can be understood as the peasant's way of bringing about a redistribution of rural property—a kind of spontaneous land reform. If his efforts, disorganized as they may be, were not interfered with by national politics and politicians, he would be likely to achieve a fair amount of success. The power of the landed interests is too great, however, to permit this to happen. Costa Rica still earns the lion's share of its wealth from agricultural enterprises, and is likely to continue to do so for many years. For this reason, the coffee aristocracy, in alliance with other landed interests, is not likely to let the squatter movement get out of hand.

The Costa Rican peasant has few allies in his struggle, and those he has have very little power. Only the left-wing parties and university stu-

[5] For the patrón, the advantage of this system is that he does not have to pay social security taxes and is not responsible for severence pay for any worker who is employed for less than thirteen weeks during the year.

dent groups have expressed solidarity with him, and neither of these counts for very much in Costa Rican politics. As was shown in chapter 5, both ITCO and IMAS have sometimes been more interested in enhancing their own institutional image than in providing the impoverished peasant with real help, while the major political parties pay only lip service to the agrarian question. They mouth their agreement with the need for reform (everybody claims to be in favor of reform), but the serious talk of politics concerns other issues. In essence then, the peasant stands alone, much in the way that the Mexican villagers of Morelos stood alone against the onslaught of the sugar growers. Will the reply of the Costa Rican elites to peasant demands echo that of the Mexican hacendado who said, "If that bunch from Anenecuilco wants to farm, let them farm in a flower pot, because they're not getting any land, even up the side of the hills" [Womack, 1968:63]?

The prognosis for the Costa Rican peasant is not good. Options have evaporated, and no sign of relief is in sight. The next twenty years are likely to see a progressive decline in his already inadequate standard of living. How will the story end? To be sure, one can expect increasing levels of violence as more and more peasants are forced against the walls of landlessness and unemployment. Full-scale revolution is, however, quite unlikely. The only hope for the peasant lies with forces that are largely beyond his control—the national political system. It can be expected that as the generation which participated in the Civil War of 1948 passes from the political scene, new issues will emerge in national politics and new parties will be formed. It would not be surprising if at least one such party were to base its platform on alleviating the deprivation of the peasantry. Such a party could certainly argue a strong case.[6] It is possible that a decade from now, if conditions in the countryside continue to worsen, a party appealing to the impoverished rural masses may achieve broad support. Although such a party is unlikely to be successful in its bid for the highest political positions, it might gain control over rural municipal governments, which have recently been granted new autonomy and fiscal authority [Vicente Castro, 1972:83-88]. Local governments have been ineffectual and moribund in the past [Baker, Fernández and Stone, 1972:83-88], but if they were peasant controlled and organized into a nationwide rural coalition, they might be revitalized, and subsequently might initiate extensive agrarian reform at the local level.[7]

---

[6] A recent study [Booth, 1974:6] has found that in 1973 the mean income in the metropolitan area of Costa Rica was nearly six times that of the rural areas.

[7] It was perhaps to counteract just such a possibility that a change in the system of

Ultimately, however, the peasant will lose: he is increasingly an anachronism in the era of the transnational agro-industrial complex with its capital-intensive, labor-saving technology. The Costa Rican countryside of the future is likely to see the almost complete disappearance of the remaining smallholding peasants, for they will be unable to compete with the industrial giants. Similarly, the landless peasants will engage in a losing struggle to obtain employment on mechanized plantations. Eventually, landlessness and unemployment will confront the peasant at a time when the escape valves of the past will have been closed. Only intensive efforts on the part of the state would be able to halt the demise of the peasantry.

---

electing deputies to the Legislative Assembly was considered in 1976. This reform would have provided for the election of the majority of deputies at the national level rather than at the provincial level, and hence would have reduced rural power in the Assembly.

Reference Matter

Appendix 1: A Note on the Definition of Peasants

It is necessary to define the concept *peasant*,[1] but this is no easy task, as is evidenced by the flood of literature which has attempted to do so. Mintz [1973:92] has pointed out that while the debate as to the "true" definition promises to be unending, some middle-range definition is possible if one limits his purposes. Since in this book the concept is used with a rather specific heuristic purpose in mind, the task of setting a middle-range definition becomes a good deal easier.

Most definitions fit into one of two frameworks of analysis [Shanin, 1971:11-14; Powell, 1971:4-11]. Perhaps the most widely used framework among American scholars grows out of the work by Kroeber [1948:284]. This view, popularized by Robert Redfield's work [1930] on Mexican peasants and immortalized by his student Oscar Lewis [1951], focuses on the cultural uniqueness of peasants and places peasant society somewhere on the *gemeinschaft-gesellschaft* continuum. The central difficulty with this approach arises when one tries to interpret observed peasant behavior as a product of that cultural uniqueness. Some of the hottest academic debates of the decade have sprung from such notions as Oscar Lewis's "culture of poverty" [1951;1959;1960;1966; Valentine, 1968], George Foster's "limited good" [1965;1970; Huizer, 1970], Edward Banfield's "amoral familism" [1958;1970; Davis, 1970; Silverman, 1968; Huizer, 1969:162], and Charles J. Erasmus's *"encogido* syndrome" [1968; Huizer, 1970]. In essence, the critics of the cultural argument all make the same point: in seeking an explanation for what is

---

[1] While I would not be uncomfortable using Womack's [1968] "people of the fields," I think it would be a disservice to other scholars to use a term stripped of its theoretical significance.

observed to be "backward," "unmodern," "irrational" behavior, one should first look at the objective conditions of economic and political exploitation which predominate in peasant societies. An examination of such conditions, critics argue, will reveal that peasant behavior is a rational response to their position as a subjected, exploited group. It is out of this critique of the "cultural" framework of analysis that the "economic" framework grows. The roots of this position are found in Marx and Engels [1950], and take on modern expression in the works of Julian Steward [1956], Eric Wolf [1966], Ernest Feder [1971b], and Barrington Moore, Jr. [1966].

Admittedly, the two-fold categorization offered above is quite broad, and without doubt, several of the authors would feel uncomfortable being placed in the same "box." Nevertheless, the distinction between the two positions is sufficiently clear-cut to make it obligatory for the student interested in defining peasants to choose between the two. The positions are not necessarily mutually exclusive, but if the definition is to possess heuristic power it will have to focus either on the cultural argument or on the economic one. I discard the cultural basis of definition because of my own experience with peasants. The researcher who first comes into contact with a peasant society is likely to find it so different from anything with which he is familiar that he is bound to encounter support for the cultural position. However, as one becomes more familiar with peasants and begins to observe more carefully exactly *why* things are done the way they are, it becomes clear that they are done in those ways for quite rational reasons, the most important of which is the peasant's "underdog status" [Wolf, 1966; Powell, 1971]. It is his recognition that he is at the bottom of the economic and political ladder that determines the outlines of his behavior. My acceptance of the economic argument to the exclusion of the cultural one is, in the end, a personal choice, and only can be defended on those grounds.

Coming to the definition itself, one has to confront another problem: how broad is it going to be? Essentially, the choice is one between limiting the definition to include only those peasants who have access to land, either owned, rented, or sharecropped [Shanin, 1971:240-45], and broadening it to include landless agricultural laborers of various types, often called rural proletarians or semiproletarians [Powell, 1971:11]. Although some would strongly disagree, it does not appear that there are any compelling arguments for choosing between the two definitions. Rather, it would appear that both landless and landed country folk could be included in the general category of peasant. As Mintz [1973:95] argues,

> peasantries commonly live in close association with landless, wage-earning agricultural workers whose economic relations incline us to

define them more as rural proletarians than as peasantries. The extent to which a rural proletariat justifiably may be segregated analytically from a peasantry will, of course, depend on many environing factors. For that part of the world with which the writer is most familiar—the Caribbean region—it is difficult to specify the characteristics of either such "type" without reference to the other. Moreover, alternating simultaneous participation of large groups of people in activities associated with each "type" raises genuine questions about the typology itself.

Since this book treats landed and landless country folk an inclusive definition would seem to be most appropriate. For this reason the definition provided by Landsberger and Hewitt [1970:560] best fits the purposes of this study. They state, ". . . we shall use the term 'peasant' to refer to any rural cultivator who is low in economic and political status." Such a definition focuses on the fact that the individual is engaged existentially, as Wolf [1966] puts it, in agricultural tasks, as opposed to the large landowner who never works the fields. It also emphasizes the underdog nature of the peasantry in both economic and political terms. Economically, the peasant has little capital, little land, and limited control of production and distribution. Politically, he has little or no access to centers of political power and therefore precious little influence on the allocation of scarce resources. The definition is sufficiently broad to include landed and landless types alike, and permits me to refer to both types with a single expression. However, as the extensive discussion in chapter 4 should make clear, my use of the term peasant does not in any way imply that I ignore important variations within the peasantry. Indeed, much of the analysis rests on the transition of Costa Rican country folk from one type of peasant (landed) to another (landless).

Appendix 2:
Rank-Order Techniques

One method of rank-ordering provides the respondent with a list of all nine types and asks him to rank them. Such a procedure is likely to be successful only with literate populations who can study a printed list and mark their responses. Since many of the respondents in this study were illiterate, the procedure had to be rejected. Furthermore, even if the respondents had been literate, it is questionable whether individuals would be capable of responding accurately to a task which requires the ordering of as many as nine items.[1] A second method deals with one category at a time, asking the respondent to place the category along a continuum (e.g., on the rungs of a ladder [Haller, Holsinger and Ulhoa Saraiva, 1972:947]). The problem with this method is that each category is examined in isolation without reference to any other type, which prevents the respondent from considering the types in relation to each other, and this is ultimately what the researcher wants to know. The third technique is that of paired comparisons [David, 1963]. This technique, also known as "forced-choice comparisons," presents the respondent with two items at a time and asks him to choose between them. The procedure is repeated over and over again until every possible combination has been examined.

The forced-choice comparisons procedure overcomes the drawbacks of the ones previously mentioned. Since there are only two objects to consider at a time, the task is much simpler and more manageable than a complete rank-ordering of all the items at once. By dealing with a pair, the technique permits the respondent to order the items in relation to each other rather than in isolation, thereby overcoming the difficulty of the single rank at a time technique. And it has the added advantage of

---

[1] In a linguistic investigation conducted by Berk-Seligson [1978], it was found that university students in Costa Rica were unable to rank-order deviations from standard speech when there were more than five deviations from a given norm.

forcing "the subject to make comparisons which he can easily overlook in a rank-ordering task" [Burton, 1972:65]. That is to say, the paired-comparison technique avoids the well-known tendency of respondents to rank a list of items without fully considering all of the implications of their ordering. For example, when asked to rank four ice-cream flavors, chocolate, vanilla, strawberry, and peach, the respondent might begin by saying to himsef, "I like chocolate better than all the others, so I will rank it first. I like vanilla better than strawberry, so vanilla gets second place, strawberry third, and peach last." That same person, however, when confronted with a paired-comparison test, might end up choosing peach over vanilla, since upon comparing these two flavors alone, he may prefer the former to the latter. The error in the first rank-ordering would be produced by his failure to consider the vanilla-strawberry pair. The failure to consider all pairs becomes more and more frequent as the number of items increases.

The only difficulty with the paired-comparison test is that when the number of items becomes fairly large, the number of pairs grows enormous, resulting in the rapid onset of respondent boredom and the consequent loss of precision in the respondent's answers. Where the number of items is large, the researcher has no choice but to artificially reduce the number of pairs by substituting conjoint judgments (those in which the number of comparisons is reduced by using tetrads rather than pairs) for disjoint (direct) judgments. Such a procedure, however, has the distinct disadvantage of making it necessary to infer the direct judgments and also to assume transitivity [Green and Carmone, 1970:54-57; Green and Rao, 1969:24-25]. Since experience has shown that numerous intransitivities appear in rank-order judgements (i.e., A preferred to B, B preferred to C, but C preferred to A), this drawback is a serious one, but one which is necessary for certain experiments. Another technique for dealing with the problem of boredom, one that was used in the present study, is dividing up the number of pairs into small groups (from eight to ten) and spacing them at widely separated points throughout the questionnaire. This technique proved to be of great assistance although it, too, has its limits, and cannot be employed too often in any single questionnaire.

Appendix 3:
The Problem of Inconsistency

While the paired-comparisons method used to elicit the data in this study has the advantage of greatly simplifying the rank-ordering task (by requiring that the respondent retain in his mind only two peasant types at a time), it does create a problem in the calculation of the rank orders. The problem arises directly out of the fact that it permits the respondent to express "inconsistent" preferences which are not possible under a rank-order method. These "inconsistent" responses arise when, for example, A is preferred to B, B is preferred to C, and C is preferred to A. In this situation each of the three stimuli would be given a point (having been preferred to one of the three stimuli), and thus all three would tie for first place. When such ties occur we obtain no useful information, whereas had we simply asked the respondent to order the three stimuli, he might well have provided a ranking.

The fact that inconsistency is possible in the paired-comparison procedure but not in the rank-order procedure would appear, at first glance, to be a factor in discouraging its use as a technique of data collection. Further consideration, however, suggests that all that is done in the rank-order procedure is to make it impossible for the respondent to provide an inconsistent response even if such a response is quite reasonable. An illustration is provided by David [1963:11]. He develops a situation in which successive pairs of three athletic teams meet in a tournament. In the first encounter team A beats team B, in the second encounter team B beats team C, but in the final match, team C beats team A. Such a situation is common, because certain strengths that one team has when playing another become weaknesses in playing a third team (for example, height may be necessary to beat one team, but speed another). David points out that the clearest illustration of this phenomenon is found in the popular game of stone, scissors, and paper.

Thus the so-called inconsistencies of judgement made in the paired comparisons situation may be a result of the fact that the respondent is focusing on different attributes of the stimuli when he examines different pairs. The responses are not genuinely inconsistent but reflect accurate evaluation on the part of the respondent, since there is more than one valid order. There are, however, other reasons why such "inconsistent" judgements can appear. One is that the judge may be guessing when he states his preferences. Such a situation could arise when the stimuli have little salience for or are unfamiliar to the respondent. It could also arise when the stimuli are in fact highly similar and therefore difficult to rank-order with precision—when respondents are asked to judge color chips in which the color differs by only one shade, for example. Of course, the *inconsistency* may have been produced by an error in judgment on the part of the respondent or by his failure to cooperate in the task at hand. These situations are perhaps the only ones to which the term *inconsistency* can be appropriately applied.

From this discussion it is clear that inconsistent judgements can occur for a number of reasons. Unfortunately, from the paired-comparison data alone the researcher is unable to determine the cause. What he is left with is a tied ranking which he can attribute to either legitimate (i.e., a rational reason for the inconsistency to appear) or illegitimate reasons. Whatever the cause of the inconsistency, the researcher needs some way of determining which respondents are so inconsistent in their responses that they should be dropped from the analysis. Such respondents may, as has been shown, have valid reasons for their inconsistent judgements, but because of the many tied ranks which several such inconsistencies produce, it is necessary to eliminate these respondents.

An objective criterion for dropping respondents with highly inconsistent pairs has been developed by Maurice Kendall [1948:121-38]. Kendall suggests a "coefficient of consistence," and a method for calculating the statistical significance of this coefficient.

The consistence coefficient for the entire sample of 531 respondents was determined, and resulted in a mean of .921. Perfectly consistent responses were given by 39.7 percent of the individuals, and 73.3 percent had consistence coefficient levels over .90. The Chi-square test of significance, which tests to see if the respondent allotted his preferences totally at random, indicates that none should be excluded from the study owing to inconsistency of response.

The difficulty with accepting Chi-square values as the criterion for rejecting inconsistent respondents is that they are not stringent enough. In order to be excluded from the study, using this criterion, the respondent would have to have produced more than 27 of a possible maximum of 30 circular triads (p = .05). Thus if the respondent has any consistency at all in his data, he would not be excluded. This would mean that the respondent who produced 23 of the possible 30 triads in this study would be considered sufficiently consistent to be included in the study. Since the Chi-square values were calculated in this study to "clean" the data of respondents who were inconsistent, the Chi-square criterion is of no use in the present situation where no respondents were completely inconsistent.

Since the Chi-square criterion proved unsuitable for cleaning the data in the present study, it was decided to use the consistence coefficient alone as the criterion and to eliminate all respondents whose coefficient was more than two standard deviations below the mean. The mean consistence coefficient is .921 and the standard deviation is 0.107. Thus respondents whose coefficient is less than 0.707 were excluded. Using this criterion for "cleaning" the data results in the elimination of 4.9 percent of the cases, or a total of 26 cases.

Appendix 4:
Attitude Scales

The series of questions designed to measure personal efficacy has been analyzed using Guttman's scalogram method and the items have been found to form a unidimensional cumulative scale (the coefficient of reproduceability is .93, and the coefficient of scalability .77). Each respondent has been assigned a Guttman scale score based on his responses to the items. The scores range from a low of 0 to a high of 5. These scores have then been standardized to make their later use in this book more readily comparable with the trust index. Three checks on the scale were conducted: the alpha reliability coefficient was calculated and yielded a value of .89; the Guttman split-half coefficient was calculated as .83; and a factor analysis was run on the six variables. A single factor (with an eigenvalue greater than 1) was produced, with loadings which ranged from a high of .92 to a low of .69. This one factor explained 62 percent of the variance in these variables.

The six items used to measure trust were not constructed so as to form a cumulative scale, and thus were not analyzed with the Guttman method. Instead, factor analysis was employed in order to determine the amount of common variance. The unidimensionality of the eight items on the trust scale was substantiated (all variables loaded on one factor, which explained 42.4 percent of the variance). The eight items were then subjected to a test of reliability and produced a Cronbach's alpha of .78, a Guttman split-half coefficient of .77, and a mean inter-item correlation of .31. Factor scores were used to assign a scale score to each respondent on the trust dimension.

Works Cited

Books, Articles, and Interviews

Aberbach, Joel D.
   1969 "Alienation and Political Behavior." American Political Science Review 63 (March): 86-99.

Acosta V., Rogelio.
   1969 Análisis de la estructura de producción del café en Costa Rica, con base en la información del registro de productores de la Oficina del Café. San José: Oficina del Café.

Adams, Frederick V.
   1914 Conquest of the Tropics: The Story of the Creative Enterprises Conducted by the United Fruit Company. Garden City, N.Y.: Doubleday.

Adams, Richard.
   1967 The Second Sowing; Power and Secondary Development in Latin America. San Francisco: Chandler Publishing Co.

Agency for International Development (U.S.).
   1970 Costa Rica Agricultural Development Program Projects. San José: U.S.A.I.D.

Aguilar Bulgarelli, Oscar R.
   1969 Costa Rica y sus hechos políticos de 1948 (Problemática de una década). San José: Editorial Costa Rica.

Alker, Jr., Hayward, and Bruce M. Russett.
   1966 "Indices for Comparing Inequality." In Richard L. Merritt and Stein Rokkan, eds., Comparing Nations. New Haven: Yale University Press.

Alvarez, Eduardo.
   1954? Condiciones económicas y financieras de la actividad cafetalera en Costa Rica. San José: Banco Nacional de Costa Rica.

Anderson, Thomas P.
   1971 Matanza: El Salvador's Communist Revolt of 1932. Lincoln: University of Nebraska Press.

de Andrade, Moretzsohn.
	1966 "Decadência do campesinato costariquenho." Revista Geographica (Brazil) 66 (June): 135-51.
Araujo, José Emilio G., ed.
	1975. La empresa comunitaria. San José, Costa Rica: Instituto Interamericano de Ciencias Agricolas.
Araya Pochet, Carlos.
	1971 "El desarrollo económico y social de Costa Rica a partir de 1821." In Oscar Aguilar Bulgarelli, ed., El desarrollo nacional en 150 años de vida independiente. Ciudad Universitaria "Rodrigo Facio": Publicaciones de la Universidad de Costa Rica, Serie Historia y Geografía no. 12.
Archivo Nacional.
	1844 Contrato Soto-Keith. San José.
Archivo Nacional, Sección Histórica-Congreso, various documents.
Archivo Nacional, Sección Legislativa, various documents.
Arias Sánchez, Oscar.
	1971 Grupos de presión en Costa Rica. San José: Editorial Costa Rica.
	1976 Quién gobierna en Costa Rica? Ciudad Universitaria "Rodrigo Facio," Costa Rica: Editorial Universitaria Centroamericana.
Arredondo Alberto and Alfredo Costales Samaniego, eds.
	1965 La realidad social de Centro América. Estudios y documentos no. 18, editado por Centro de Estudios y Documentación Sociales, A.C. Mexico.
Arroyo, Victor Manuel.
	1973 Carlos Luis Fallas. San José: Ministerio de Cultura, Juventud y Deportes.
Asamblea Legislativa.
	1971 "Informe de mayoría—expediente No. 4355—Investigación venta de terrenos del I.T.C.O. en Chambacú. San José: Archivo Asamblea Legislativa. (typescript)
Avila Bolaños, Olger.
	1972 "La Sociedad Itineraria de Costa Rica, 1843-1854." Ciudad Universitaria "Rodrigo Facio": Tesis de Grado, Universidad de Costa Rica.
Backer, James.
	1974 La Iglesia y el Sindicalismo en Costa Rica. San José: Editorial Costa Rica.
Baker, Christopher E., Ronald Ferńandez Pinto, and Samuel Z. Stone.
	1972 El gobierno municipal en Costa Rica: sus características y

funciones. San José: Instituto de Fomento y Asesoría Municipal (IFAM).
Balch, George I., and Lyman A. Kellstedt.
  1975 "Trust in the Political System: A Construct Validation." Paper presented at the Annual Meeting of the American Political Science Association in San Francisco, September 2-6.
Banco Central de Costa Rica.
  1960 Memória Anual 1960. San José.
Banfield, Edward C.
  1958 The Moral Basis of a Backward Society. New York: The Free Press.
  1970 "Reply to J. Davis." Comparative Studies in Society and History (July): 354-59.
Barlett, Peggy F.
  1973 "El tabaco y el pasto—Respuestas del campesino a los cambios económicos locales, nacionales e internacionales: análisis del cambio en el uso del suelo en una comunidad en el cantón de Puriscal." San José: Ministerio de Agricultura y Ganadería. (mimeographed).
  1975 "Agricultural Change in Paso: The Structure of Decision Making in a Costa Rican Peasant Community." Ph.D. diss., Columbia University.
Barrenechea Consuegra, Fernando.
  1956 "Una organización para empresarios del café." San José: Escuela Superior de Administración Pública de América Central. (mimeographed).
Beeche, Octavio.
  1935 Indice general de la legislación vigente en Costa Rica, Tomo Primero. San José: Imprenta Nacional.
Bell, John Patrick.
  1971 Crisis in Costa Rica; The 1948 Revolution. Austin: University of Texas Press.
van den Berghe, Pierre L.
  1974a Class and Ethnicity in Peru. The Netherlands: E. J. Brill.
  1974b "The Use of Ethnic Terms in the Peruvian Social Science Literature." In Pierre L. van den Berghe, ed., Class and Ethnicity in Peru. The Netherlands: E. J. Brill, 1974.
van den Berghe, Pierre L., and George Primov.
  1977 Inequality in the Peruvian Andes: Class and Ethnicity in Cuzco. Columbia: University of Missouri Press.
Berk-Seligson, Susan.
  1978 "Phonological Variation in a Synchronic/Diachronic Sociol-

Works Cited

inguistic Context: The Case of Costa Rican Spanish." Ph.D. diss., University of Arizona.

Berk-Seligson, Susan, and Mitchell A. Seligson, eds.
1978 El hombre de Agua Buena: Un campesino costarricense (manuscript).

Biesanz, John and Mavis.
1944 Costa Rican Life. New York: Columbia University Press.

Bilderback, Loy, Marcos Bogan, and Hermógenes Hernández.
1976 "Cambio en los limites de los cantones costarricense, 1950 a 1974: Plan de IDESPO para comparabilidad cantonal. Heredia: Universidad Nacional, Instituto de Estudios Sociales en Población (IDESPO).

Block, Jeanne H., Norman Haan, and M. Brewster Smith.
1973 "Activism and Apathy in Contemporary Adolescents." In James F. Adams, ed., Understanding Adolescence: Current Developments in Adolescent Psychology. 2nd ed. Boston: Allyn and Bacon.

Bonilla Genaro Duarte, Mario.
1973 "Cooperativa Gil Tablada Corea." In Instituto Mixto de Ayuda Social, Memoria del primer laboratorio experimental para formar cuadros constructores de empresas comunitarias. Bataán, Costa Rica: IMAS, ITCO, CONAI.

Booth, John A.
1974 Características socio-gráficas de las regiones periféricas de Costa Rica. San José: Instituto de Fomento y Asesoría Municipal.

Booth, John A., Miguel Mondol, and Alvaro Hernández C.
1973 Tipología de Comunidades, vol. 2. San José, Costa Rica: Dirección Nacional de Desarrollo de la Comunidad-Acción Internacional Técnica.

Booth, John A., and Mitchell A. Seligson.
1978a "Images of Participation in Latin America." In Political Participation in Latin America, vol. 1: Citizen and State. New York: Holmes and Meier.
1978b Political Participation in Latin America, vol. 1: Citizen and State. New York: Holmes and Meier.
1979 "Peasants as Activists: A Reevaluation of Political Participation in the Countryside." Comparative Political Studies 12 (April):29-59.

Brown, Albert L.
1973 "The Agricultural Credit Project of the Agricultural Sector Program of Costa Rica." In Agency for International Devel-

opment, Small Farmer Credit in Costa Rica, A.I.D. Spring Review of Small Farmer Credit, vol. 2 (February).

Bryce-Laporte, Roy Simon.
- 1974 "Intergenerational Relations in a 'Jamaican' Village in Limón, Costa Rica." Caribbean Studies.

Buitrage Ortíz, Carlos.
- 1972 "The Development of Agrarian-Commercial Capitalism in Puerto Rico: Some Aspects of the Growth of the Coffee Hacienda System; 1857-1898." Paper presented at the Symposium "Landlord and Peasant in Latin America and the Caribbean," Cambridge, England (December 19-20).

Busey, James L.
- 1958 "Foundations of Political Contrast: Costa Rica and Nicaragua." Western Political Quarterly 11 (September): 627-59.
- 1967 Notes on Costa Rican Democracy. Boulder: University of Colorado Press.

Calvo Saenz, José Roberto.
- 1969 "Estudio agro-económico para la explotación bananera de una finca en la zona Atlántica." Ciudad Universitaria "Rodrigo Facio": Tesis de Grado, Universidad de Costa Rica.

Carcanholo, Reinaldo
- 1978 "Sobre la evolución de las actividades bananeras en Costa Rica." Estudios sociales centroamericanos 19 (enero-abril): 143-203.

Cardoso, Ciro Flamarion S.
- 1973 "La formación de la hacienda cafetalera en Costa Rica (Siglo XIX)." Estudios sociales centroamericanos 6 (September-December): 22-48.
- 1975 "Historia económica del café en Centro América (Siglo XIX): Estudio Comparativo," Estudios sociales centroamericanos (April): 10-55.
- 1977 "The Formation of the Coffee Estate in Nineteenth-Century Costa Rica." In Kenneth Duncan and Ian Rutledge, eds., Land and Labour in Latin America. Cambridge: Cambridge University Press.

Cartano, David.
- 1968 "Social Integration and Conflict in a Developing Community of the Colombian Interior." Ph.D. diss., Ohio State University.

Castillo, Carlos M.
- 1954 "Análisis exploratorio del sistema de tenencia de la tierra en Costa Rica." Problemas Agrícolas e Industriales de México 2 (no. 1): 97-106.

Centro de Estudios Democráticos de América Latina (CEDAL).
 1971 Cooperativa de caficultores latinoamericanos. La Catalina, Costa Rica: CEDAL.
 1974 Costa Rica: Empresas comunitarias campesinas, vol. 2. San José: CEDAL.
Centro de Estudios sobre Alcoholismo.
 1973 "Encuesta nacional sobre hábitos de ingestión de alcohol." Serie de monografías no. 1. San José.
Cerdas Cruz, Rodolfo.
 1972 La crisis de la democracia liberal en Costa Rica. San José: Editorial Universitaria Centroamericana (EDUCA).
Certificado de Prenda.
 n.d. San José: Federación de Cooperativas de Caficultores.
Chacón Pacheco, Nelson.
 1975 "Reseña de nuestras leyes electorales." San José: Litografía e Imprenta LIL.
Cháves Camacho, Jorge.
 1969 "Evolución demográfica de la población de Costa Rica." Revista de la Universidad de Costa Rica 27 (December): 37-42.
Clark, David S.
 1971 Renting, Sharecropping and Other Indirect Land Tenure Forms in Costa Rica: A Legal and Economic Analysis. Ciudad Universitaria "Rodrigo Facio." University of Costa Rica School of Law Agrarian Project.
Clarke, James W.
 1973 "Race and Political Behavior." In Kent S. Miller and Ralph M. Dreger, eds., Comparative Studies of Blacks and Whites in the United States. New York: Seminar Press.
Coatsworth, John.
 1974 "Railroad, Land Holding and Agrarian Protest in the Early Porfiriato." Hispanic American Historical Review 54 (February): 48-71.
Cockcroft, James D., André Gunder Frank and Dale L. Johnson, eds.
 1972 Dependence and Underdevelopment: Latin America's Political Economy. Garden City, N.Y.: Doubleday & Company.
Colby, Benjamin N., and Pierre L. van den Berghe.
 1969 Ixil Country: A Plural Society in Highland Guatemala. Berkeley: University of California Press.
Comisión Económica para América Latina.
 1973 Tenencia de la tierra y desarrollo rural en Centroamérica. San José: Editorial Universitaria Centroamérica (EDUCA).

Comisión especial encargada de investigar el cumplimiento por parte de la United Fruit Company de ley No. 3 de 4 de septiembre, 1930.
    1933   "Informe de la Comisión Especial." Archivo Nacional, Sección Histórica-Congreso.
Comisión Nacional Campesina.
    1965   El I.T.C.O.; La ley de tierras y colonización y el problema agrario nacional. San José: Imprenta Elena.
Convención Colectiva de Trabajo.
    1971   "Convención Colectiva de Trabajo celebrada entre La Compañía Bananera de C. R. y el Sindicato de Trabajadores Bananeros Unidos Independientes (SITRABUNI) y el Sindicato Unión de Trabajadores de Golfito (UTG). San José:Imprenta Borrase.
Cooley, William W., and Paul R. Lohnes.
    1971   Multivariate Data Analysis. New York: Wiley.
Costales Samaniego, Alfredo.
    1965   "Las condiciones de trabajo en el campo." In Alberto Arredondo and Alfredo Costales Samaniego, eds., La realidad social de Centro América. Estudio y documentos no. 18, editado por Control de Estudio y Documentación Sociales, A.C. Mexico.
Costa Rica.
    1868   Censo General de la República de Costa Rica (27 de noviembre de 1864). San José: Imprenta Nacional.
    1885   Censo de Población 1883. San José: Ministerio de Fomento, Sección de Estadística.
    1893   Censo general de la República de Costa Rica de 1892. San José: Tipografía Nacional.
Costa Rica, Ministerio de Agricultura y Ganadería.
    1972   "Informe sobre la actividad cafetalera de Costa Rica: aspectos agronómicos del cultivo." San José: Oficina del Café.
Craig, Jr., Wesley W.
    1969   "Peru: The Peasant Movement of La Convención." In Henry A. Landsberger, ed., Latin American Peasant Movements. Ithaca: Cornell University Press.
Creedman, Theodore.
    1971   "The Political Development of Costa Rica, 1936-1944: Politics of an Emerging Welfare State in a Patriarchical Society." Ph.D. diss., University of Maryland.
Da Cunha, Euclides.
    1944   Rebellion in the Backlands (Os sertões). Chicago: The University of Chicago Press.

Dammers, Kim.
   1965 "An Introduction to the Labor Union Movement of Costa Rica." San José: Associated Colleges of the Midwest—Central American Field Program. (mimeographed)

David, Herbert A.
   1963 The Method of Paired Comparisons. N.Y.: Hafner Publishing Company.

Davies, James C.
   1969 "The J-Curve of Rising and Declining Satisfaction as a Cause of Some Great Revolutions and a Contained Rebellion." In Hugh Davis Graham and Ted Gurr, eds., Violence in America. New York: Bantam Books.

Davis, J.
   1970 "Morals and Backwardness." Comparative Studies in Society and History 12 (July): 340-53.

Denton, Charles F.
   1969 "Bureaucracy in an Immobilist Society: The Case of Costa Rica." Administrative Science Quarterly 14 (September): 418-25.
   1971 Patterns of Costa Rican Politics Boston: Allyn and Bacon.

Departmento Nacional de Estadística.
   1905 Segundo censo agrícola general. San José: Tipografía Nacional.

Diéz años del ITCO.
   1972 Supplement to La Nación, 29 October 1972: 19-35.

Dirección General de Estadística y Censos.
   1941 Boletín de Exportaciones de Café, Cosecha 1939-1940. San José: Imprenta Nacional.
   1966a Censo Agropecuario, 1963. San José.
   1966b Censo de Población, 1963. San José.
   1966c Censo de Vivienda, 1963. San José.
   1966d Fincas Menores de una manzana. San José.
   1968 Encuesta de Hogares por Muestreo: Julio de 1966 a Junio de 1967. San José.
   1972 Población de la República de Costa Rica por Provincias, Cantones y Distritos, estimación al: 1 de julio de 1972. San José.
   1973a Anuario Estadístico de Costa Rica, 1971. San José.
   1973b Comercio Exterior de Costa Rica. San José.
   1974a Censos nacionales de 1973, Agropecuario. San José.
   1974b Censos nacionales de 1973, Vivienda. San José.
   1974c Comercio exterior de Costa Rica, 1973. San José.

1975 Censos nacionales de 1973, Población, vols. 1 and 2. San José.
1977 Estadística Vital—1975. San José.
Dobles, Fabian.
1970 El sitio de las abras. San José: Editorial Costa Rica.
Downing, T. Edmond, and E. Jean Matteson.
1965 "Squatters: A Form of Spontaneous Colonization in Costa Rica." San José: Tropical Science Center. (mimeographed)
Duncan, Kenneth and Ian Rutledge, eds.
1977 "Land and Labour in Latin America: Essays on the Development of Agrarian Capitalism in the Nineteenth and Twentieth Centuries." Cambridge: Cambridge University Press.
Dunlop, Robert Glasgow.
1847 Viajes en Centroamérica. In Ricardo Fernández Guardia, ed., Costa Rica en el siglo XIX, 2nd ed. Ciudad Universitaria "Rodrigo Facio": Editorial Universitaria Centroamericana, 1970. (Translation of Travels in Central America, 1847.)
Durham, William H.
1977 "Scarcity and Survival: The Ecological Origins of Conflict between El Salvador and Honduras." Ph.D. diss., University of Michigan.
Edelman, Jacob M.
1964 The Symbolic Uses of Politics. Urbana: University of Illinois Press.
Egginton, Everett and Mark Ruhl.
1974 "The Influence of Agrarian Reform Participation on Peasant Attitudes: The Case of Colombia." Inter-American Economic Affairs 28 (Winter): 27-43.
Equipo Técnico Interinstitucional.
1970 "Zona Bananera Atlántico Norte." San José: Oficina de Planificación. (mimeographed)
Erasmus, Charles J.
1968 "Community Development and the Encogido Syndrome." Human Organization 27 (Spring): 65-74.
van Es., J. C., and Robert L. Whittenberger.
1970 "Farm Ownership, Political Participation and Other Social Participation in Central Brazil," Rural Sociology 35 (March): 15-25.
Facio Brenes, Rodrigo.
1942 Estudio sobre economía costarricense. San José: Editorial Soley y Valverde. Reprinted in Facio, Obras de Rodrigo Fa-

cio, vol. 1. San José: Editorial Costa Rica, 1972.
1943 "Ensayos cooperativos en Costa Rica." Originally in El Surco 31 (January), and reprinted in Facio, Obras de Rodrigo Facio, vol. 1. San José: Editorial Costa Rica, 1972.
1972 Obras de Rodrigo Facio, vol. 1. San José: Editorial Costa Rica. (Originally published in 1942.)

Fallas, Carlos Luis.
1934 "Cómo se hizo la huelga de la zona atlántica." El Trabajo (2 September): 3.
1947 Gentes y gentecillas. San José: Imprenta Trejos Hnos.
1960 Don Bárbaro. San José: Imprenta Elena.
1970 Mamita Yunai. San José: Imprenta y Litografía Lehmann.

Fallas, Marco Antonio.
1972 La factoría de tabacos de Costa Rica. San José: Editorial Costa Rica.

Feder, Ernest.
1971a "Latifundia and Agricultural Labour in Latin America." In Teodor Shanin, ed., Peasants and Peasant Societies. Middlesex, England: Penguin Books.
1971b The Rape of the Peasantry: Latin America's Landholding System. Garden City, N.Y.: Doubleday & Company.

Fernández, Mario E., Anabelle Schmidt, and Victor Basauri.
1976 La Población de Costa Rica. San José: Editorial Universidad de Costa Rica.

Fernández Bonilla, León.
1886 Colección de documentos para la historia de Costa Rica, vol. 5. Paris: Imprenta Pablo Dupont.

Fernández Guardia, Ricardo.
1967 Cartilla histórica de Costa Rica, 43rd ed. San José: Antonio Lehmann.

Fishel, John T.
1979 "Political Participation in a Peruvian Highland District." In Mitchell A. Seligson and John A. Booth, eds., Political Participation in Latin America, vol. 2: Politics and the Poor. New York: Holmes and Meier.

Flores, Edmundo.
1963 Land Reform and the Alliance for Progress. Princeton: Princeton Center for International Studies.

Ford, Thomas R.
1955 Man and Land in Peru. Gainesville: University of Florida Press.

Form, William H.
   1974 "The Politics of Distrust: Field Problems in Comparative Research." Studies in Comparative International Development 9 (Spring): 20-48.
Forman, Shepard.
   1975 The Brazilian Peasantry. New York: Columbia University Press.
   1979 "The Significance of Participation: Peasants in the Politics of Brazil." In Mitchell A. Seligson and John A. Booth, eds., Political Participation in Latin America, vol. 2: Politics and the Poor. New York: Holmes and Meier.
Foster, George.
   1965 "Peasant Society and the Image of the Limited Good." American Anthropologist 66 (October): 293-315.
   1970 "Comment." Human Organization 29 (Winter): 313-14.
Frank, André Gunder.
   1972 "Sociology of Development and Underdevelopment." In James D. Cockroft, André Gunder Frank, and Dale L. Johnson, Dependence and Underdevelopment: Latin America's Political Economy. Garden City, N.Y.: Doubleday & Company.
Freire, Paulo.
   1971 "Education as Cultural Action: An Introduction." In Louis M. Colonnese, ed., Conscientization for Liberation. Washington, D.C.: Division for Latin America, United States Catholic Conference.
Gamson, William A.
   1968 Power and Discontent. Homewood Ill.: The Dorsey Press.
   1971 "Political Trust and Its Ramifications." In Gilbert Abcarian and John W. Soule, eds., Social Psychology and Political Behavior: Problems and Prospects. Columbus, Ohio: Charles A. Merrill.
Garrido Guerrero, Jorge Isaac.
   1968 El cultvo del banano en Costa Rica. San José: Litografía Lehmann.
Gibson, Jeffrey R.
   1970 "A Demographic Analysis of Urbanization: Evolution of a System of Cities in Honduras, El Salvador and Costa Rica." Ithaca, N.Y.: Cornell University Latin American Studies Program Dissertation Series.
Goldkind, Victor.
   1961 "Sociocultural Contrast in Rural and Urban Settlement

Types in Costa Rica." Rural Sociology 26 (December): 365-80.

Gómez, Miguel.
1970 "El rápido descenso de la fecundidad en Costa Rica." In Asociación Demográfica Costarricense, Quinto seminario nacional de demografía. San José.

González, Yamileth.
1973 "El problema agrario en Costa Rica." Ciudad Universitaria "Rodrigo Facio": Conferencia no. 9 de la Cátedra de Historia de las Instituciones de Costa Rica.

González Flores, Luis Felipe.
1933 "El desenvolvimiento histórico del desarrollo del café en Costa Rica y su influencia en la cultura nacional." As reprinted in Hector Rojas Solano, El Café en Costa Rica. San José: Oficina del Café, 1972. (Originally in Jorge Carranza Solís, Monografía del Café, vol. 1. San José, 1933.)

González Muñóz, Antonio.
1966 "Necesidad del fuero sindical en Costa Rica." Ciudad Universitaria "Rodrigo Facio": Tesis de grado, Universidad de Costa Rica.

González-Vega, Claudio.
1973 "Small Farmer Credit in Costa Rica: The Juntas Rurales." A.I.D. Spring Review of Small Farmer Credit, vol. 2., Washington, D.C.: Agency for International Development.

González Víquez, Cleto.
1914 "Impréstitos ingleses." Anales del Atero de Costa Rica (no. 4). (Reprinted in Cleto González Víquez, Capítulos de un libro sobre historia financiera de Costa Rica. San José: Editorial Costa Rica, 1965. Also reprinted as Cleto González Víquez, Historia financiera de Costa Rica. San José, Editorial. Costa Rica, 1977).
1933 "Origen del café de Costa Rica." In Hector Rojas Solano, ed., El café en Costa Rica. San José: Oficina del Café, 1972.

Greaves, Thomas C.
1972 "The Andean Rural Proletarians." Anthropological Quarterly 45 (April): 65-83.

Griffin, Keith.
1976 Land Concentration and Rural Poverty. London: MacMillan.

Grupo de Estudio en Tenencia de la Tierra y Desarrollo Rural.
1972 Costa Rica: Características de uso y distribución de la tierra. San José: CEPAL, FAO, OIT, SIECA, IICA (mimeographed: published in 1973 as Tenencia de la tierra y

desarrollo rural en centroamérica. San José: Editorial universitaria centroamericana).
Grupo de Productores Bananeros de la Provincia de Cartago.
1929 Los dictámenes sobre el impuesto bananero. San José: Imprenta Alsina.
Guerrero, José, Octavio Jiménez, Eduardo Carrillo, and Julio Padilla.
1927 "Exposición enviada al soberano congreso constitucional al 6 de enero de 1927 por La Sociedad Económica de Amigos del País." San José: Archivo Nacional, Sección Legislativa; and La Gaceta, 1 February 1927.
Guier, Enrique.
1971 William Walker. San José: Litografía Lehmann.
Gutiérrez, Joaquín.
1973 Murámonos, Federico. San José: Editorial Costa Rica.
Hall, Carolyn O.
1972 "Some Effects of the Spread of Coffee Cultivation upon the Landscape of Costa Rica in the Nineteenth and Twentieth Centuries. Ph.D. diss., St. Hugh's College, Oxford, England.
1976 El Café y el desarrollo histórico-geográfico de Costa Rica. San José: Editorial Costa Rica y Universidad Nacional.
Hall, Douglas.
1959 Free Jamaica, 1838-1865: An Economic History. New Haven: Yale University Press.
Haller, Archibald O., Donald B. Holsinger, and Helcio Ulhoa Saraiva.
1972 "Variations in Occupational Prestige Hierarchies: Brazilian Data." American Journal of Sociology 77 (March): 941-56.
Havens, A. Eugene.
1966 "Some Recent Issues in Survey Research in Latin America." Madison, Wisconsin: Land Tenure Center, University of Wisconsin. (mimeographed)
Heath, Dwight B.
1969 "Bolivia: Peasant Syndicates among the Aymara of the Yungas—A View from the Grass Roots." In Henry A. Landsberger, ed., Latin American Peasant Movements. Ithaca: Cornell University Press.
Hennessy, Alistar.
1969 "Latin America." In Ghita Ionescu and Ernest Gellner, eds., Populism, Its Meaning and National Characteristics. New York: MacMillan.
Hernández, Edward Dennis.
1975 "Modernization and Dependency in Costa Rica during the Decade of the 1880s. Ph.D. diss., University of California at Los Angeles.

Hernández Rodríguez, Alvaro.
> 1970 "La reforma agraria y el caso de Costa Rica." Ciudad Universitaria "Rodrigo Facio": Tesis de grado.

Herrera García, Adolfo, Enrique Mora V., and Francisco Gamboa G.
> 1971 Partido Vanguardia Popular: Breve esbozo de su historia, 2nd ed. San José: Imprenta Elena.

Hill, George W.
> 1964 "The Agrarian Reform in Costa Rica." Land Economics 40 (February): 41-48.

Hill, George W., Manuel Gollás Quintero and Gregorio Alfaro.
> 1964 Un área rural en desarrollo: sus problemas económicos y sociales, Costa Rica. San José: Instituto Universitario Centroamericano de Investigaciones Sociales y Económicas.

Hinton, William.
> 1966 Fanshen: A Documentary of Revolution in a Chinese Village. New York: Vintage Books.

Hobsbawm, E. J.
> 1959 Primitive Rebels: Studies in Archaic Forms of Social Movement in the 19th and 20th Centuries. New York: W. W. Norton & Company.
> 1967 "Peasants and Rural Migrants in Politics." In Claudio Veliz, ed., The Politics of Conformity in Latin America. London: Oxford University Press.

Huizer, Gerrit.
> 1969 "Community Development, Land Reform and Political Participation: Preliminary Observations on some Cases in Latin America." American Journal of Economics and Sociology 28 (April): 159-78.
> 1970 " 'Resistance to Change' and Radical Peasant Mobilization: Foster and Erasmus Reconsidered." Human Organization 29 (Winter): 303-13, 321-22.
> 1972 The Revolutionary Potential of Peasants in Latin America. Lexington, Mass.: Lexington Books.

Huntington, Samuel P.
> 1968 Political Order in Changing Societies. New Haven: Yale University Press.

Illich, Ivan D.
> 1971 Deschooling Society. New York: Harper and Row.

Institute for the Comparative Study of Political Systems.
> 1966 Costa Rican Election Factbook. Washington, D.C.: Operations and Policy Research.
> 1970 Costa Rican Election Factbook, supplement. Washington,

D.C.: Operations and Policy Research.
Instituto de Defensa del Café.
 1940 Informe sobre la situación del café. San José.
Instituto Mixto de Ayuda Social.
 1973 Memoria del primer laboratorio experimental para formar cuadros constructores de empresas agrícolas comunitarias. Bataán, Costa Rica: IMAS.
Instituto de Tierras y Colonización (ITCO).
 1967 Programa para la solución del problema de ocupantes en precario. San José: ITCO. (mimeographed)
 1972 Boletín informativo sobre actividad realizada por el I.T.C.O. San José: Fotolitografía nacional.
 1973 "El Jobo, lucha sin tregua." San José: n.p.
 1974 "Ponencias en el Seminario de Asentamientos Campesinos, en Costa Rica: Empresas Comunitarias Campesinas." Vol. 1. San José: CEDAL (Centro de Estudios Democráticos de América Latina).
 1975 Labor realizada por el I.T.C.O. a 1974: Informe estadístico. San José: ITCO, Departamento de Planificación.
Jaguaribe, Helio.
 1973 Political Development: A General Theory and a Latin American Case Study. New York: Harper and Row.
Jiménez Castro, Alvaro.
 1971 Leyes y reglamentos usuales sobre café(segunda edición). San José: Antonio Lehmann.
Jiménez Castro, Wilburg.
 1953 Movimientos migratorios internos en Costa Rica y sus causas. Washington, D.C.: Pan American Union.
Jiménez Veiga, Danilo.
 1971 "Para el análisis de algunos problemas y perspectivas del movimiento sindical costarricense." In Centro de Estudios Democráticos de América Latina (CEDAL), El movimiento sindical costarricense. San José: Biblioteca CEDAL No. 28.
Johnson, Allen W.
 1971 "Security and Risk-Taking Behavior among Poor Peasants." In George Dalton, ed., Studies in Economic Anthropology. Washington: American Anthropoloigical Association.
Johnson, Dale L.
 1972 "Dependence and the International System." In James D. Cockcroft, André Gunder Frank; and Dale L. Johnson, eds., Dependence and Underdevelopment: Latin America's Political Economy. Garden City, N.Y.: Doubleday & Company.

Jones, Chester Lloyd.
   1935   Costa Rican Civilization in the Caribbean. New York: Russell and Russell.
Kalnins, Arvids.
   1972   Tributos municipales costarricenses: análisis crítico y perspectivas. San José: Instituto de Fomento y Asesoría Municipal.
Karnes, Thomas L.
   1961   The Failure of Union: Central America 1824-1960. Chapel Hill: University of North Carolina Press.
Kepner, Jr., Charles David.
   1936   Social Aspects of the Banana Industry. New York: Columbia University Press.
Kepner, Jr., Charles David, and Jay Henry Soothill.
   1935   The Banana Empire: A Case Study in Economic Imperialism. New York: Vanguard Press.
Klaren, Peter.
   1977   "The Social and Economic Consequences of Modernization in the Peruvian Sugar Industry." In Kenneth Duncan and Ian Rutledge, eds., Land and Labour in Latin America. Cambridge: Cambridge University Press.
Kroeber, A. L.
   1948   Anthropology. New York: Harcourt, Brace & Co.
Lambert, Jacques.
   1971   Latin America: Social Structures and Political Institutions. Berkeley: University of California Press.
Landsberger, Henry A.
   1969   Latin American Peasant Movements. Ithaca: Cornell University.
Landsberger, Henry A., and Bobby M. Gierisch.
   1979   "Political and Economic Activism: Peasant Participation in the Ejidos of the Comarca Lagunera of Mexico." In Mitchell A. Seligson and John A. Booth, eds., Political Participation in Latin America, vol. 2: Politics and the Poor. New York: Holmes and Meier.
Landsberger, Henry A., and Cynthia N. Hewitt.
   1970   "Ten Sources of Weaknesses and Cleavage in Latin American Peasant Movements." In Rodolfo Stavenhagen, ed., Agrarian Problems and Peasant Movements in Latin America. Garden City, N.Y.: Doubleday & Company.
Leiva Rojas, Orlando.
   n.d.   "IMAS—Qué es IMAS? Por qué existe IMAS? Cómo Trabaja IMAS?" San José: Gráfica Litho-offset.

Lewis, Oscar.
- 1951 Life in a Mexican Village. Urbana: University of Illinois Press.
- 1959 Five Families; Mexican Case Studies in the Culture of Poverty. N.Y.: Basic Books.
- 1960 Tepoztlán: Village in Mexico. N.Y.: Holt, Rinehart and Winston.
- 1966 La Vida; A Puerto Rican Family in the Culture of Poverty: San Juan and New York. N.Y.: Random House.

Lindo Bennett, E.
- 1970 "La actividad cacaotera en Costa Rica." Ciudad Universitaria "Rodrigo Facio": Tesis de Grado.

Lizano Fait, Eduardo.
- 1973 Personal interview, August 24, San Pedro de Montes de Oca, Costa Rica.

Lorenz, M. O.
- 1905 "Methods of Measuring the Concentration of Wealth." Publications of the American Statistical Association 9, nos. 65-72. Boston: American Statistical Association.

Lundberg, Donald E.
- 1968 Costa Rica. San José: Juan Mora.

McClintock, Cynthia.
- 1976 "Socioeconomic Status and Political Participation in Peru: The Impact of Agrarian Cooperatives, 1969-1975." Paper presented to the seminar "Faces of Participation in Latin America: A New Look at Citizen Action in Society," San Antonio, Texas, November 12-13.

McGovern, Joseph J.
- 1966 "The Costa Rican Labor Movement: A Study in Political Unionism." Public and International Affairs 4 (Spring): 88-116.

MacLeod, Murdo J.
- 1973 Spanish Central America: A Socioeconomic History, 1520-1720. Berkeley: University of California Press.

Macune, Jr., Charles W.
- 1963 "The Building of the Atlantic Railroad of Costa Rica, 1821-1891." Master's thesis, George Washington University.

Malloy, James M.
- 1970a Bolivia: The Uncompleted Revolution. Pittsburgh: University of Pittsburgh Press.
- 1970b "El MNR Boliviano: Estudio de un movimiento popular nacionalista en América Latina." Estudios Andinos 1 (no. 1): 57-92.

Works Cited

    1971   "Generation of Political Support and Allocation of Costs." In Carmelo Mesa-Lago, ed., Revolutionary Change in Cuba. Pittsburgh: University of Pittsburgh Press.

Marx, Karl, and Frederick Engels.
    1950   Selected Writings, vol. 1. Moscow: International Publishing House.

Mathiason, John R.
    1972   "Patterns of Powerlessness among Urban Poor: Toward the Use of Mass Communications for Rapid Social Change." Studies in Comparative International Development, 7 (Spring): 64-84.

Mathiason, John R., and John D. Powell.
    1972   "Participation and Efficacy: Aspects of Peasant Involvement in Political Mobilization," Comparative Politics 4 (April): 303-29.

May, Stacy, et al.
    1966   Costa Rica: A Study in Economic Development. New York: Twentieth Century Fund.

May, Stacy, and Galo Plaza.
    1952   Costa Rica, a Study in Economic Development. N.Y.: Twentieth Century Fund.
    1958   The United Fruit Company in Latin America. Washington, D.C. National Planning Association.

Mejía M., Francisco.
    1973   Taped interviews.

Meléndez, Carlos.
    1966   "Aspectos sobre la historia del cultivo del trigo en Costa Rica durante la epoca colonial." Anales de la Academia de Geografía e Historia de Costa Rica: 25-49.
    1972   "Aspectos sobre la inmigración jamaicana." In Carlos Meléndez and Quince Duncan, El negro en Costa Rica. San José: Editorial Costa Rica.
    1977a   "Formas en la tenencia de la tierra durante el regimen colonial." In Carlos Meléndez Ch., ed., Costa Rica: Tierra y poblamiento en la Colonia. San José: Editorial Costa Rica.
    1977b   "Los origines de la propiedad territorial en el valle central durante el siglo XVI." In Carlos Meléndez Ch., ed., Costa Rica: Tierra y poblamiento en la colonia. San José: Editorial Costa Rica.

Migdal, Joel S.
    1974   Peasants, Politics and Revolution: Pressures toward Political and Social Change in the Third World. Princeton: Princeton University Press.

Miller, Arthur H.
  1974 "Political Issues and Trust in Government, 1964-1970," American Political Science Review 68 (September): 951-72.
Ministerio de Agricultura y Ganadería.
  1973 Boletín estadístico agropecuario del MAG, no. 8. San José.
Mintz, Sidney W.
  1953 "The Culture History of a Puerto Rican Cane Plantation, 1876-1949." Hispanic American Historical Review 33 (May): 224-51.
  1973 "A Note on the Definition of Peasantries." The Journal of Peasant Studies 1 (October) 91-106.
Mitchell, Edward J.
  1968 "Inequality and Insurgency: A Statistical Study of South Vietnam." World Politics 20 (April): 421-38.
  1969 "Some Econometrics of the Huk Rebellion." American Political Science Review 63 (December): 1159-71.
Molina, Marcelino, Juan J. Rivera and Carmen Lyra.
  1934 "Historia de la United Fruit Company y de sus rapacidades." Series in El Trabajo (January 7, 14, February 24).
Monge Alfaro, Carlos.
  1966 Historia de Costa Rica (13th ed.). San José: Imprenta Trejos Hnos.
Montealegre R., Mariano.
  1948 "Comentario al discurso de George Gordon Paton 'Cuando volverá el café a los standards antes de la guerra?' " Revista del Instituto de Defensa de Café 19 (June, no. 163): 69-71.
Montoya, J. F., and L. A. Reuss.
  1960 "Changes in Occupation and in Size of Land Holdings—with some Father-Son Comparisons—Selected Rural Households, Cantón of Atenas, 1959." San José: Ministry of Agriculture and Industries. (mimeographed)
Moore, Barrington, Jr.
  1966 Social Origins of Dictatorship and Democracy: Lord and Peasant in the Making of the Modern World. Boston: Beacon Press.
Moore, Richard J.
  1979 "The Urban Poor in Guayaquil, Ecuador: Modes, Correlates, and Context of Political Participation." In Mitchell A. Seligson and John A. Booth, eds., Political Participation in Latin America, vol. 2: Politics and the Poor. New York: Holmes and Meier.
Moraes, Clodomir.
  1970 "Peasant Leagues in Brazil." In Rodolfo Stavenhagen,

Agrarian Problems and Peasant Movements in Latin America. Garden City, N.Y.: Doubleday & Company.

Muller, Edward M.
  1979 Agressive Political Participation. Princeton: Princeton University Press.

Muñóz Castro, J.
  1962 "La actividad del tabaco en Costa Rica." Ciudad Universitaria "Rodrigo Facio": Tesis de Grado.

Murdock, George Peter.
  1963 Outline of World Cultures, 3rd ed. New Haven: Human Relations Area Files.

Norris, Thomas L.
  1952 "Decision-Making on a Costa Rican Coffee Estate." Ph.D. diss., Michigan State College.

Nunally, J.
  1967 Psychometric Methods. New York: McGraw Hill.

Núñez M., Francisco María.
  1971 "La Moneda y la banca en ciento cinquenta años de independencia (síntesis)." In Oscar Aguilar Bulgaelli, ed., El desarrollo nacional en 150 años de vida independiente. Ciudad Universitaria "Rodrigo Facio": Publicaciones de la Universidad de Costa Rica, Serie Historia y Geografía no. 12.

Nunley, Robert E.
  1960 The Distribution of Population in Costa Rica. Washington, D. C.: National Academy of Sciences.

Obregón Loria, Rafael.
  1971 De nuestra historia patria: los primeros días de independencia. Madrid: Imp. Suc. de Vda. de Galo Séz (Publicaciones de la Universidad de Costa Rica, Serie Historia y Geografía, no. 10).

Oficina del Café.
  1954 Recopilación de leyes relativas al café(desde el año 1825). San José: Imprenta Las Américas.
  1972 Informe de Labores 1971. San José.
  1973a Informe sobre la actividad cafetalera de Costa Rica. San José. (mimeographed)
  1973b "Registro de beneficiadores." Circular no. 480, 16 January. San José. (mimeographed)
  1973c "Registro de exportadores." Circular no. 495, 3 July. San José. (mimeographed)

Oficina Internacional de Trabajo.

1972 Situación y perspectivas del empleo en Costa Rica. Geneva: OIT.

Oficina Nacional de Estadísticas.
1912 Resúmenes estadísticos años 1883 a 1910: comercio, agricultura, industria. San José: Imprenta Nacional.

Olien, Michael D.
1967 "The Negro in Costa Rica: The Ethnohistory of an Ethnic Minority in a Complex Society." Ph.D. diss., University of Oregon.
1968 "Levels of Urban Relationships in a Complex Society: A Costa Rican Case." In Elizabeth M. Eddy, ed., Urban Anthropology: Research Perspectives and Strategies. Athens, Georgia: University of Geogia Press.

Paige, Jeffrey M.
1971 "Political Orientation and Riot Participation." American Sociological Review 36 (October): 810-20.
1975 Agrarian Revolution: Social Movements and Export Agriculture in the Underdeveloped World. New York Free Press.

Pan-American Coffee Bureau.
1972 Annual Coffee Statistics, no. 36. New York: Pan American Coffee Bureau.

Pearson, Neale J.
1969 "Guatemala: The Peasant Union Movement, 1944-1954." In Henry A. Landsberger, ed., Latin American Peasant Movements. Ithaca: Cornell University Press.

Perlman, Janice E.
1976 The Myth of Marginality: Urban Poverty and Politics in Río de Janeiro. Berkeley: University of California Press.

Petras, James, and Hugo Zemelman.
1972 Peasants in Revolt: A Chilean Case Study. Austin: University of Texas Press.

Petras, James, and Maurice Zeitlin.
1970 "Agrarian Radicalism in Chile." In Rodolfo Stavenhagen, Agrarian Problems and Peasant Movements in Latin America. Garden City, N.Y.: Doubleday & Company.

Powell, John Duncan.
1971 "Peasants in Politics." (manuscript)

PROCCARA (Programa de Capacitación Campesina para la Reforma Agraria).
1975 Las empresas asociativas campesinas Tegucigalpa, D.C.: PROCCARA.

Rawson, Ian.
1974 "The Campesino of Costa Rica as Peasant; Indications from

a Community Study." San Ramón, Costa Rica (mimeographed).
1975 "Cultural Components of Diet and Nutrition in Rural Costa Rica." Ph.D. diss., University of Pittsburgh.

Ray, James Lee, and J. David Singer.
1973 "Measuring the Concentration of Power in the International System." Sociological Methods and Research 1 (May): 403-38.

Redfield, Robert.
1930 Tepoztlán: A Mexican Village. Chicago: University of Chicago Press.
1956 Peasant Society and Culture: An Anthropological Approach. Chicago: University of Chicago Press.

Revista del Instituto de la Defensa de Café (RIDC).
1937 "Cuentas de venta," 5 (August, no. 34): 327-36.
1940 "Embarques de café de Costa Rica," 10 (November, no. 73): 332-37.
1940 "Lista de beneficiadores de café," 10 (November, no. 73): 338-44.

Reynolds, Jack.
1972 Costa Rica: Midiendo el impact demográfico de los programas de planificación familiar. Ciudad Universitaria "Rodrigo Facio": Centro de Estudios Sociales y de Población (CESPO).

Riggs, Fred W.
1964 Administration in Developing Countries; The Theory of Prismatic Societies. Boston: Houghton Mifflin.

Riismandel, John.
1972 "Costa Rica: Self-Images, Land Tenure and Agrarian Reform." Ph.D. diss., University of Maryland.

Riismandel, John, and James H. Levitt.
1976 "Un estudio cuantitativo de algunos aspectos de la esclavitud en Costa Rica en tiempos de la colonia." Revista del pensamiento centroamericano (July-September): 101-16.

Robinson, John P.
1973 "Toward a More Appropriate Use of Guttman Scaling." Public Opinion Quarterly 37 (Summer): 260-67

Robinson, John P., and Philip R. Shaver.
1974 Measures of Social Psychological Attitudes, rev. ed. Ann Arbor: Survey Research Center, Institute for Social Research.

Rodríguez Vega, Eugenio.
1974 Los días de Don Ricardo. San José: Editorial Costa Rica.

Rowles, James.
    1973   "Instituto de Tierras y Colonización vs. Sociedad Stewart Hermanos, Ltda." In Oscar Salas Marrero and Rodrigo Barahona Israel, Derecho Agrario. San José: Publicaciones de la Universidad de Costa Rica.

Russett, Bruce Mark.
    1964   "Inequality and Instability: The Relation of Land Tenure to Politics." World Politics 16 (April): 442-54.

Russett, Bruce Mark, Hayward R. Alker, Karl W. Deutsch, and Harold Lasswell.
    1964   World Handbook of Political and Social Indicators. New Haven: Yale University Press.

Sabean, David Warren.
    1972   Landbesitz und Gesellschaft am Vorbend des Bauernkriegs: Eine Studie der sozialen Verhaltnizze im sudlichen Oberschwaben in den Jahren vor 1525. Stuttgart: Gustave Fischer Verlag.

Saenz, Alfredo.
    1929   Contratos y actuaciones de las compañía del Ferrocarril de Costa Rica y la United Fruit Company, en Costa Rica. San José: Imprenta "La Tribuna."

Saenz P., Carlos Joaquín.
    1969   "Population Growth, Economic Progress, and Opportunities on the Land: The Case of Costa Rica." Ph.D diss., University of Wisconsin.

Saenz P., Carlos Joaquín, and C. Foster Knight.
    1971   Tenure Security, Land Titling and Agricultural Development in Costa Rica. Ciudad Universitaria "Rodrigo Facio": University of Costa Rica School of Law Agrarian Law Project.
    1972   "Aspectos jurídicos y económicos de la titulación de tierras en Costa Rica." Revista de Ciencias Jurídicas 20-21 (October): 129-236.

Saenz Ulloa, Rolando.
    1973   "Derecho y legislación agraria en Costa Rica." Speech made to the Ciclo de Conferencia Sobre Derecho Agrario, San José, April 27-28.

Salas Marrero, Oscar A. and Rodrigo Barahona Israel.
    1973   Derecho agrario. Ciudad Universitaria "Rodrigo Facio": Publicaciones de la Universidad de Costa Rica, Serie Ciencias Jurídicas y Sociales, no. 22.

Salazar Navarrete, José Manuel.
    1962   Tierras y colonización en Costa Rica. Ciudad Universitaria:

Publicaciones de la Universidad de Costa Rica, Serie Tesis de Grado y Ensayos, no. 15.
1973 "Las empresas bananeras nacionales." Lecture delivered to the Ciclo de Conferencias de la Cátedra de Historia de las Instituciones de Costa Rica. Ciudad Universitaria "Rodrigo Facio."

Salazar Navarrete, José Manuel, Ennio Rodríguez, and José Manuel Salazar X.
1977 "An Innovative Agrarian Policy: The Case of Costa Rica." Paper presented to the International Seminar on Agrarian Reform and Institutional Innovation in the Reconstruction and Development of Agriculture: Major Issues in Perspective. Madison: Land Tenure Center, University of Wisconsin (Published in Estudios sociales centroamericanos 20 (May-August, 1978): 47-110).

Salguero, Miguel.
1976 "Agente de policía." Gentes y Paisajes, various issues.

Sandner, Gerhard.
1960 Turrubares. San José: Instituto Geográfico de Costa Rica.
1962 La colonización agrícola de Costa Rica, vol. 1. San José: Instituto Geográfico.
1964 "Cot de Oreamuno: Herencia colonial, uso de la tierra y problemas socioecónomicos en una población antigua del valle central costarricense." Informe Semestral 7 (January-June): 11-82.

Santos de Morais, Clodomiro.
1971 La organización campesina y el desarrollo rural. Ciudad Universitaria, Costa Rica: Cooperativa Universitaria de Libros.
1972 Estudio de la movilidad de la mano de obra en Centro-America. Guatemala. (typescript)

Sauers, Bernard J.
1974 "Peasant Migration in Latin America: A Survey of the Literature in English." Peasant Studies Newsletter 3 (April): 19-25.

Schulman, Sam.
1966 "A Proposed Schema of Latin American Tenure Classes." Southwestern Social Science Quarterly 37 (September): 122-36.

Schultz, Theodore W.
1964 Transforming Traditional Agriculture. New Haven: Yale University Press.

Scott, James C.
   1976   The Moral Economy of the Peasant: Rebellion and Subsistence in Southeast Asia. New Haven: Yale University Press.
Scott, W.
   1970   "Attitude Measurement." In G. Lindzey and E. Arronson, eds., Handbook of Social Psychology. Reading, Mass: Addison-Wesley.
Seligson, Mitchell A.
   1973   "Transactions and Community Formation: Fifteen Years of Growth and Stagnation in Central America." Journal of Common Market Studies 11 (March): 173-90.
   1975   Agrarian Capitalism and the Transformation of Peasant Society: Coffee in Costa Rica Buffalo. State University of New York Special Studies Series, no. 69.
   1977a "Agrarian Policy in Dependent Societies: Costa Rica." Journal of Interamerican Studies and World Affairs 19 (May): 201-32.
   1977b "Prestige Among Peasants: A Multidimensional Analysis of Preference Data," American Journal of Sociology 83 (November): 632-52.
   1979a "The Impact of Agrarian Reform: A Study of Costa Rica." The Journal of Developing Areas (January, in press).
   1979b "Trust, Efficacy and Modes of Political Participation: A Study of Costa Rican Peasants." British Journal of Political Science (October), forthcoming.
   1979c "Unconventional Political Participation: Cynicism, Powerlessness, and the Latin American Peasant." In Mitchell A. Seligson and John A. Booth, eds., Political Participation in Latin America, vol. 2: Politics and the Poor. New York: Holmes and Meier.
   forthcoming-a "A Problem-Solving Approach to Measuring Political Efficacy," Social Science Quarterly 60 (March, 1980).
   forthcoming-b "Public Policies in Conflict: Land Reform and Family Planning in Costa Rica." Comparative Politics (October, 1979).
Seligson, Mitchell A., and Susan Berk-Seligson.
   1978   "Language and Political Behavior: A Methodology for Utilizing the Linguistic Component of Socio-Economic Status." American Journal of Political Science 22 (August): 712-41.
Seligson, Mitchell A., and John A. Booth.
   1976   "Political Participation in Latin America: An Agenda for

Research." Latin America Research Review 11 (Fall): 95-119.

1979a "Structure and Levels of Political Participation in Costa Rica: Comparing the Countryside with the City." In Mitchell A. Seligson and John A. Booth, eds., Political Participation in Latin America, vol. 2: Politics and the Poor. New York: Holmes and Meier.

1979b Political Participation in Latin America, vol. 2: Politics and the Poor. Holmes and Meier.

Seligson, Mitchell A., and José Manuel Salazar X.

1979 "Political and Interpersonal Trust Among Peasants: A Reevaluation." Rural Sociology, 44 (Fall):505-524.

Shanin, Teodor.

1971 "Introduction." In Teodor Shanan, ed., Peasants and Peasant Societies. Middlesex, England: Penguin Books.

Sharpe, Kenneth Evan.

1977 Peasant Politics: Struggle in a Dominican Village. Baltimore: Johns Hopkins University Press.

Shaw, Paul.

1976 Land Tenure and Rural Exodus in Chile, Colombia, Costa Rica, and Peru. Gainesville: The University Presses of Florida, Latin American Monograph no. 9.

Sierra Cantillo, Gonzalo.

1973 Taped interview, San José, August 23.

Silverman, Sydel.

1968 "Agricultural Organization, Social Structure, and Values in Italy: Amoral Familism Reconsidered." American Anthropologist 70 (February): 1-20.

Simpson, Lesley Bryd.

1952 Many Mexicos. Berkeley: University of California Press.

Slater, Patrick.

1969 "The Analysis of Personal Preferences." British Journal of Statistical Psychology, vol. 13: 119-35.

Smith, T. Lynn.

1970 "The Structure of Rural Society in Colombia: The Case of Tabio." In Smith, ed., Studies in Latin American Societies. Garden City, New York: Doubleday & Company.

Soles, Roger.

1972 Rural Land Invasions in Colombia. Ph.D. diss., University of Wisconsin-Madison.

Soley Guell, Tomás.

1940 Compendio de historia económica y hacendaria de Costa

Rica. San José: Editorial Soley y Valverde.
1947 Historia económica y hacendaria de Costa Rica, vol. 1. San José: Editorial Universitaria.

Squatters.
1972 Anonymous taped interviews with squatters.

Stavenhagen, Rodolfo, ed.
1970 Agrarian Problems and Peasant Movements in Latin America. Garden City, N.Y.: Doubleday.

Stephens, John Lloyd.
1841 "Incidents of Travel in Central America, Chiapas and Yucatán." In Ricardo Fernández Guardia, ed., Costa Rica en el siglo XIX. Ciudad Universitaria Centroamericana, 1970.

Steward H., Julian et al.
1956 The People of Puerto Rico. Urbana: University of Illinois Press.

Stewart, Watt.
1964 Keith and Costa Rica. Albuquerque: University of New Mexico Press.

Stinchcombe, Arthur L.
1961 "Agricultural Enterprise and Rural Class Relations." American Journal of Sociology 67 (September): 165-76.

Stone, Samuel Z.
1969 "Los cafetaleros." Revista de Ciencias Jurídicas (Costa Rica) 13 (June): 167-217.
1971a "Algunos aspectos de la distribución del poder político en Costa Rica." Revista de Ciencias Jurídicas (Costa Rica) 17 (June): 105-30. In translation in Dwight B. Heath, ed., Contemporary Cultures and Societies of Latin America, 2nd ed. N.Y.:Random House, 1973.
1971b "Suplemento." Revista de ciencas jurídicas 17 (June). A supplement to Stone (1971a), but issued as a separate volume.
1973 "Inversiones industriales en Costa Rica." Revista de Ciencias Sociales (Costa Rica) 7 (April): 67-89.
1975 La dinastía de los conquistadores: La crisis del poder en la Costa Rica contemporánea. San José: Editorial Universitaria Centroamericana.

Tanter, Raymond and Manus Midlarsky.
1967 "A Theory of Revolution." Journal of Conflict Resolution 11 (September): 264-90.

Tawney, R. H.
1966 Land and Labor in China. Boston: Beacon Press.

Taylor, Charles Lewis and Michael C. Hudson.

1972 World Handbook of Political and Social Indicators. New Haven: Yale University Press.

Thiel, Bernardo Augusto.
1902 "Monografía de la población de la República de Costa Rica durante el siglo XIX." Revista de Costa Rica en el siglo XIX.

Thiesenhusen, William C.
1974 "Chile's Experiments in Agrarian Reform: Four Colonization Projects Revisited." American Journal of Agricultural Economics 56 (May): 323-30.

Thome, Joseph R.
1965 "Gathering Survey Data for Agrarian Legal Studies in Latin America." Madison, Wisconsin: Land Tenure Center, University of Wisconsin. (mimeographed)

Tinoco, Luis Demetrio.
1945 "Panorama económico de Costa Rica a principios del siglo XVI." Revista de la Universidad de Costa Rica 1 (September): 46-56.

Torres Rivas, Edelberto.
1971 Interpretación del desarrollo social centroamericana. San José: Editorial Universitaria Centroamericana. 46-56.

Trudeau, Robert H.
1971 "Costa Rican Voting: Its Socio-Economic Correlates." Ph.D. diss., University of North Carolina.

Tullis, F. LaMond.
1970 Lord and Peasant in Peru: A Paradigm of Political and Social Change. Cambridge: Harvard University Press.

Union leaders.
1973 Anonymous taped interview with leaders of the Union de Trabajadores de Golfito, January 18.

United Fruit Company.
1932 Letter replying to the Comisión Especial del Congreso, dated August 22. Archivo Nacional, Sección Histórica-Congreso.

United Nations.
1977 Yearbook of International Trade Statistics, 1976. New York: U. N. Department of Economic and Social Affairs.

United States Department of Agriculture.
1970 Crop Production and Country Policies, special issue on Costa Rica, February.

Ureña, Gabriel.
1972 "Factores determinantes en la vida colonial costarricense." Ciudad Universitaria "Rodrigo Facio": Tesis de Grado, Universidad de Costa Rica.

Urróz Escobar, Jamil.
   1966 "Algunos aspectos del sindicalismo y su desarrollo en Costa Rica." Ciudad Universitaria "Rodrigo Facio": Tesis de Grado, Universidad de Costa Rica.

Valentine, Charles A.
   1968 Culture and Poverty: Critique and Counter-Proposals. Chicago: University of Chicago Press.

Valerio Rodríguez, Juvenal.
   1953 Turrialba, su desarrollo histórico. San José: Editorial Torma.

Vega Carballo, José Luis.
   1972 "Bases para un periodización de la evolución agraria centroamericana." San José: Programa Centroamericana de Desarrollo de las Ciencias Sociales. (mimeographed)
   1973 "El nacimiento de un regimen de burguesía dependiente: el caso de Costa Rica (II)." Estudios sociales centroamericanos 6 (September-December): 83-118.

Vicente Castro, Carlos Manuel.
   1972 Nuestro gobierno y el régimen municipal. San José: Imprenta Nacional.

Víquez, Gerardo H. and Leonida López Guzmán.
   1971 "Informe de Costa Rica." In Centro de Estudios Democráticos de América Latina, Caficultura y Cooperativismo en América Latina. La Catalina, Costa Rica: CEDAL.

Vogel, Robert C.
   1978 "Repayment of Agricultural Credit in Developing Countries: What Do Low Delinquency Rates Really Show?" (manuscript)

Vogel, Robert C., and Claudio González-Vega.
   1969 Agricultural Credit in Costa Rica. San José: Agency for International Development.

Volio, Marina.
   1972 Jorge Volio y el Partido Reformista. San José: Editorial Costa Rica.

Wagner, Moritz, and Carl Scherzer.
   1856 Die Republik Costa Rica en Central-Amerika. Leipzig. Translated and published as La República de Costa Rica en la América Central. San José: Ministerio de Cultura, Juventud y Deportes, 1974.

Waisanen, Frederick B., and Jerome T. Durlak.
   1966 A Survey of Attitudes Related to Costa Rican Population Dynamics. San José: Programa Interamericano de Información Popular.

Weisskoff, Richard, and Adolfo Figueroa.
 1976 "Traversing the Social Pyramid: A Comparative Review of Income Distribution in Latin America." Latin American Research Review 11 (no. 2): 71-112.
White, Robert A.
 1969 "Mexico: The Zapata Movement and the Revolution." In Henry A. Landsberger ed., Latin American Peasant Movements. Ithaca: Cornell University Press.
Whittenburg, James P., and Randall G. Pemberton.
 1977 "Measuring Inequality: A Fortran Program for the Geni [sic] Index, Schutz Coefficient, and Lorenz Curve. Historical Methods Newsletter 10 (Spring): 77-84.
Wilson, Charles M.
 1947 Empire in Green and Gold: The Story of the American Banana Trade. New York: Holt, Rinehart and Winston.
Wolf, Eric.
 1955 "Types of Latin American Peasantry: A Preliminary Discussion." American Anthropologist 57 (June): 452-71.
 1966 Peasants. Englewood Cliffs, N.J.: Prentice-Hall.
 1969 Peasant Wars of the Twentieth Century. New York: Harper and Row.
Womack, John Jr.
 1968 Zapata and the Mexican Revolution. N.Y.: Random House.
Woodbridge, Paul A.
 1961 "El contrato ley." Ciudad Universitaria "Rodrigo Facio": Tesis de Grado.
Young, Forrest W.
 1970 "Nonmetric Multidimensional Scaling: Recovery of Metric Information." Psychometrica 35 (December): 455-73.
Young, Forrest W., and Warren S. Torgerson.
 1967 "TORSCA, A Fortran IV Program for Shepard-Kruskal Multidimensional Scaling Analysis." Behavioral Science 12 (September): 498.
Zagoria, Donald.
 1971 "The Ecology of Peasant Communism in India." American Political Science Review 65 (March): 144-60.
Zeitlin, Maurice.
 1966 "Political Generations in the Cuban Working Class." American Journal of Sociology 71 (March): 493-508.
Zúñiga Huete, Angel.
 1928 "La cuestión ferroviaria y bananera del atlántico y el derecho positivo costarricense." In Cooperativa Bananera Costarri-

cense, trabajos y opiniones sobre las cuestiones agraria y ferrocarrileras, en relación con los concesionarios extranjeros en Costa Rica. San José: Imprenta "La Tribuna."

Newspapers

Diario de Costa Rica (San José).
La Gaceta (San José).
La Libertad (San José).
La Nación (San José).
El Pueblo (San José).
La República (San José).
El Trabajo (San José).
La Tribuna (San José).
La Voz del Atlántico (Limón).

Index

Acosta, Tomás de. *See* de Acosta, Tomás
Afrecanische and Laeisz, 76
Agrarian capitalism: and rebellion, xxv, 154; creating new opportunities, xxvii; in Guatemala, 153; and Indians, 157; in El Salvador, 159
Agrarian reform. *See* Land reform
Agricultural colonies: for coffee production, 15
Aguinaldo: United Fruit Company refuses to pay, 74-75
Alajuela, 52
Alcoholism, 22
Alliance for Progress, 126
Amoral familism, 173
Aparcería. *See* Sharecropping
Asociación Nacional de Productores de Café: establishment of, 36
Astua Pirie: ITCO project, 149
Attitude scales: of efficacy, 117, 141-43; trust in government, 117, 139-41
Attitudes: of land reform beneficiaries, 136-44; of future orientation, 144-45; of measurement techniques, 181
Authoritarianism: in Brazil, xxx

Banana cultivation: as escape valve for peasants, xxxi, 63-64, 154
Banana industry: as potential source of wealth, 48; low rate of taxation on, 94
Banana workers: and migration, 29; and history of strikes, 73; housing conditions of, 93; description of, 93-95; status ranking of, 97

Bananas: early development of, 53; exports, 53, 54; Gros Michel variety, 53; production, 54, 76; differential railroad rates, 55; number of farms in 1884, 55; preferential treatment for on railroad, 55; comparison with coffee production, 56-64; local growers, 57; profits of, 58; local planters in conflict with United Fruit Company, 58; Soto-Keith contract, 58; tax on, 59-61; comparison with coffee taxes, 60-61; diseases of, 67-68, 76; decline in production in 1930s, 68; new companies initiate production in Atlantic zone, 76; discovery of disease-resistant varieties, 164; mentioned, 47
Banco Internacional: and coffee financing, 39-40
Banco Nacional: and coffee cooperatives, 37; and coffee financing, 39-40; and Rural Credit Boards, 124
BANDECO: initiates banana cultivation in Atlantic zone, 76
Banks: control of, 25; and coffee financing, 39-40
Barbilla: and cacao, 11
Barranca: railroad to, 50
Bautista Quirós, Juan, 58
Beef: marked expansion of in Costa Rica, 164
Beneficios: early installation of, 19; credit, 24; number of, 32, 40; geographic distribution of, 32-33; decline in the number of, 33; interlocking directorates of, 33; history of, 33-34; competition between, 34

213

Index

Blacks: numbers of in colonial Costa Rica, 4; as slaves, 8; prevented from migrating within country, 65; impact of Depression on, 68; advantages of in banana zone, 69-70
Bloque de Obreros y Campesinos: new name taken by Communist Party, 70
Bolivia: agrarian reform in, xxx; peasants in, 155; Revolution of 1952, 155, 160; Indians in, 160
Boston Fruit Company, 54
Brazil: authoritarianism in, xxix; sharecroppers in, 98; peasants of, 116; peasant movement in, 121; coffee in, 164; mentioned, 38

Cacao: as legal tender, 9; in the Atlantic region, 11; failure of, 12; land grants for cultivation of, 12; as medium of exchange in colonial period, 17; replaced by currency, 17; cultivation by ex-banana workers, 73
CACM. See Central American Common Market (CACM)
Caldera: transportation of coffee to, 17
Calderón Guardia, Rafael Angel, 47
California, United States, 22
Cañas, Juan Manuel de. See de Cañas, Juan Manuel
Carnegie, Andrew, 55
Carrillo, Braulio: coffee land grants, 15
Cartago: colonial population of, 7; home of colonial elite, 10; land grants in, 15; coffee profits help improve, 17; population of, 43; mentioned, 11, 42, 67
Castle and Cook, 76
Cattle industry: and poor peasants, 102; mentioned, 47
Census: of 1905, 22; of 1864, 23; of 1883, 23; of 1935, 27; agricultural, of 1963, 144, 146; agricultural, of 1973, 144-46
Central American Common Market (CACM): and new industrial sector, 47; Costa Rica joins, 162-63
Central American Federation, 18
Centro Para el Estudio de Problemas Nacionales, 47
CGTC. See Confederación General de Trabajadores Costarricenses (CGTC)
Chambacú ITCO project, 149
Chile: exports of coffee to, 15; imports of wheat from, 22; peasant movement in, 121, 161; agrarian reform compared to Costa Rica, 136-37
Chinese: prohibition of immigration of, 65; work on railroad, 65
Chiriquí Land Company, 74
Civil War of 1948: and peasants, 125; mentioned, 47, 63, 73, 168
Class distinctions: in colonial period, 9-10
CNP. See Consejo Nacional de Producción (CNP)
COBAL: initiates banana cultivation in Atlantic zone, 76
Coefficient of consistence: explained, 179
Coffee: expansion before 1820, 14; introduction of, 14; government control of, 15, 16, 36-38, 41-42; export of, 16, 19-20, 35; production costs of, 16, 20; profits of, 16, 20, 41-42; transportation of, 16, 17, 50, 53; profits used to make infrastructure improvements, 17; taxes on, 17, 45; early production techniques of, 18; beneficios, 19; mechanization of, 19; credit for production, 20, 38-40, 56; and monetarization of economy, 22; decline in food production caused by, 22; and proletarianization, 23; growing regions, 24; and land concentration, 27; and population growth, 27; and colonization, 31; concentration of production of, 32; and recibidores, 33; brands, 34-35; impact of World War II on, 34-36; minimum wage law established, 36; pricing of, 36, 44; German interests, 37; number of cooperatives, 37; impact of price declines, 38, 44; number of exporters, 40-41; Officina del Café, 41; comparison with banana production, 56-64; comparison with banana taxes, 60-61; and escape valves, 154; in El Salvador, 159; sales to Soviet Union, 163
Coffee aristocracy: power declining, 47
Collective bargaining, 75
Colombia: peasants of, 116; and communal enterprise reform programs, 134
Colonia La Trinidad: success of, 129
Colonial period: poverty in Costa Rica, 4-10
Colonization: spontaneous, 28; as payment of public debts, 31; description of, 92-93; costs of, 127; data on, 127; lessons learned from program, 129; selection of colonists, 129

Index

Communal enterprise (Empresas comunitarias de autogestíon): description of, 134-35; attitudes of members, 135; problems of, 135; and human fertility, 166

Communist Party: and unions, xxxi; founded, 47, 70; changes name, 70; and riots of 1933, 70; ruled illegal, 70; dissolved, 73; role of, in banana strike, 75-76; leadership of, 104; and peasant organizations, 104

Confederación General de Trabajadores Costarricenses (CGTC): formed in 1952, 74; membership of, 74

Conference of Punta del Este: and land reform, 126

Consejo Nacional de Producción (CNP): requires proof of title for loans, 92; created in 1949, 123; function of, 123; establishment of general stores, 124; provides high quality seed, 124

Contract laws (*contrato-leyes*): with United Fruit Company, 62, 68

Contrato-leyes. See Contract laws (*contrato-leyes*)

Cooperatives: coffee, 37; representation on coffee board, 41

Cortés-Chittendon contract: signed in 1938, 73

Costa Rica Coffee House, 40

Costa Rica Railway Co. Ltd., 52, 55

Credit: for coffee, 20, 38-40; and loss of land, 24; to untitled landowners, 92; granted by the CNP, 123; and Banco Nacional, 124. *See also* Bananas; Coffee

Cuba: revolution in, 125

Culture of poverty, 173

Day laborers: described, 94
de Acosta, Tomás, 14
de Cañas, Juan Manuel, 14
de Lesseps, Ferdinand, 64
de Sojo, Diego, conqueror of Talamanca, 11
Del Monte Corporation, 76
Dependency: on coffee, 38; and development, 48; and banana enclave, 56-64
Depression of 1930s: and conditions in banana zone, 67; in El Salvador, 159
Desamparados, 15
Díaz, Porfirio, 159
Discriminant analysis: used to predict group membership, 119

Dominican Republic, xxix

Echandi-Hitchcock law, 59
Efficacy: and theory of peasant activism, 114; of peasants, 141-43. *See also* Attitude scales
El Jobo: squatting incident in, 107
El Salvador: 1932 rebellion in, 156, 159-60; coffee in, 159; population pressure in, 162, football war in, 163
Emerald mines, 11
Empresas comunitarias de autogestión. *See* Communal enterprise (Empresas comunitarias de autogestión)
Encomiendas: laws governing, 7; break up of, 8
Encogido syndrome, 173
England, 12
Epidemics, 4-5
Escazú: coffee planting in, 15
Esparta: colonial population of, 7
Esquilmo. *See* Sharecropping
Ethnic discrimination. *See* Ethnic homogeneity; Racism
Ethnic homogeneity: defined, 156; and treatment of peasants, 156; and nonrebellion, 157. *See also* Racism
Europe: and market for coffee, 34-36

Fallas, Carlos Luis: jailed and exiled, 70; lead banana workers strike, 71; mentioned, 67, 76
Federación de Artesanos, Panaderos, Construccionistas y Carpinteros: early union organization, 66
Federación de Obreros Bananeros (FOBA): formed in 1952, 74
Federación de Trabajadores Bananeros Anexos (FETRABA): formed in 1950, 74
Federación Unitaria Nacional de los Trabajadores Agrícolas de Campesinos (FUNTAC): organization of, 105; purpose of, 105-6
Ferdinand de Lesseps: builds Panama Canal, 64
Fernández, Santiago: coffee exporter, 16
FETRABA. *See* Federación de Trabajadores Bananeros Anexos (FETRABA)
Figueres Ferrer, José: raises income tax, 63; and land invasions, 106; and ITCO, 107
Finca Coyolar: ITCO project, 149

FOBA. *See* Federación de Obreros Bananeros (FOBA)
Food production: impact of coffee cultivation on, 22; and wheat, 23
Football War: between El Salvador and Honduras, 163; impact on CACM, 163
France, 12, 30
Fremont, John C., 50
FUNTAC. *See* Federación Unitaria Nacional de los Trabajadores Agrícolas de Campesinos (FUNTAC)
Future orientation: of peasants, 144-45. *See also* Attitude scales

Gamson's hypothesis: and theory of peasant activism, 114
Germany, 56
Gilliat, John K. and Co. Ltd., 60
Gini index: applied to income distribution, 138; of land distrubution in 1963 and 1973, 147-48; calculation of, 148; mentioned, 27
Gold mining: in colonial period, 5; in Talamanca, 11; source of wealth, 18
Golfito: strikes in, 73
González Flores, Alfredo, 58
Grecia: coffee cooperative in, 37
Guanacaste: and migration, 29; sharecropping in, 92; mentioned, 65
Guardia Guitiérrez, Tomás: arranges first railroad construction, 50-51
Guatemala: independence of, 14; land prices in, 24; impact of agrarian capitalism on peasants, 153-54; vagrancy laws in, 156; peasant rebellion in, 156-57; ethnic groups in, 157; mentioned, 18
Guevera, Ernesto Ché, 155
Guttman scale, 181

Hacienda: colonial, 7
Hacienda workers: description of, 93; housing conditions of, 93; treatment of, 93; unionization of, 93. *See also* Land tenure
Hatillo: coffee planting in, 15
Homestead Acts: and migration, 30; history of, 32
Honduras: gold mines in, 5; and communal enterprise reform programs, 134; football war, 163

IMAS. *See* Instituto Mixto de Ayuda Social (IMAS)

Immigration, 18
Inconsistency: measurement of, 178
Independence: of Costa Rica, 14; and Pacto de Concordia, 14
Indians: numbers of in Colonial Costa Rica, 4, 7; in Atlantic coast region, 11; of Talamanca region in colonial period, 11; reservations (*reservas indigenas*), 130; and capitalism, 157; in Mexico, 157-58; in El Salvador, 159; in Bolivia, 160; in Peru, 160
Instituto de Tierras y Colonización (ITCO): and peasant movements, 107-10; and Miravalles expropriation, 110; and squatting, 113; program described, 127-36; problems in delivering services to colonies, 128; problems in road construction, 128; settles squatter conflicts, 130-31; titles granted by, 130-31; and formation of agricultural enterprises, 131; impact of reform programs, 136-52; future projects of, 149; land distribution of, 149-52; titling program of, 152; and assistance to peasants, 168
Instituto Mixto de Ayuda Social (IMAS): and peasant movements, 107-10; and assistance to peasants, 168
Instituto Nacional de Aprendizaje (The National Job Training Institute), 107
Instituto Nacional de Defensa del Cafe establishment of, 36-37. *See also* Coffee
Instituto Nacional de Vivienda y Urbanism (INVU): and service to ITCO colonies, 128; and Río Cañas Model, 132
INVU. *See* Instituto Nacional de Vivienda y Urbanismo (INVU)
Italians, 67. *See also* Banana workers
ITCO. *See* Instituto de Tierras y Colonización (ITCO)

Jamaica: conditions in 1860s, 64; migration, 64; mentioned, 68
Jiménez, Joaquín, 50
Jiménez Oreamuno, Ricardo: elected president, 47; attempts to tax United Fruit Company, 59; mentioned, 71
Jiménez Viega, Danilo, 73
John K. Gilliat and Co., Ltd. *See* Gilliat, John K. and Co. Ltd.
Junta de Liquidaciones: control of, by large growers, 36; establishment of, 36. *See also* Coffee

Index

Keith, Henry Meiggs, 51
Keith, Minor C.: railroad builder, 52-56; and banana plantings, 53
Kurtze, Francisco, 50

Labor: scarcity of, 19; development of, 44
Lacheur, William Le. *See* Le Lacheur, William
La Cruz Guanacaste: and squatting, 107
Land: and security, xxvii, 91-95, 97, 98, 99, 155, 156; availability of, 8-9; concentration of, 23-26, 144-49; inheritance of, 24, 28; price of, 24, 25-26, mortgage foreclosures on, 24-27; as a factor of production, 25; purchases of, 25-26; purchases of 1700-1849, 25-26; value of 1700-1849, 26; grants of in Matina, Térraba, and San Ramón, 31; and legal code of 1841, 31; and legal code of 1886, 31; titling problems, 31-32, 91; given to Minor Keith, 52; owned by peasants, 89-91; amount of untitled, 91; legal position of untitled owners, 92; difficulties of poor peasants acquiring, 102; titling program, 103-31, 136, 152; and Miravalles expropriation, 110; invasion of, 115; attitudes of tenure types, 118; and population pressure, 162. *See also* Agrarian reform; Instituto de Tierras y Colonización (ITCO); Sharecropping
— distribution: and rural violence, xxvii
— grants: to cacao planters, 12; to coffee growers, 15
— invasions: and peasant types, 120; and impact of organization, 121
— ownership: peasant love for, xxvii
— reform: and rebellion, xxvi, xxx; in Bolivia, xxx; in Peru, xxx; first efforts, 125; in the 1940s, 125; and Oficina de Colonización y de Distribución de Tierras del Estado, 125; agrarian reform law passed, 126; criticisms of, 126; goals of the reform law, 126; and Río Cañas Model, 132; impact on income, 136-38; impact on attitudes, 138-44; future projects, 149; problems of, 165
— tenure: and the development of the yeoman, 6-10; and Royal taxation, 8; and Spanish law, 8; patterns of, 88-95
Landed peasants: as allegiant activists, 120
Landless laborers: as alienated apathetics, 120

Landowners with title: status ranking of, 97
Latifundios: development of, 8
Latin America: as a dual society, 3; wealth of colonies, 3
Legislative assembly: control of, by elites, 43
Le Lacheur, William, 16
Lesseps, Ferdinand de. *See* de Lesseps, Ferdinand
Ley de Gracias: and movement of United Fruit Company to the Pacific Coast, 68
Leyes de Cabezas: and migration, 30
Leyes de Terranos Baldíos: and migration, 30
Limited good, image of, 173
Limón: as port for coffee, 50; railway to, 55-56; conditions in 1892, 67; mentioned, 58, 69, 73
London, England: coffee exchange of, 19; and coffee financing, 39

Madríz, Castro (president), 50
Mata Redonda: coffee planting in, 15
Matina: and cacao, 11; roads to, 17; land grants in, 30; railway to, 55
MDPREF: computer program, 100; explanation of, 100-1
Meiggs, Henry, 51
Meseta central: definition of, 5
Mexico: peasant rebellion in, xxviii, 156-159; ethnic groups in, 157; Porfirio Díaz in, 159; mentioned, 10
Middle class: development of, 44
Migrant workers: described, 95; insecurity of, 98; and security, 155
Migration: as alternative to rebellion, xxx; from Andalucía, Spain, 9; motivation for, 9; affected by coffee, 27-31; and Homestead Acts, 30; and Leyes de Cabezas, 30; and Leyes de Terranos Baldíos, 30; of Jamaicans, 64-65; law prohibiting black, 66; of peasants to cities, 163
Minifundios: increase of, 148
Minimum wage: on coffee haciendas in 1973, 93
Ministerio de Obras Públicas: and services to ITCO colonies, 128
Ministry of Labor: and supervision of haciendas, 94
Miravalles: and ITCO, 110
Modernization: impact on traditional society, 3

Moin: roads to, 17
Mora, Juan Rafael: struggle against William Walker, 25; exports of coffee, 40
Mora Fernández, Juan, 15
Mora Porras, Juan Rafael, 50
Morelos, Mexico, 168
Morgan, Henry: piracy of, 12
Morice, Eugenio, 65
Morice, Luis: and land acquisition, 107; and murder of Gil Tablada Corea, 109-10
Municipal governments, 168

National Job Training Institute, The. *See* Instituto Nacional de Aprendizaje (The National Job Training Institute)
National Production Council. *See* Consejo Nacional de Producción (CNP)
Negroes. *See* Blacks
New Orleans, Louisiana, 54
Nicaragua: threats of invasion from, xxvi; gold mines of, 5; colonial road to, 17; agricultural development of, 163; mentioned, 72
Nicoya: sugar refinery near, 65
Northern Railroad: history of, 55. *See also* Bananas

Occupational structure: in 1864, 43
Oduber, Daniel, 106
Oficina de Colonización y de Distribución de Tierras del Estado: and land reform, 125
Oficina del Café: composition of the board, 41; control of exporters' profits, 41-42. *See also* Coffee

Pacto de Concordia: independence, 14
Pacheco-Hoadley contract, 55
Panama: colonial road to, 17; impact of canal on railroad, 53; and communal enterprise reform programs, 134; agricultural growth in, 163
Panama Disease: 67-68, 76
Partido Agraria: and land reform, 126
Partido Reformista: and minimum wage law, 66
Parrita: strike in, 73
Pavas: coffee planted in, 15
Peasants: as demographic surpluses, xxx; types of, 88-103; earnings of, 89-90; education of, 89-90; landed type described, 89-91; titled landowner described, 89-91; legal position of the untitled owners, 92; day laborers, 94; migrant workers, 95; methodology for determining social stratification of, 95-96; ranking of types, 96-99; arrested in La Cruz, 108; reported to have been tortured by police, 108; attitudes of, 116; and Revolution of 1948, 125; definition of, 173-75; cultural characteristics of, 174
— leagues: comité campesino, 105; fomented by the Communists, 105; and FUNTAC, 105; success and failure of, 106; led by government agencies, 107-10; spontaneous, 111
— organizations: types of, 104; weaknesses of, 155
— Types: ranks, 97; and security, 100; and legal-illegal dimensions, 102
Peru: agrarian reform in, xxx; and tobacco monopoly, 12; ethnic groups in, 157; peasant rebellion in, 157; Indians in, 160; mentioned, 10, 51
Plantation workers: status ranking of, 97-99
Population: in colonial Costa Rica, 4-5; epidemics in colonial period, 4-5; distribution in early colonial period, 6; colonial settlement, 7; occupatios in 1864, 23; growth rate in 1751-1892, 27; distribution in 1824, 28; distribution in 1864, 29; distribution in 1892, 29; distribution in 1927, 29-30; urbanization, 42-44; of Cartago, 43; of San José, 43, 47; composition of 1883, 44; rural-urban division, 44; birth rate, 102; and pressure on land, 102; and peasant rebellion, 161-62; fertility among landed and landless peasants, 166
Problem-solving efficiency scale: use of, 117
Proletarianization: caused by coffee production, 23
Public employees: increase of, 47
Public policy: and coffee, 16
Puerto González Víquez: strike breaks out in, 74. *See also* Banana workers
Puntarenas: transportation of coffee to, 17, 49, 52

Quepos: strikes in, 73

Index

Racial discrimination: and United Fruit Company contracts, 68-69; against Blacks, 69-70; in banana zone, 69-73. *See also* Ethnic homogeneity; Racism

Racism: laws restricting entry of minorities, 65-66; towards Jamaicans, 65-66; towards Blacks, 161

Railroad: need for, 49-50; financing, 50-51, 52-54; construction difficulties, 50-53; loss of lives in construction, 52; competition between lines, 55; differential railroad rates, 55; Northern Railroad established, 55; various contracts, 55; and shortage of labor, 64

Rank-ordering: methods of, 176

Rebellion: in a peasant society, xxiv; absence of, xxv; causes of, xxv; and adaptive strategies, xxvi; and social banditry, xxvi; risks of, xxvi-xxviii; and escape valves, xxix, 154; peasants as victims, xxix; self-help as alternative, xxix; migration as alternative to, xxx; and agrarian capitalism, 154; factors which militate against, 154; and non-rebellion, 154; reasons for non-rebellion, 155; and ethnicity, 156-61; in El Salvador, 159-60

Reilly, Edward, 50

Renting: risks of, 98

Repression: in El Salvador, 162

Revolution of 1948. *See* Civil War of 1948

Río Banano: railway to, 55

Río Cañas model: of agrarian reform, 131-32

Risks: of coffee production, 21; of renting or sharecropping, 98; of squatters, 98

Rivas, Nicaragua: cacao haciendas, 12

Roads: impact on, of coffee transportation, 17; Sociedad Económica Itineraria, 17; and colonization program, 127-28

Rockefeller, John D., 55

Roman Catholic Church: and colonial settlements, 7

Salvador, El. *See* El Salvador

San José: coffee profits help improve, 17; transportation of coffee to, 17; population of, 43; distrust over railroad, 52; 1932 special municipal elections, 70

San Juan de Murciélago: coffee planting in, 15

San Ramón: land grants in, 31

Santa Cruz, Guanacaste: and Río Cañas model, 132

Sarapiquí: roads to, 17; land grants in, 31

Security: of hacienda work, 21; of middle class, 44; alternative routes to, 98; and peasant types, 99, 154-55; relationship to legal-illegal dimensions, 102

Self help: as alternative to rebellion, xxix

Servicio Nacional de Acueductos y Alcantarías (SNAA): and ITCO colonies, 128

Sharecropping: description of, 92; risks of, 98

Sigatoka: banana disease, 67-68

Sindicato de Pequeños Productores Agricolas de Limón: peasant union, 106

Sindicato de Trabajadores Bananeros Unidos Independientes (SITRABUNI): signs collective bargaining contract, 75

Sindicato Nacional de Calzado: militant unions, 66

Siquirres, 62

SITRABUNI. *See* Sindicato de Trabajadores Bananeros Unidos Independientes (SITRABUNI)

Sixaola River, 11

Slave labor: discussed, 8

SNAA. *See* Servicio Nacional de Acueductos y Alcantarías (SNAA)

Social stratification: in rural Costa Rica, 88-103; dimensions of, 100-2

Sociedad de Artesanos: early union organization, 66

Sociedad Económica de Amigos del País, La: pressure for favorable banana contract, 60

Sociedad Económica Itineraria: and road improvements, 17

Sociedad Mutualista de Artesanos de Panadería: early union organization, 66

Sociedad Mutualista de Tipógrafos: early union organization, 66

Sociedades de Socorro: early union organization, 66

Soto-Keith contract: terms of, 52; tariffs for rail transport, 58

Soviet Union: coffee sales to, 163

Spain: and gold in Central America, 5; monopoly of tobacco in Peru, 12; war with England and France, 12; in Costa Rica, 42; mentioned, 38

Squatters: and rebellion, xxvi; and 1942

Squatters (*Cont.*)
law, 32; description of, 90-93; risks of, 98; disputes among, 105; and violence, 106-7; in El Jobo, 107; explanation of motivations for, 116; as highly cynical and highly efficacious, 120; as alienated activists, 120; ITCO and settlement conflicts, 130-31; number of, 167; as makers of spontaneous land reform, 168
Standard Fruit Company, 76
Status incongruity: of colonial elites, 11
Steady plantation workers: treatment of and unionization of, 93; description of, 93-94
Strikes: of shoemakers, 66; of Italian railroad workers, 67; 1934 banana strike, 71-73; of 1938, 73; of 1943, 73; of 1949, 73; of 1953, 74; of 1955, 74; of 1971, 75; motivations for, 94. *See also* Banana workers
Suerre: and cacao, 11
Sugar: sales to North American market, 163; mentioned, 47

Tablada Corea, Gil, 109
Talamanca: gold mines in, 11
Taxes: and encomienda, 7; on tobacco, 13; on coffee, 17, 45; on land, 46; on bananas, 59-61, 94
Technology: and unemployment, 164
Tenure type: and human fertility, 166. *See also* Peasants
Térraba: land grants in, 30
Tinoco Granados, Frederico, 58
Tobacco, 12, 13
Trabajadores Agrícolas de Heredia, 76
Tropical Trading and Transport Company, 53, 55
Trust in government: and theory of peasant activism, 114; and land reform, 139-41
Turrialba: colonization in, 31; and migration of Blacks, 66, 70

Unemployment, 164
Unión, La: land grants in, 15
Unión de Pequeños Productores Agrícolas de Guanacaste: peasant union, 106
Unión de Pequeños Productores Agrícolas de Pérez Zeledón: peasant union, 106
Unión de Pequeños Productores Agrícolas de Villa Neilly: peasant union, 106
Unión de Trabajadores Agrícolas de Limón: became engaged in dispute with banana companies, 76
Unión de Trabajadores de Golfito (UTG): formed in 1950, 74; history and membership of, 75
Union movement: first major strike, 66; FETRABA formed, 74; UTG formed, 74
United Fruit Company: establishment of, 54; benefits of, 57; contracts with, 59-64; taxes paid by, 60-61; congressional committee investigates, 61; helped establish a pattern of dependency, 63; moved to Pacific Coast, 68, 73; racial discrimination, 68-69; strikes against, 72-75; and Cortés-Chittendon contract, 73; refuses to pay aguinaldo, 74-75; signs collective bargaining contract, 75; production volume of, 76; and treatment of workers, 94; compared to hacienda employment, 99; housing conditions, 99
United States: and Big Stick policy, 58; encourages agrarian reform, 125; land titling program, 136; mentioned, 41
University of Michigan survey, 117
University of Santo Tomás, 17
Unsteady day workers: and security, 155-56
Urinama Indians, 11
Uruca, La, 15
UTG. *See* Unión de Trabajadores de Golfito (UTG)

Vagrancy laws, 156
Vargas-Schutt contract, 55
Vásquez de Coronado, Juan, 43
Vázquez de Coronado, Gonzalo, 11
Venezuela, 117
Volio, Jorge, 66

Wages: on haciendas, 22
Walker, William, 25, 31
Wheat. *See* Food production
World War I: and wheat prices, 23
World War II: and coffee financing, 38-40; and coffee exports, 40

Yeoman: origin of, 6-10

Zambos-Mosquitos Indians: and cacao, 12
Zapata, Emiliano: and rebellion, xxviii; role of ethnicity in rebellion, 158-59; mentioned, 27
Zapote: coffee planting in, 15